Our Lives Are But Stories

Our Lives Are But Stories

NARRATIVES OF TUNISIAN-ISRAELI WOMEN

ESTHER SCHELY-NEWMAN

Wayne State University Press   Detroit

06   05   04   03   02   5   4   3   2   1

Library of Congress Cataloging-in-Publication Data

Schely-Newman, Esther, 1948–
Our lives are but stories : narratives of
Tunisian-Israeli women / Esther Schely-Newman.
p. cm.—(Raphael Patai series in Jewish folklore and anthropology)
Includes bibliographical references and index.
ISBN 0-8143-2876-8
1. Jews, Tunisian—Israel—Biography.   2. Jewish women—Israel—Biography.
3. Immigrants—Israel—Biography.   4. Jews, Tunisian—Israel—Social life
and customs—20th century.   5. Storytelling.   I. Title.   II. Series.
DS113.8.T83 S34 2002
305.48'9691—dc21   2001008612

CONTENTS

CONTENTS

PREFACE

The work on this book began when I was born. I avidly listened to stories told by family members, other elders, and friends. The stories told of former days in Tunisia prior to emigrating to Israel and of building a new community. But most of all, the stories told how people established their own lives in a changing world. The stories present an Israeli life different from what I was taught in school and different from what is portrayed in the media. The incongruity is the basis of this book, which attempts to analyze the way women create their own lives through their stories against the backdrop of a patriarchal system, ethnic prejudice, and a modern rapidly changing world. The book examines stories of now-frail elderly women who tell of themselves as they were in their prime, carrying the world—their families—on their shoulders. These stories do not dwell on their weaknesses, but rather are told in the flattering light chosen by the tellers themselves.

Storytelling does not end with the writing of a book; only life itself provides closure. Although death puts an end to individual stories, other people take up the task of telling the stories of their lives. I now tell my daughter, Devora, many of the stories my mother used to tell me. Telling family stories soothes the pain of loss and ensures continuity of ethnic and gender identity.

The book has benefited from the contributions of many people: the narrators, particularly the women and men of *moshav* Gilat, but also the people I talked to in Aminadav and Givat Yearim. All offered important insights into the work. Most appreciated are the comments provided by colleagues who read parts or all of the work in different stages: Yoram Bilu, Shoshana Blum-Kulka, James Fernandez, Harvey H. Goldberg, Don Handelman, Galit Hasan-Rokem, Tamar Katriel, and Michael Silverstein, who introduced me to the challenge and excitement of studying oral discourse. Special thanks to Dan Ben-Amos, general editor of the Raphael Patai Series and Adela Garcia, project editor at Wayne State University Press, for the time and advice given me. I also wish to thank The Levi Eshkol Institute for Economic, Social and Political Research, The Memorial Foundation for Jewish Culture, The Smart Family Foundation for Communication Research, The S. A. Schonbrunn Research Endowment Fund, and The Shaine Center for Research in Social Science for their support at different stages of research and writing.

To my daughter, Devora, who provided my motivation and to Stanley M. Newman, my husband and partner, whose constant support and critique enabled me to complete the endeavor: this book is yours as much as it is mine.

INTRODUCTION

And that's it. The whole world is stories
u-akuwa. e-denya kula xrayef

When, in 1992, a student went to interview Odette about her life in Israel, she was told, "Do you want me to tell you thirty-seven years in half an hour?" Indeed, one cannot condense a whole life into a single interview, but the stories people tell about their lives are time capsules, concentrating and distilling their experiences. These narratives are a mode of creating, working out, and affirming individual female identity as negotiated within the constraints of particular settings.[1] Emerging within culturally defined interactions, narratives are salient phenomena in the study of culture and identity, performance and interactions. The content (narrated events) is flexible and can be adjusted to a variety of narrative events, and the resulting texts of such interactions are polysemic—open to multiple explanations.

This study treats stories elderly Tunisian-Israeli women tell about themselves, and thus the value of narratives is measured in terms of performance and in the construction of a coherent life story within its context(s) (Peacock and Holland 1993). The biographies of the elderly women do not pretend to present life as lived in the daily round of everyday problems, complaints, bickering, and jealousies, or a chronology of what actually happened to them as individuals or as a group. What is presented are the lives the women wish known to their audiences. Central to the analysis, therefore, are the dialogues maintained between verbal exchanges in specific settings, between participants, and between cultural norms, and the constraints inherent in narrative events (Bakhtin 1986, 68–69; Voloshinov [1929] 1986, 94, 102).

9

The life stories of four women, Fortuna, Biya, Ghaliya, and Odette, all of whom reside in small agricultural communities (*moshavim*), serve as the basis for the study, creating a virtual group biography of the Tunisian-Israeli grandmother, from childhood through migration and old age. The individual narratives are used here both to tell this larger story and to examine storytelling itself as a cultural phenomenon. The women tell and retell ancestral anecdotes, using storytelling to negotiate and reconcile conflicting situations, to socialize and warn the younger generation, to praise themselves, and to criticize others. These stories reflect ambivalence about leaving the familiar for the unknown, apprehension over changing cultural values, and processes of adaptation to a new reality. Above all, these stories are about the narrators themselves, negotiating and reaffirming their identities as daughters, wives, mothers, and grandmothers, searching and finding their individual voices in doing so. To understand this gendered discourse, one must consider not only formal features of narratives but also immediate contextual aspects and the social and communicative goals of the interactions. The ethnography of communication combined with personal-female-intimate narratives provides the theories required to study the interactions.[2] Together these methodologies highlight the gendered discourse, as evident in the context(s) of narration and discourse strategies; the analysis of the content within its cultural setting allows for a better understanding of the many layers of symbolic meanings.

Researching the stories of family and neighbors means studying one's own group. The study of family narratives also involves shifts in my personal position, between participant and observer, at times letting my professional gear "observe" while I participated. The women were aware of my research interests, frequently telling me about events because they knew that I would like to hear or record them. Furthermore, the narrators were aware of my knowledge of their stories, as well as of my belonging to a particular family in the community; intertextuality therefore is significant in the study. As a biological daughter and a sociocultural "daughter of the community," I was also subject to greater scrutiny as an addressee of the narratives, expected to learn the lessons implied. Information was conveyed to me not merely to satisfy my ethnographic

curiosity, but to encourage me, as a member of the frequently criticized younger generation, to benefit from and act upon the lessons
contained in that information.

In this story of my mother, Fortuna, and her cohorts I address questions of entitlement to use data I am privy to by virtue
of being a member of the community. I use the real names of
people and places, in keeping with the stated preferences of the
women, who feel that "we have no reason to hide our actions or
identity."[3] I believe that the data are not mine but belong to the
narrators, who want to be heard, and that representing their experiences requires giving a voice to each individual woman within
the interaction exactly as it occurred. As most narratives were not
elicited, the choices the women make during the emerging interactions become interpretive keys, since the women are using shared
aesthetic criteria of eloquence and tellability (Bauman 1992, 182;
Briggs 1988, 8–9). The dialogic nature of performance—the fact
that it is an ongoing negotiation of meanings—suggests that the
presentation of interaction should include the surrounding utterances in addition to the narratives themselves. My analyses and
interpretations attempt to locate the functions of each narrative
as it pertains both to the life of the narrator and the dynamics
of the narrative event. The interpretations are mine, and therefore I cannot be certain that the women meant what I say they
meant or that they are aware of the implications I have assigned
their words. The cultural knowledge I bring to the analysis, however, gives emic validity, allowing me to view the individual stories
as representative of the lives of other women who share similar
experiences.

In addition to analyzing life stories, this book addresses a
number of theoretical issues pertaining to the study of personal
narratives: (1) combining analyses of form and content; (2) the
dialogic relations between life and story in personal experience
narratives; (3) the construction of female gendered identity; (4) the
construction of ethnic identity by the selection of various elements
of Tunisian-Muslim, Jewish, and Israeli cultures; (5) my dual role
as participant and observer in the creation of text and its analysis;
and (6) the mode of writing that best represents the combination
of my voice and that of other individual women.

Setting the Scene: Contextualization

The interpretation of texts demands their full contextualization. This involves not merely the time, place, and identity of the participants in the interaction, but also other data which may include local or remote circumstances, the idiosyncratic tendencies of participants, global events, and previous utterances (Ben-Amos 1993; Goodwin and Duranti 1992; Schiffrin 1994; Silverstein 1992). The difficulty in grasping or defining context results from the fact that context exists only in relation to other focal points; text and context are ongoing dialogical processes, mutually feeding into each other in dynamic and complex relationships (Georgakopoulou 1997, 29–30; Schiffrin 1994, 362). Not all factors are equally relevant, and participants negotiate meaning and assess the significance of contextual elements ("cues") within the emerging discourse. In my analysis I attempt to follow the leads and interpretation of cues of the participants, as signals of referential and indexical meanings (Bauman and Briggs 1990, 69; Gumperz 1982, 131). The number of contextual elements referred to in any specific interaction depends upon the circumstances and on the familiarity of the participants with the topic. When stories are decontextualized—lifted from their original discourse—a translation on different levels is required in order to fill the gaps between the addressees in the original setting(s) and the new audience/reader (Bauman and Briggs 1990; Silverstein, in press). The following sections attempt to do just this, to familiarize the reader with the historical and cultural backgrounds, the methodology and the theories employed for the collection and analysis of the data.

The stories in this study are recollections of past events, individual memories set against the backdrop of the collective memory of Tunisian Jews as a distinct group within the larger conglomerate of ʿedot hamizrah (communities of the East) in Israel. Unlike the collective memory, which may be contested by different voices—politics, media, and academe—and constantly reshaped by them, individual memories are less restricted. Personal narratives do not require an authority beyond the entitlement of the experience and do not purport to influence the official voices, at least not in the initial intimate settings of narration. Nevertheless, a dialectical relation exists between individual and collective memory: individual recollections have a ripple effect. Stories told in family settings sometimes translate into other media and eventually participate in the struggle for authoritative voice in the collective remembrance of the past.[4] The following historical chapter is based both on narratives collected and on "official" sources.

Remote Context: History and Culture

The women of this study were born between 1917 and 1932 and spent their formative years in Tunisia, migrating to Israel as married women. Though born in different towns, and possessing individual histories, they share the same cultural and religious values, and their experiences in Tunisia and in Israel bear many similarities. By the time I began recording their stories, in 1987, all of these women were well established in their communities: they were grandmothers, past childbearing age, and their husbands had already retired from their primary occupations. The differences between Fortuna, then seventy years old, and Biya, fifteen years her junior, were thus minimal. The term "elderly" is used throughout the book to describe this group of women, who in their own culture are considered 'ajawez (old people), having different responsibilities—and privileges—than their juniors.

The women migrated from Tunisia, a French colony on the verge of independence, in 1949 (Fortuna and Ghaliya) or 1955 (Biya and Odette). Like that of other North African countries, Tunisian culture is male-centered, the pattern of residence predominantly patrilocal in extended family settings, and the division of labor and space based on gender (Dwyer 1978; Hejaiej 1996; Mernissi [1975] 1987). Jews have been living in Tunisia for hundreds of years, perhaps since Phoenician times (Abramski-Bligh 1997; Hirschberg 1974). Though Jews maintained a separate religious identity and resisted assimilation into the larger Muslim society, their culture was influenced by the surrounding society, particularly in terms of everyday life and mores. With time, a Judeo-Islamic cultural symbiosis emerged, mainly in non-normative areas.[5] Jews and Muslims in Tunisia share many of the same patterns of residence and courtship, folk religion, oral folklore, folkways, and a belief in jnoun (demons) (see, for example, Bahloul 1996; Patai 1986; Valensi 1989). However, as noted by Goldberg, studies of Muslim societies have tended to overlook Jewish life, and studies of Jews in Israel tend

13

to "downplay the significance of the Islamic setting within which these communities lived their lives" (1990, 3). The interaction between the Jewish, the Muslim, the Israeli, and the female aspects of identity are considered in this study, as well as issues of entitlement to genres of speech, in an attempt to add to the understanding of female identity in changing times (cf. Abu-Lughod 1986, 1990; Gal 1991).

Emigration

The coexistence of Jews in Arab countries ended in the middle of the twentieth century with the creation of the State of Israel in 1948 and the subsequent waves of migration, which essentially depleted the Arab countries of their Jewish populations. The Tunisian Jewish population, estimated in 1949 as over 105,000, was reduced by the middle of the 1990s to about 2,500, mostly living in the capital, Tunis, and on the island of Jerba (Deshen 1997; DellaPergola 1992). The Jewish population of Tunisia generally was urban and consisted of merchants, artisans, professionals, or workers; Jewish farmers were a very small minority.[6] Migrating to Israel for many meant, among other things, adjusting to living in a farming community, a *moshav. Moshavim* are cooperative agricultural villages, consisting of a small number of individual family farms (generally between 50 and 150) with certain activities, such as marketing and purchasing, controlled by the community (see Lees 1995). Settling in *moshavim* frequently meant a change in patterns of residence from extended to nuclear family. Many Tunisian Jews still lived in extended family settings in 1950, either within the same compound or in close proximity to relatives. This pattern had to change simply because the farms in *moshavim* are intended to support individual families, and as a result many families were scattered among different communities.[7] In the first decade of Israeli statehood, about three hundred *moshavim* were established, for both ideological and practical reasons (J. Reinharz 1991). Working the land was perceived as a way to redeem the Jewish people from their urban bourgeois nature, to transform them from "exilic" Jews to Hebrews rooted in their own land (see Handleman 1998; Katriel 1993, 1997; Katriel and Shenhar 1990). It was also part of a policy of population dispersion and security arrangements: most of the new *moshavim* were established near the borders or in areas with a large Arab population.

14

New immigrants, then, were sent to build agricultural communities as a way of enculturating themselves and also fulfilling state and security needs.

In addition to these changes in occupation and residence patterns and the adjustments to a new country and culture, non-European immigrants also had to cope with the prevailing perceptions of the socio-economic-cultural cleavage between Jews from different ethnic backgrounds. These cultural distinctions still exist, especially between Ashkenazim and Sephardim, popularly understood as Jews originating from Europe and those from Middle Eastern countries.[8] The Eurocentric bias of the government leadership was far more obvious in the early years of the state than it is today, as indicated in reports about that period (Chafets 1986; Segev 1986). A quote from a brochure of the late 1950s by the Jewish United Fund (designed to raise money for social projects in the State of Israel) illustrates the dominant attitude toward Sephardi Jews:

> During recent years, we have had a large influx of Jews from the Near East and Africa. . . . Most of the people who come to Israel from these countries have darker skin. . . . Many of the countries from which they come are underdeveloped. Some of these darker-skinned Jews lived in the Casbah in Casablanca in ghettos under the most miserable conditions. . . . The lighter-skinned Jews who came from Eastern Europe include professionals, tradesmen, and those who have been exposed to the sciences, the arts and the professions. (Elazar 1989, 8–9)

Despite the increasing demographic and political power of Sephardim and the weakening of the Ashkenazi hegemony, social, economic, and educational gaps continue to exist at the present time. The growing number of Sephardi Knesset (Israeli Parliament) members notwithstanding, access to power and economic resources still remain limited for non-Ashkenazi in Israel (Kimmerling 2001; Smooha 1993; Shuval 1989). This hegemony is interpreted by some as a necessary part of the process of nation building (Bar Yosef 1968; Shuval 1989), while others view it as cultural colonization (Shohat 1997). The issue of Israeli identity and the role played by the Ashkenazi establishment remains vital in contemporary Israeli discourse in literature and film (Loshitzky 1996) as well as politics.[9]

Prejudice against non-Europeans did not affect all immigrants in a similar manner. People of the same ethnic origin settled most *moshavim* with minimal contact with the "other," but prejudice was shown, explicitly or implicitly, by representatives of the government sent to help the immigrants in their initial process of adjustment. Women counselors were sent to assist women in acclimating to a new diet stressing local ingredients and with advice on childcare and on how to challenge a husband's demands. These counselors, who in some cases were younger than the immigrants' children, often denigrated traditional knowledge and behavior, even in exclusive female spheres such as child rearing. Nevertheless, these contacts with other Israelis allowed the immigrant women to gain some knowledge of Israeli society, independent of that of their husbands. Working and gaining new knowledge gave women greater responsibilities in family matters, in turn reducing male authority and hastening the breakdown of the traditional social structure (Katzir 1984).

The lives of these Tunisian-Israeli women have been significantly altered from that of their mothers and grandmothers. They migrated to a new country, with different patterns of residence and occupations. Israel confronted them with a different perception of gender roles: the Israeli women they encountered were active in the public sphere and held positions of authority and power. They had to learn a new language to communicate with their children and grandchildren; some had to work for wages to support their families. They helped their children gain an education and achieve a profession, and witnessed their daughters gaining an independence they never thought possible. Their children married into other ethnic groups, and their families are scattered throughout Israel and around the world.

Changes notwithstanding, the focus of these women's lives stays constant: their primary roles continue to be those of wife and mother, and the domestic sphere their primary arena. Women are officially eligible to vote and be elected to *moshav* committees, but in ethnically homogeneous *moshavim* it is rare to find women in positions other than teacher, secretary, or nurse.[10] Traditional ways of reaching decisions—by the husband or father—are slowly being altered, however, and women are finding ways to voice their needs and wishes.[11] The elderly women continue to exercise traditional methods of influencing their spouse and kin offspring by employing the power of storytelling. Narration thus becomes a lifeline of presenting, maintaining, and asserting, as well as challenging, gender and ethnic identities (cf. Langellier 2000).

Narration and Narrative Events

For Tunisian men and women, Jews and Muslim alike, narration is a medium of socialization and sociability, used for entertainment and education in different contexts and on different occasions (Bascom [1954] 1965; Hejaiej 1996; Noy [1966] 1968; Webber 1991). Narrative events in a variety of speech genres occur frequently on both formal and informal occasions; I have witnessed narrations in sermons in the synagogues, in men's casual discussions during interludes in religious services, in family settings, and during women's visitations. People tell stories while waiting for the doctor at the local clinic, while shopping in the local store, or when they meet friends on the bus or in the open market. Although contemporary media and changes in leisure time have reduced opportunities, narrating continues to be a favorite activity among the older generation of Tunisian Israelis. Their repertoire includes traditional genres, such as stories about historical figures, biblical legends, and fairy tales, as well as personal-experience narratives. This latter genre is gradually replacing other traditional genres as the dominant choice (Schely-Newman 1997).

Jews and Muslims share many of the same stories, but differences exist between men and women in narrative style, in narrative genres, and in the contexts appropriate for narration. Tunisian Jewish women, like their Muslim counterparts, were relegated to the private sphere. Silence vis-à-vis their male relatives was basic to their normative behavior. However, women's imagination was not confined; they shared their concerns with each other and told folktales, *xurayef,* fictional representations of reality. Men, on the other hand, told stories, *hikayat,* representing life experiences (Webber 1984; 1985). The recounting of events from the daily life of women was not considered a genre unto itself, but simply as the *klam* (words) or *duwa* (speech) *taʿ nsha* (of women). Yet, female *xurayef* (fictional tales) are laden with themes inspired by their personal experiences, and through them women may express their emotions without actually violating cultural norms (Hejaiej 1996, 47–60).[12] The major themes in women's folktales are family life—marriage, birth, and relations with kin; explicit, or more frequently, implicit sexuality is at the basis of many tales. These themes continue to be a major concern in the discourse of Tunisian Israeli women, though the fictional is now gradually being replaced by "real" stories—their own, their neighbors', or those gleaned from the media.[13] These personal narratives continue to serve as an enculturation tool, and though the narrators are modest in their demeanor and traditional in their views, their narratives are nevertheless pregnant with sexual meanings and symbolism. Within the context of changing cultures, personal narratives can be interpreted as subversive. The women may explicitly support the hegemonical patriarchal structure of society, while their stories and narration may at the same time challenge and even reject the same social order. This double role of narration and narratives is exemplified and stressed in a variety of ways throughout the book.

Immediate Context: Settings of Performance

Fieldwork for this study was carried out in informal settings, with stories told as a part of conversations. Interviews were conducted in private homes or sitting around the central table in the *moʿadon kshishim,* the community center for elderly people. Sometimes I asked general questions, but let the women answer at their own pace, freely associating, helping or interrupting each other. My familiarity with the women and their languages helped maintain this informality; they did not have to change their speech on my behalf but could continue to mix Hebrew, Arabic, and French lexemes in the same utterances, a common code among noneducated immigrants (see chapter 1). I visited *moʿadonim* (centers) and talked with the group before bringing in my tape recorder and camera. During these early visits the women and I negotiated our mutual identities according to our respective roles and values: I wanted to know why they lived on a *moshav,* or what they remembered about their first encounters with the locale, and they, in turn, asked who I was married to and why I had only one child, reaffirming my identity in traditional terms of origins defined by location and familial relations (L. Rosen 1984). Once I had satisfied their interest, I was able to participate in their interactions and tape and photograph them.

The data most frequently consists of conversational narratives, stories meshed into their surrounding discourse. In this genre the importance of co-textuality (as well as intertextuality) is enhanced. Although narrators may tell stories that are new to the audience, more frequently the audience is familiar with the events, and the result is polyphonic or even competing narration (Blum-Kulka 1997, 122–24). The mutual dependence of text and context is therefore considered in this book: narrative texts are presented within their surrounding utterances, to allow for an analysis of how stories emerge, form, and shape the conversations in which they are embedded (Peterson and Langellier 1997, 136). The stories discussed belong to the amorphous genre of personal narratives, "the mundane happenings of an ordinary day and extraordinary events that mark our lives" (Langellier 1989, 243). Each story used in this book has a narrative structure and an implied assertion of truth value. The main character in the story is the narrator, or sometimes the narrator tells of an event that she has personally witnessed (Stahl 1989, 15). Whether the details of the story are accurate or not is unimportant; people always tell about their concerns so that the stories reveal the "truth of [their] experiences," even when they bend the truth or simply lie about events (*Interpreting Women's Lives* 1989, 261). The familiar and informal contexts of narration minimized the importance of distinction between true and false. Stories and narrators are judged (by the audience) in relation to the narrative event—competence in performance, entitlement to the story, poetic structure, or relevance to the conversation—rather than by the accuracy of the narrated events (Bauman 1986; Bauman and Briggs 1990).

These conversational narratives tell about events in the lives of the narrators: discontinuous units, told over time and on different occasions, comprising the life story of the individual and/or her family. The meaning(s) of these cumulative stories is primarily related to the narrator's evaluation of her life (Linde 1993, 4, 21). Though the stories tell about individual lives, the memories conjured up are embedded in a common social setting (Weissberg 1999, 13). Individual memories are thus couched in the collective memory. As they tell about specific weddings or migration routes, the meanings of their stories emerge not only from the individual events being narrated, but also from what cultural norms determine as a "proper marriage" or as legitimate reasons for migrating. This interaction between the individual's recollections and group memory enables me to segment the narratives told by each woman and to reconstruct them into a continuous story.

The stories were selected for their "narrative" quality, rather than for their accurate representation of women's lives (Peacock and Holland 1993, 368–69). Most of these stories were marked as significant by the narrators, and their importance is not based on the grandeur of the events they describe but on their structures and the dynamics of interaction from which they derive. Stories are presented within their surrounding discourse, allowing the voices of the women to be heard. My words are intertwined with the women's, setting them in chronological order and combining them into a coherent biography of the elderly Tunisian-Israeli women living on a *moshav*. At the same time, my words interpret the women's voices, providing them with literal and symbolic meanings by translating them from oral to written analytical discourse.

The conversational narratives studied here deal with personal experiences comprising the life stories of the women told in intimate family settings. The approach to such data cannot fall within the traditional structure of any specific academic knowledge. Following Langellier and Peterson (1993) and Sawin (1999), I, too, view the stories as a discursive practice that produces a culture, in this case an engendered culture of Tunisian Israelis. To do so, the stories must be considered not only as artifacts (texts), transmitting information about particular events and culture, but also as performances within specific contexts. These contexts—from the remote cultural background to the immediate interaction and audience participation—shape the content and the overall meaning of the narratives. The challenge in analyzing the data lies in the dynamics of narration within the cultural background, and the multiplicity of meanings in narratives that intersect gender, ethnicity, and age. My particular roles and identities as a daughter-ethnographer provide a perspective on how storytelling functions as a means for ethnic survival.

Structure of the Book

The organization of the book follows the main events in the course of a lifetime, divided into meaningful stages in the life of a Tunisian-Jewish-Israeli woman (cf. Rosenwald and Ochberg 1992, 2; Kirshenblatt-Gimblett 1989, 124–25). It does not therefore necessarily follow the order in which the stories were told; none of the women related a comprehensive life story in a chronological autobiography. The study combines two major axes: content— the life story of the women—and form—the role of engendered narration in the lives of these women. Each chapter both presents a particular stage in women's lives and discusses pertinent theoretical issues. Chapter 1, on childhood, examines the process of acquiring narrative competence: the language(s) used and family storytelling. Chapter 2, on marriage, treats the position a narrator chooses in creating a coherent story and the issue of participatory rights in narrative events. Chapter 3, on motherhood, looks at the female discourse of procreation and the emergence of narratives in conversations. The fourth chapter, on migration, examines role changes and the effect they have on narrative genres. Chapter 5, on old age, treats the discourse of nostalgia and counternostalgia and the poetic structure of oral narratives. The concluding chapter takes a reflexive turn, treating the problematics of conducting fieldwork "at home" and the modes of writing such a study. In a broader view, the study follows the process by which Tunisian-Israeli women acquire a voice, and the process of translating *les cris de la vie* (the cries of life) into *l'écrits de la vie* (the writing of life). [14]

Prior to telling their aggregate life story, I introduce the four women whose lives are the basis for the study.

Main Narrators

1. *Fortuna,* my mother, was born in 1917 in Sfax, the second-largest city in Tunisia, and raised (not adopted) by a childless maternal aunt. In 1941 she married a second cousin, Noro, a Jewish Tunisian French citizen just released from his army service. In 1942, Noro volunteered for service in the Free France Army, under the French general Charles de Gaulle, serving in the Middle East until the end of World War II. When he returned to Tunisia in 1945, my father began planning to return with his family to Israel (then Palestine, under the British Mandate). The emigration was delayed, however, until May 1949, six months after I was born. In Israel Noro joined friends who were planning to settle in a new agricultural

Fortuna, April 1999

community, *Moshav Gilat*. Because of the primitive conditions in the *moshav* and the lack of medical treatment, Fortuna had several miscarriages and other health problems. Noro, who was a barber in Sfax, became a construction worker and a farmer, working nights as a guard, and later as attendant in a nearby gas station.

The division of labor in my family was clear: Noro took care of almost everything—working for wages, shopping, and helping with the children and grandchildren, even with the cooking. In fact, my mother did very little outside the house: the neighbors still remember my father waiting in line with the women to get food during the early years in the community, while other husbands left such chores to their wives. Noro was an acclaimed raconteur, always entertaining people with jokes and stories—a bon vivant and an avid reader of adventure stories. All this abruptly ended in the summer of 1987, when my father suffered a stroke and his speech and mobility were seriously impaired; his condition worsened over time. My mother, who had been pampered all her life, now became the head of the household, in charge of everything from finances to the daily care of an invalid husband. With his death in February 1997, Fortuna, like other elderly widows, learned to adjust to yet a new role. She continued to live on the *moshav*, next door to

Biya, July 1989

her son, daughter-in-law, and grandchildren, visited the *mo'adon kshishim* (old people's club) regularly, and made new friendships. She died in June 1999.

2. *Biya* was born in 1932 in Sousse, a large city near the sea, which served as a railroad center.[15] Her father sold *brik* (fried pastry) in the town market, but had financial difficulties raising four girls and four boys, necessitating that Biya work in a factory to support her family and assemble a dowry. In 1955 she married Shimon, and the couple, together with her husband's parents, migrated to Israel and settled in Gilat, where her brother lived. They soon had their own house, which they shared with Shimon's parents, and raised three sons and three daughters. In Tunisia, Shimon worked with his father, who owned a restaurant, but in Israel his situation changed and Shimon tried his hand at farming and later in a variety of other jobs. Biya, in addition to raising the family, found ways to assist financially—watching the neighbors' children, tending a kiosk, and selling home-cooked goods.

Located across from my parents' home, Biya's yard is a favorite site for social gatherings, and consequently for my fieldwork. Her children and siblings frequently visit, and friends stop by almost daily, particularly on Saturday. One of Biya's brothers was a well-known storyteller, and many of his stories have been recorded and collected for the Israeli Folklore Archives.[16] The family frequently

Ghaliya, July 1990

talk about his large collection of books and recall the stories with which he entertained them. Biya prides herself on having been an excellent student and on her ability to read and write in French. Given these accomplishments, she sees herself as my helper, or partner, in scholarly work—assisting me by providing her own stories and by introducing me to her family and prompting them to tell me stories as well.

3. *Ghaliya* was born in 1924 in Gabes, a small town in the south of Tunisia, near the island of Jerba.[17] The southern area of Tunisia was less influenced by French colonialism than the north. Jerba was a major Jewish center, considered far more traditional and pious than the northern towns. Ghaliya's mother died when she was only three years old, and Ghaliya was raised by wealthy grandparents. The extended family lived in a large house with running water and even a private *mikvah* (ritual bath). Ghaliya says that there were never fights between the women, who spent their days together caring for the house and the family. She attended school for a few years and can still read some French. When she was fourteen her grandparents married her to Michael, an orphan cousin, and the couple lived with his paternal grandfather, a rich goldsmith who was more strict than her own grandfather. In 1949,

Ghaliya and Michael, with their three children, decided to immigrate to Israel. It was an opportunity, according to Ghaliya, to create their own independent life. The family joined Michael's brother in *Moshav Gilat,* and Michael began to work for *Solel Boneh,* a large construction company. While Michael continued to work in the same place until retirement, Ghaliya stayed at home, raising eleven children. At present, she spends much of her time visiting children and grandchildren living in different parts of Israel.

Coincidentally, my family and Ghaliya's arrived at the *moshav* at approximately the same time and were allotted neighboring houses. Because Ghaliya's three older children are the same ages as my siblings and I, the six of us were inseparable during our childhoods. Growing up with Ghaliya's children, I, too, became a target audience for family tales. Ghaliya is an outgoing woman, who likes to visit people, listen to stories, and share her own. Like Biya, she is in charge of the household and family matters, leaving to her husband the responsibility of providing financial support for the family.

4. *Odette* was born in 1925 in the capital, Tunis. She, too, had to help her family, and struggled with the desire to study.[18] She worked in a doctor's office for some years and acquired nursing skills that became useful in Israel. In 1943 she married Gabriel, a Jew who had fled Tripoli during the war and settled in Tunis. The family immigrated to Israel with their children in 1955 and settled in *Moshav Aminadav,* a frontier community (at the time) on the outskirts of Jerusalem, where they still live. In Israel they had three more children, all now living in Jerusalem and its suburbs. Although Gabriel was well-to-do in Tunisia, his fate changed in Israel and Odette was forced to leave the house and work to help support the family, in addition to raising her children and working the family farm.

While my relationship with the other women was predefined —I was the daughter of Fortuna and Noro—the relationship with Odette had to be negotiated on different terms. I first met her in 1993, during fieldwork in a *mo'adon kshishim* with other women from Morocco, Iraq, and Yemen. An outgoing woman, as well as the only Tunisian woman in the club, Odette took me as her protégé and gladly agreed to be interviewed and even to come to talk to my university class. I continued to visit the *mo'adon* to conduct fieldwork and frequently spend time with Odette in her home.

25

Odette, January 1993

In addition to the stories of these women, the book includes events and stories from the lives of other friends and neighbors of my parents. These are *Jeani,* who was born in a small town in central Tunisia (Sidi Bu Zid) and emigrated to Israel with her husband in 1949, where they became founding members of Gilat. *Alice* and *Thérèse* were born in Sfax and emigrated with their husbands and young children in 1954; both families joined relatives who lived in Gilat, and both have remained there. *Miḥa* came from the northern town of Bizerte and emigrated with her family in 1955. They, too, joined relatives in Gilat and have lived there ever since. Additional data were collected during visits to other *moʿadonim* in *moshavim* in the vicinity of Jerusalem.

Note on Texts

The narratives in this study appear in different formats. Synopses of stories are given to illustrate the issue under discussion. These are stories told about the lives of women other than the narrator herself. Life stories of the four women (Biya, Fortuna, Ghaliya, and Odette) that were told with minimal responses or comments from the audience are printed as continuous text, without line segmentation. The analysis of these stories focuses on their content, rather than their performance. Other stories, those told in a polyphonic style, are segmented into lines corresponding to patterns of interaction, or to "breath groups," equivalent to complete sentences. Most of these stories appear in the appendix.

I have translated all of the narratives from Hebrew, Arabic, French, or a combination of the three languages (see chapter 1). The shift in languages is noted only where the practice of code switching is interpreted as meaningful.

In memory of my mother,

So my daughter won't forget.

CHAPTER 1

Childhood

He who has no daughters, what caused his death?
illi ma ʿandush lə bnat, ʿalash mat?

Among Jews in Tunisia the birth of a daughter was met with much less enthusiasm than that of a son. In his collection of oral Judeo-Arabic texts describing everyday life, Cohen (1964) begins with a text that shows the preference: "From the moment a woman has happily delivered, a *martba* is prepared in the house.[1] If she had a girl, we do a *shabaʿ*, and that's it. But if, praise God, it's a boy, the rules are much more complicated." (24)[2]

The only rite for the birth of a girl is the *shabaʿ* (seven), a family gathering on the seventh day after birth, in which the infant is given a name. The rituals for the birth of a boy are numerous and involve more time, effort, money, and preparation.[3] A girl's birth may be accompanied by mocking remarks about the father's manhood, and comfort to the mother in the form of ʿam e-jay yikun ʿendak ouliyed (next year you'll have a son).

The different value given to boys and girls is expressed in a variety of ways: mothers fearing the evil eye may dress a boy as a girl; women may inadvertently count only their sons as their offspring, adding their daughters only as an afterthought. Furthermore, the birth of a girl more seriously "pollutes" the mother, doubling the time during which she is ritually impure, which requires conjugal avoidance (Leviticus 8:2–6). Virilocal residence after marriage means that male children will continue to share the parental home, thus ensuring financial support for elderly parents in their declining years.[4] As for girls, they must be sheltered and cared for until they can be married off at great expense, due to the custom of paying the groom large amounts of money as dowry (Awret 72). A common Tunisian proverb underscores the attitude toward girls: *illi ma ʿandush lᵊ bnat, ʿalash mat?* (He who has no daughters—what caused his death?).[5]

Compared with memories and stories about marriage, motherhood, or emigration, the women told few stories about their childhood. This paucity of memories can be explained by the little value the culture put upon childhood as a distinct period in one's life (cf. Kirshenblatt-Gimblett 1989, 124–25; S. Reinharz 1994; Rosenwald & Ochberg 1992, 2). The stories women do tell—the onset of menarche and going to school—suggest that the narrators attribute specific importance to them. These events and stories about them need to be explained both in cultural and idiosyncratic terms (Rosenthal 1993).

Becoming a Woman

There is no term in Judeo-Arabic for a virgin—the meaning is included in the terms *"bint"* (daughter), *"sbbiya,"* or *"tofla"* (pubescent, unmarried).[6] In fact, there is no age limit to being a *bint;* only when she marries does a *bint* become *mra* (woman, wife).[7] In all stages of life the woman is referred to in kinship terms, as daughter of, wife of, or mother of; the individual identity of a woman is less emphasized than that of men (Abu-Lughod 1988, 152). Young females are expected to remain in the company of other women in the household, secluded and protected from the outside, male world. The girl is waiting for her *shaʿad* (fortune, fate)—that is, her predestined husband—to give her social status and the opportunity to fulfill her female potential. Girlhood is a transitory stage for Muslim and Jewish girls alike, a time of expectations, observing and learning before becoming a member of the society by marrying, a time for indirect socialization through watching and listening.[8] The women recall being with female relatives and participating in or watching their activities: cleaning, cooking, or visiting relatives. There was, however, one occasion when attention was given to the individual girl: at the onset of menarche. Because in Muslim societies menstruation is perceived as a woman's secret, not shared with little girls, menarche became the opportunity for instruction and for welcoming the girl into the women's world (Delaney 1988, 78–79; Awret 1984, 156).

Biya was in school when she first menstruated, and she ran home, frightened. She was embarrassed but her mother insisted upon hearing what had happened. Once her mother was reassured about the source of bleeding, after repeatedly inquiring if Biya had been touched by anyone or if she had been injured in any way, Biya was reassured that this was normal and was a positive sign that now she was like all women, able to bear children. She was also made aware of some connection between conduct and procreation: "If a man touches you, you'll become pregnant," Biya was warned.[9] Fortuna had a different experience: she was not even aware she was bleeding, but her aunt Hanna, whom she was helping wash laundry, noticed her stained garments. Hanna told her quickly to get up, reassured her that this was all women's way, and instructed her what to do.

Explanations and warnings were accompanied by a ceremonial practice using oil. The girl was told to observe her reflection in a bowl of olive oil for some time, and to smile at her reflection, then her face was rubbed with the oil. Biya and Ghaliya were told that the observation of their reflection would set their visage so that it would always remain as it was on that day, and ensure a happy life.[10] These customs resemble those involving the use of a mirror as a love charm by fixing one's gaze on someone particular.[11] According to Fortuna, the oil would smooth a woman's passage into womanhood, as did the custom of painting the palms of the menstruating girl with *henna*, "to bless her path into womanhood" (Awret 1984, 156). The concentration on the face and appearance of the girl is somewhat similar to a rite among Eastern European Jews in which the mother slaps her daughter on both cheeks so that the rush of blood to the face will make the girl "have a wonderful color all [her] life" (Zborowski and Herzog 1952, 347–48).[12] In addition to the calming effect of the slap, as in cases of hysteria, slapping may also bear some warning to the young woman, as if reminding her of the consequences of being an adult. The Tunisian oil ceremony was

31

accompanied by a festive meal of couscous with chicken, unusual during midweek, or by special honey-dipped, oil-fried cakes. A related custom existed in Algeria, where the menstruating girl was dressed in an apron and kerchief and prepared a meal for the family, serving it in miniature dishes.[13]

This North African Jewish ritual in its variations seems to emphasize woman's roles and place. The physiological change was celebrated in a female setting, within the private sphere, using materials belonging to the female world. The oil and bowl, both used for cooking, join other household items used as female metaphors, such as pots or the house itself (Schely-Newman 1996b). The red *henna* is used in a large number of feminine rites of passage ceremonies. Marking the passage of a girl from childhood to maturity was an exclusive female affair in which the close network of women accompanied the girl on her path to womanhood. Women played a similar role in the elaborate wedding ceremonies (see following chapter) and when a woman gave birth.

As important as the onset of menarche is for the individual woman, this is not a commonly described event. I do not recall the specific occasion on which my mother told me her own story, but it was in recent years, when I was in my mid-forties. Other women were cooperative and told me in detail what had happened to them only when I asked specifically about this topic. If other women were present, they joined the conversation and shared their own memories.[14] This omission is related not to coyness but to the low degree of importance given to specifically female experiences, since married women talk freely about signs and symptoms of menstruation, pregnancies, childbearing, and menopause, though not explicitly about sexual relations. It is as if womanhood per se is not important enough to be individualized or publicly celebrated in the traditional Tunisian-Jewish culture. Womanhood is publicly recognized and celebrated by elaborate rites of passage only when the potential for bearing children is legitimized through marriage. The ten-year age difference between Ghaliya and Fortuna is negligible; both reached social maturity when they married and had children, be it at the age of fourteen or twenty-four. Until that time the girl was an appendage of her mother or close female relatives, who bore the responsibility for her behavior, a responsibility transferred to her husband's kin once she married. The connotation of menstruation with impurity, and the fact that it is a "women's issue," probably add to the reluctance to openly talk about the ceremony. Furthermore, the onset of menarche, like menstruation, belongs to the female private sphere, which has little, if any, prestige, and the discourse thereof is thus limited to women (S. Reinharz 1994). Therefore, while the female-exclusive discourse of menstruation and procreation empowers women (see chapter 3), it also contributes to the ambivalence about sharing these stories and retaining the traditional ceremonies. The onset of menarche remains an individual experience, possibly shared with daughters, but not part of the "life story" a woman tells other people.

In Israel these forms of acknowledging menarche have almost totally disappeared. Biya and Thérèse performed them for their oldest daughters, but did not continue with their other daughters. Fortuna, Ghaliya, and Odette did nothing to mark the transition in their daughters' lives. Several factors may account for the abandonment of the rite. For instance, sex education in school and the greater exposure of young people to the "facts of life" may have diminished the "mystery" of menstruation. In addition, the general devaluation of traditional ethnic customs in Israel has led to the discarding altogether of some informal and private rites which are not supported by formal religion. Not the least of the factors involved is the changes in male and female societies: young women in Israel are not secluded from male society, and other females are not their exclusive support group, but are second to the peer group. Even though women continue to help each other, there is a growing preference for privacy and individualism. Changes in women's roles and activities have resulted in two distinct ways of marking a girl's coming to maturity today. Puberty is celebrated publicly in the girl's bat mitzvah at the age of twelve. Parallel to boys' bar mitzvah at age thirteen, the ceremony may include religious elements or simply be celebrated as a party. In addition, however, some women continue to mark their daughters' maturation on a private-individual level. For example, several Tunisian women raised in Israel told me that they gave the daughter a piece of jewelry on the occasion. The traditional customs marking the introduction of the girl to the exclusive female world have been abandoned, but women may retain the custom of celebrating the occasion by creating some intimate moment of mother-daughter bonding.

Going to School

While the stories about onset of menarche were shared only with other women and only when specifically asked about, the women frequently talked about their education; school days memories and stories are recounted over and over again by the women and their husbands. Unlike other girlhood events, this is an individual experience that occurs in the public sphere. It is not related to traditional female roles, but is a sign of modern times. Women describe in detail the black aprons they wore, the books they read, the stories they heard, and their preparation of homework. Jewish boys in Tunisia received religious education and learned to read Hebrew for ritual purposes, but girls generally were not literate in Hebrew. Even in enlightened and modern Europe, Jewish religious schools for girls were opened only in 1917 (Elor 1994, 66).

Secular education and literacy for Jewish girls (and boys) in North Africa and the Arab world was accomplished through the involvement of the Alliance. The Alliance Israélite Française school network was founded in Paris in 1860. These schools had a civil mission to expand French middle-class culture and to "remake Middle Eastern Jewry in its own emancipated image" (Goldberg 1996, 14). The influence of modernity was stronger in the northern part of Tunisia than in the south, as a result of the objection of Jerban rabbinical authorities, which prevented the opening of an Alliance school on the island (Tobi 1996). The first Alliance school for boys opened in Tunis in 1878, and the first for girls in 1912. Secular education gained importance, and by the 1920s and 1930s many Jewish girls studied either in the Alliance schools or in the école laique funded by the French colonial government. Religious classes continued to be taught to boys in the kuttab (Jewish religious school), and Modern Hebrew was taught as part of the activity of Zionist groups (Saadon 1999; Tsur 1996).

Education stood in conflict with traditional roles of women. On the one hand education was positively evaluated: schooling was a sign of modernity and a recognizable asset for a girl who was to be married. Education enabled better employment and increased earning. Yet, on the other hand, girls were not supposed to work outside their home for wages.[15] Among Tunisian Jews, as among their Muslim counterparts, even when girls' education was seen

34

favorably, the purpose was general and not vocational, as was the case for boys (Zamiti-Horchani 1986, 113). Nanette was born in 1913 and is proud of attending high school for several years and having worked for wages, but her family wanted to make certain her reputation would not be tarnished, so she worked with her brothers. Fortuna finished primary school but was not allowed to continue to high school. The objection came from her maternal uncle, who asked, "What does she need school for? Are we going to send her out to work?"

Education nevertheless was a source of concern for the parents: attendance at school meant that girls were removed from the immediate supervision of their families. In addition, the content of the material taught in schools was unknown, and might have raised fears about the loss of traditional values.[16] What seems to be lacking in the stories is parents' fear of the freedom provided by literacy. Yet the conflict inherent in education is revealed in the stories women tell about their education.[17] A clear example of the contradiction between tradition and the menace of modernity through education is found in Odette's story: "I finished school at the age of eleven, received a scholarship. The principal saw my grades and schoolwork and invited my father to school. He told him: 'You have a special child and we want to send her to France to become a secretary.' My father told him: 'God forbid! According to our customs—we have an Arab education—we do not give our daughters away, only to a husband or to the grave.'"[18]

When Odette first told me what her father supposedly said to the French principal, she spoke in Hebrew, using a rendition of a Tunisian Arabic proverb *il bint l-el dkar ow l-el qbar* (the girl [is] for the male or for the grave).[19] This was a proverb that was not common among Jews, though the differences between modern (French) and traditional (Judeo-Arab) values were well known. I later inquired what the father actually said to the principal, and this time Odette spoke in French, saying that her father was unusually explicit, using the verb *découcher* (to sleep elsewhere than one's residence) and insisting that a daughter would leave her father's home only to her husband's house or in a coffin.[20] Tunisian Jews were able to accept and reject elements of both traditions: Odette's father and other Jewish families allowed their daughters to have a modern French education, but only as long as other values were not affected. The opportunities of a better education and a full scholarship could not be measured against the values of modesty. Note that Odette's perception of the female role is attributed to a "less sophisticated" tradition, Arab education; in this manner Odette removes herself (and even the Jewish tradition) from a mode of behavior she was forced to follow. The process of choosing between modern and traditional is evident in another example: Odette said that she studied in the *école laique,* not the Alliance, because in the Alliance school they were apparently using Tunisian Arabic, while in her school they taught the "real language," French.

Education sets the women apart from their mothers, thus creating two models of identification: the "modern" father who is proud of his daughter's achievements and supports her learning a new language, and the mother, who sometimes attempts to pressure her daughter to remain within the traditional boundaries. About half an hour after reporting the conversation between her father and the school principal, Odette returned to the story of her education,

> My mother would tell me, "There is no school. You need to learn to sew, do this and that, and clean the floor." . . . My mother did not go to school, not even for one day, but she was very smart. My father, . . . he loved me and was proud of me. . . . Every month I was first in my class. One day an Italian girl, a good Christian friend, improved her grades and we both reached first place. I came home proud. My father liked that girl, but he said, "Why does Anna have this position?" . . . "Next month she'll surpass you, you'll be second," and he slapped me. I asked why and he said, "It cannot be that someone else will be better than you."

Odette's mother was concerned with traditional roles, while her father encouraged her competitiveness, though within the limits of the community.[21] The competition is based on ethnic grounds; it is not clear whether the father would have been as upset if the other girl had been Jewish. Mentioning the ethnicity of the other girl may reinforce Odette's perception of her own ability: she is smarter than the modern European girls in her class.[22]

Competition with others and traditional values were not the only obstacles preventing girls from continuing their education. There were also financial concerns, so that stories about school frequently include mention of the sacrifices that had to be made, particularly in comparison with wealthy girls. Biya tells, for example, how the teacher gave her books in exchange for domestic help and how a rich girlfriend, Denise, gave her a daily sandwich in return for doing her homework and carrying her books.

The paucity of childhood memories other than school stories may derive from a combination of cultural perceptions and other individual factors. Viewing childhood as a time of waiting for adulthood (i.e., marriage) reduces it to an "empty" period, as if there is nothing in particular worth telling about, nothing that can serve to mark the individual life story. School, on the other hand, was an occasion for proving one's own value, an individual achievement measurable against that of others, male and female, Jews and non-Jews. The importance of school in the lives of the women is also evident by the stories about school as their earliest memories. As noted by Lieblich et al. (1998, 84) first memories are a key in understanding life stories from a holistic approach. Education brought pride and status to the family itself: Odette's father was invited by the French school principal to hear praises of his daughter. Fortuna mentioned that her entire family was as anxious as she was to find out the results of her exams for the *cerificat d'étude*. Furthermore, education is an experience that the women can share with the younger generation: grandchildren may not identify with daily life in the old country, but school is something they themselves are experiencing. School-day stories allow women to compare their experiences with those of others and to have a subject in common with their grandchildren.

Personal Narrative in Family Settings

Narration is telling stories to others, in a language the group shares and in a manner the group appreciates. The analysis of performance therefore begins with the language and narration within the family setting.

Language Use

Tunisians live in a diglottic and bilingual situation: they speak different variants of Arabic (classical, modern, and Tunisian-Arabic) and French, introduced by colonialism as the language of modernity and the intelligentsia (Walters 1996, 526–31; Walters 1999).

The linguistic repertoire of Tunisian Jews includes Hebrew and Judeo-Tunisian Arabic in addition to French. Judeo-Tunisian Arabic is based on Tunisian-Arabic but includes a significant number of borrowed Hebrew words and is written in Hebrew characters (see Cohen 1964, 1975). Hebrew was a holy language, used for prayers and liturgy, and it served as a lingua franca in contacts with Jews from other countries. Most men learned sufficient Hebrew in the *kuttab* to be able to participate in religious services. Modern Hebrew, as a language for everyday use, was introduced in the 1930s and taught in afternoon classes by teachers sent from Israel, mainly to members of Zionist groups (Saadon 1999). Knowledge of the Hebrew letters and fluency in spoken Judeo-Arabic allowed people to read texts with little practice beyond what was learned in the *kuttab*. The availability of religious and secular texts in Judeo-Arabic— prayers, commentaries, newspapers, novels, and folktales—made literacy an asset.[23]

The first language of the women in my study is spoken Judeo-Arabic; they learned French in school as children, and encountered Hebrew as a modern, everyday language only when they migrated. As women, they had little access to religious texts: few knew the holy language, Hebrew, nor could they read Judeo-Tunisian-Arabic. Since none of the women in this study knew Hebrew before immigrating to Israel, "literacy" for them meant knowing French. A similar attitude toward French as the equivalent to literacy, and hence, modernity, exists among elderly men as well as among Muslim Tunisians. Tunisian Arabic is seen as less prestigious than modern standard Arabic or classical Arabic. Similarly, literacy in Hebrew among elderly men and women remains limited, just as literacy among Tunisian Muslim women born in the 1930s or earlier is almost nonexistent (Walters 1999).

The status and use of Judeo-Arabic sharply declined in the twentieth century. Colonialism made French the language of the educated and a symbol of modernity, while Zionism and the emigration to Israel changed the status of Hebrew from a language of ritual to a secular, everyday language. As is the case with other Jewish languages, such as Yiddish or Ladino, Judeo-Arabic currently is spoken mainly by older people and is a subject of academic research. There are speakers of Judeo-Arabic in Tunisia, in France, and in Israel, but the language is not being formally transmitted to the younger generations. Zionist negation of experiences and cultures outside of Israel, and the requirement that all immigrants fit into the mold of the "new Hebrew" (as opposed to "Jew") were central factors in the erasure of all exilic languages (Ben-Rafael 1994a, 1994b). In addition, the Eurocentric position in Israel (particularly) during the first two decades of statehood viewed immigrants from non-Western countries as ignorant and lacking "culture" (Katriel 1994; Shohat 1997). Finally, the Israeli-Arab conflict created an identification of Arabic with the enemy. Even though Arabic is an official language in the State of Israel and is taught in schools, it is not considered to be a language with positive values, and only a small number of students continue to study Arabic beyond what is required in school (Ben-Rafael 1994a).

Modern Hebrew is the main official language in Israel and is a major marker of statehood and solidarity among its Jewish citizens. The authority and prestige of Hebrew derives from its status both as the ancient holy language of Judaism and as the language of national revival, Zionism. The revival of Hebrew as a daily language was an important part of the Zionist movement, which was also based on a powerful negative stance toward everything that was part of the old Jewish existence (Harshav 1993, 17–18). The teaching of Hebrew to new immigrants continues to be heavily funded by the state; nevertheless, native languages are forgotten at a much slower rate than Hebrew is acquired, and many Israelis of the migrating generation continue to be bilingual (Ben-Rafael 1994b, 182). In their everyday discourse the women in this study use Arabic, Hebrew, and French—more accurately, a combination of the three languages.

Moshav Gilat as a Speech Community

Gilat, a community with a population made up of Tunisian immigrants and their descendants, is a multilingual community in which Arabic, French, and Hebrew are spoken. Like other small homogeneous communities, Gilat can be defined as a speech community in itself, distinguished from its neighboring communities (Gumperz [1968] 1972, 29). A description of the communicative activities engaged in by those living in Gilat, in everyday discourse and particularly in performance, reveals its unique set of rules for language shifts (Duranti 1997, 82).

Proficiency in Hebrew, the state language, depends on age; number of years lived in Israel, gender, and education (Cooper 1985). In Gilat the older people, who emigrated as adults, are fluent in Judeo-Arabic and in French (in variable degrees). The men are usually more fluent in Hebrew because they studied in religious schools and in Israel had interactions with officials who spoke only Hebrew. The women were less exposed to Hebrew: within the community, knowledge of Judeo-Arabic was sufficient. The younger members of the community, those who emigrated as children or were born in Israel in the 1950s, are also fluent in Judeo-Arabic, which was their first language, but unlike their parents they are products of the Israeli school system and are therefore fluent and literate in Hebrew. Their own children have grown up in a Hebrew-speaking environment; they may understand their grandparents but they speak mainly Hebrew. The younger people also learn English in school and improve their English language skills through television shows, popular music, and, currently, the Internet.

Judeo-Arabic, like most other Jewish languages, suffers from a lack of prestige. The articulated linguistic position (ideology) is that Judeo-Arabic is the language of the uneducated and nonmodern—of the grandparents. It is rare to hear people raised in Israel speak to each other in Arabic, whereas this choice is quite common with older people, especially women. Cross-generational conversations depend on the proficiency of the participants, frequently resulting in the use of as much Hebrew as possible by the older people or as much Arabic as possible by the younger ones.

In Gilat, the conversations of elderly women are generally held in Arabic. Odette, who is the only Tunisian woman in Aminadav and who worked outside her house for many years, is more fluent in Hebrew than the women in Gilat, but she too seemed to enjoy speaking Arabic. When I took Fortuna to visit her, they conversed in Arabic, although they could as well have communicated in Hebrew or in French. The older people in Gilat speak among themselves and with their family members in a mixture of Arabic, Hebrew, and French. Though switching is an unmarked code, speakers are aware that they are using different language systems (Myers-Scotton 1993; Siegel 1995, 95). This awareness becomes explicit when the speaker feels he or she is expected to be eloquent, such as during taped interviews,

(A) *nedwi qelma ida uqelma ida,*
(F) *ça ne fait rien?*
I'll say a word like this and a word like that,
it won't matter?

asked Fortuna during an interview in March 1988. Yet, despite the explicit concerns, code switching does not always indicate less than full linguistic competence (Woolard and Schieffelin 1994, 63). The awareness of mixing and the differential value attributed to each of the three languages allow speakers to use language shifts as contextualization cues, and to mark group boundaries (Gal 1988, 247, 260; Maschler 1994, 208; Walters 1996, 529; Walters 1999, 204).

My interviewees, regardless of age and education, are able to communicate orally in Hebrew in everyday use, but their reading skills are limited. Many women learned to read Hebrew in special classes at the *mo'adon;* they are able to read headlines in the newspaper or roughly follow subtitles on television. Most of the elderly people, particularly women, are less eloquent in Hebrew than in Arabic or French; their competence is thus hampered when performing complex texts, a situation common to emigrants in other communities as well. Their awareness sometimes becomes explicit, as when Odette, speaking to the students in my class, in substandard Hebrew, asked for the same tolerance children give their migrant parents: "I make mistakes in Hebrew, you forgive me, right? You are my children" [*ani ossa shgia be'ivrit, tislehu li, naxon? atem yeladim sheli*].[24] The actual use of languages and the patterns of language shifts in conversation, and particularly in narrative, indicate that in fact Arabic is much more valued than people admit. On the affective level, the languages carry different connotations, even though it is not possible to assign a single social interpretation to each case of code switching (Burt 1994, 556). French has high prestige among the elderly, separating the educated from the non-educated. Hebrew is more formal and is used for official business. Arabic is the language in which the older generation was raised, the language that best represents their traditional experiences, and the language of intimacy, used for eating and drinking together and for terms of endearment. Arabic in Gilat became a private code, replacing, to a certain extent, the functions of Hebrew in Tunisia as the in-group code (Bentolila 1994). Even young people whose primary language is Hebrew use Arabic expressions as a sign of solidarity or ethnic belonging—for insider jokes and ritual insults, as well as segments of prayers and chants in the synagogue (cf. Haviland 1979). This ideological framework—which implicitly appears in the use of language—endows the unmarked code of mixing with additional meaning in verbal performance: language shifts are potential nonreferential markers, particularly in narrative performance. Shifts enable narrators to add levels of meaning to their stories, to align themselves with specific characters and to distinguish between different levels of performance—reported speech and metanarrative comments, for example—through the choice of language (Schely-Newman 1998).

The different value of the languages is reaffirmed in Biya's summary of her school days, uttered in a trilingual mode (appendix 1, lines 55–56):

> (Arabic) *u-a kuwa, e-danya kula xrayef*
> And that's it, the world is all stories
> (Hebrew) *behayay,*
> by my life [truly]
> (French) *mais moi j'ai trop souffert*
> but I did suffer a lot

The common knowledge, the experience of tradition, is conveyed in Arabic, the language of the heart. Yet this assertion is reaffirmed with a solemn declaration in the holy language, making the statement valid even for the present. The personal angle, reaffirmed by the Hebrew vow, relates to a personal experience and is uttered in the prestigious French. These examples (and others in the following chapters) demonstrate the common use and distribution of languages in Gilat. As members of the same speech community, the speakers are aware of the differential value carried by the various languages and know which language better indexes the tone, era, or topic being discussed (Hymes 1972).

A Joint Venture

Personal narratives, like family stories, are told in intimate circumstances and do not require a special time or place. As personal narrative, the stories are assumed to be true; no challenge is posed, generally, as to their factuality, even though their "truth" may be questionable (Stahl 1989, 15). These stories are part of the female sphere of experience, shared by the women who keep the family tradition (Stone 1988, 18; Hall and Langellier 1988). Because they may not qualify as "stories" worth telling to outsiders, mundane childhood memories are frequently fragmented and not always well formulated, nor do they contain much in the way of new information; through repetition the events become common knowledge, leading to shared ownership (Blum-Kulka 1997, 122–23). Indeed, family stories are frequently told jointly, are referred to in the form of undeveloped kernel stories, and are even recited by members other than the person who experienced them (Kalčik [1975] 1986). Knowledgeable participants may interrupt each other in order to support, object to, or correct a story, and the resulting text is sometimes harmonious, sometimes contentious (Moerman 1988, 82; Ochs 1997, 200). Therefore, stories that emerge from conversations do not always proceed in a linear progression from beginning to end. In such cases narrative texts are meshed into their context and cannot be perceived as separate entities (Peterson and Langellier 1997, 136).

The pattern of support/interruption/intervention in a joint narration is demonstrated in two examples of stories about childhood. The first took place in Biya and Shimon's front yard on a summer night.[25] Several people were present: Biya; Shimon; Shimon's father, Ḥayim; Biya's brother Jacob; Rachel (a neighbor); and myself. The conversation was informal, and all participated, talking in the common mixture of languages—Arabic, French, and Hebrew. Biya, supported by Shimon, talked about having been a hard worker all her life, even while in school. Her story was told mainly in French, with switching to Hebrew and Arabic (see full text in appendix 1):

1. Biya (French): I was a very good student, a brilliant student at school. The teacher,

43

2. (Arabic): what did she do
3. (French): I was studying in school,
4. (A): and when I finished classes she would send me to her mother to clean for her.
5. (F) that teacher. Miss Sitbon
6. Shimon (French): There, in Fran—in Tunisia, whoever had money could be something.
7. Esther/Biya: Yes.
8. Shimon (F): Not here. If you're smart, even if you don't have money, they'll help you.
9. (F): But not there. Poor—
10. Biya [overlapping] (A): By God, if I had been in Israel, I would have turned out
    (H) something special.
11. Shimon (F): Because she was always first in her class
12. Biya (F): Always first in class.
13. (H) [solemnly swears]: By the truth of the Torah
14. Shimon (F): She was—
15. Biya (F): A very, very good student.

Shimon's support stresses Biya's potential and the opportunities she missed. Yet the text shows that the two narrators have different agendas: Biya stresses her abilities and the social gap between herself and the rich people she worked for, while Shimon emphasizes the institutional injustice. In Israel a person with Biya's potential would not have been "left behind" but would have been supported by the state to fulfill her potential and become *mashehu-mashehu* (something-something, Hebrew slang for "great").

Note how Biya's choice of language reinforces the distinction between narrative and metanarrative comments (lines 1,2,3). School experiences belong to the realm of modernity and intelligence, and are thus related in French. Yet when Biya talks about traditional roles and the lower status attached to such activities, she shifts to Arabic (line 4): "And when I finished classes she would send me to her mother to clean for her." The use of Hebrew in this segment of speech indexes two different levels meanings. It is the holy language used for solemn swearing: *be-emet atorah* (by the truth of the Torah, line 13) and the language of modern Israel, used in a slang expression to describe the unfulfilled potential.

The personal versus institutional attitudes taken by Biya and Shimon become clearer in the following segment from the same interaction (lines 35–43 in appendix 1) in which Biya talks about her relationship with her rich friend Denise. Shimon's participation is minimal and the story is related in a more monologic manner. Perhaps the subject is perceived as belonging to the domestic female sphere, or perhaps it is information to which only Biya has access (Blum-Kulka 1997, 123).

> Biya: She [Denise] prepares a slice of bread for me, because my mother [didn't] we were poor. So she fixes a slice of bread for me with a piece of chocolate, to go to school. And I would carry her bag and prepare her homework [laughter].
>
> And she [Denise] gets up in the morning saying—she sleeps in a very nice bed, she had a dresser, and her own room—and she says, "Mother . . ."
>
> Shimon interjects: And you, where were did you sleep in Moknine?
>
> Biya (in singsong): *ya diwani ʿaliya* (woe is me!)
>
> And she says, "Mommy, prepare me a dress. What will I put on today?" and I say to myself, "Damn her, look how many dresses she has, and she doesn't even give me one."
>
> Appendix 1, lines 35–43

The contrast between Biya and Denise involves not only the past school days. It is a story about social injustice finally made right by the present-day change of fortune (Ochs 1997, 182). Rich, spoiled, and lazy, Denise is now divorced and ekes out a meager living in the markets of Paris by selling doughnuts (*brik*), the same *brik* that Biya's father sold for a living in Sousse while struggling to support his family. Biya, on the other hand, is happily married to Shimon, the son of a restaurant owner, whom she "earned" by her adroitness and dexterity, as told in the story which immediately follows (see next chapter). Thus the conversation as a whole provided the audience not only with stories about childhood but with a social map of life in Tunisia and Israel.

Strategies of Contention

Shimon's intervention in his wife's story complimented Biya's personal abilities, adding background information. Joint narration, however, is not free of contention and may include various challenges, relating both to the narrated and to the narrative event, as well as to the entitlement of participants to the knowledge (Briggs 1988, 24; Shuman 1993b). The following text (appendix 2) demonstrates a joint competitive narration in which language is used as a means of challenging. I interviewed Noro, my father, about the history of the community, and my mother, Fortuna, constantly interjected comments.[26] While he related some of the practical jokes he played on his neighbors Thérèse and Albert, Fortuna lamented in Arabic,

1. Alas, alas, what he did to them!

Without responding, Noro continued with yet another event, speaking in Hebrew:

2. One day in Tunisia, when Thérèse was little, she fell into a well.

I was not familiar with this event, and asked in Hebrew,

3. Really?

Fortuna affirmed in Arabic,

4. She tells about it.

Noro reaffirmed in Hebrew,

5. Yes, she tells about it.

At this point I went to bring my notebook and the story continued in a polyphonic manner:

8. Fortuna (Arabic): A well, without water, in Sfax. An empty well.
9. (Hebrew) She was a year and a half,
    (Arabic) I think or
    (H) two years old.
10. (A) They say
    (H) she fell into a well.
11. Noro (H): Fell into a well.
12. Fortuna (A): They started looking for her, didn't find her.

46

13. Some Arab man found her—
14. Noro [overlap]: (H)—then they found an Arab who told them,
15. "You want me to take her out of the well—"
16. Fortuna [overlap]: (A)—said, "do you want
    (H) to take her out?"
17. Noro: (H) "Give me five francs."
18. Fortuna [corrects]: Duro, duro [rising tone].
19. Noro: Duro [old Tunisian currency].
20. Esther: (H) It's a lot of money.
21. Fortuna: Duro, (F) it's nice [the sound of the word].
22. Esther: (H) Was that a lot of money?
23. Noro: (H) At the time, yes.
24. Fortuna: (H) Yes.
25. Noro: (H) They had no choice; he took her out of—
26. [unclear comment]
27. (H) So when her father came—
28. Fortuna: (A) No, not like that.
29. (F) You don't know how to tell it.
30. The grandmother was with them.
31. (H) She said, "What's that? He asks for duro for such a—"
32. Esther: (H) girl?
33. Fortuna: (H) "Little, like this, we give a duro? That's too
    much."
34. (H) No. Her mother
    (A) said
35. (H) "Yes, yes, why, why, I want to bring her out, enough."
36. (H) When her father came
    (A) They told him,
    (H) What's a duro?
37. Esther: (H) Isn't it a waste of money?
38. Fortuna: (H) Yeah, a waste of money.
39. (F) The grandmother
    (A) told them.
40. Noro [turns to another subject]: (H) I used to do all sorts of
    nonsense.
41. Fortuna [continues the story]: (A) He told them
    (H) "Yes, yes, it's ok, take her out."
    [two-second pause]

47

42. Esther [addresses Noro, in Hebrew]: There were other things
    you did with them, with the melons?
    (Another story unfolds).

The story reaffirms the view that girls are of little value.[27] I had
never heard this particular story before, which may account for the
enthusiastic desire of both Noro and Fortuna to tell me the "real"
version. In addition to its content, the joint narration is typical of
family settings, but it also reveals types of interference that are more
contentious than in the previous example by Biya and Shimon.

Fortuna's confirmation of the veracity of events (line 4) is
used as entitlement for her to tell the story, in spite of the fact that
it was Noro who initiated it. Fortuna continues to interrupt and
challenge Noro's narration, expropriating the floor and uttering
the last word (line 41). Implicit challenges range from one speaker
ignoring the contribution of the other (line 14, 38), to actually
correcting the other's facts (lines 17–18). Ignoring a contribution
may be employed when outright disagreement is not acceptable: as
a rule, women do not challenge their husbands in public. During
the conversation presented earlier (appendix 1) several people were
present, including neighbors and Shimon's father. This may be the
reason why Biya did not openly challenge Shimon's intervention,
but rather continued to stress her personal story, simply ignoring
his input on the difference between Israel and Tunisia. The story
about Thérèse in the well was told by Noro and his wife Fortuna
to me, their daughter; in this family setting challenge by a wife may
be more acceptable.

Another mode of implicit competition for the floor is the
exploitation of the differential status of languages. Shifting from
Arabic to Hebrew in line 2 allowed Noro to open a new frame
and introduce another story. Similarly, in line 39 Noro attempted
to begin a new story by telling about something else ("I used to
do all sorts of nonsense"), a topical shift highlighted by a change
of language, from Arabic to Hebrew. The higher status of Hebrew,
however, does not give Noro any advantage in this case, as Fortuna disregards his comments and continues to narrate. The use of
language shift as a challenging mechanism appears again in lines
27–29: Noro's Hebrew statement "When her father came . . ."
is challenged both in regard to content—"No, not like that," in

Arabic, and to form—*tu [ne] sais pas raconter toi* (line 29: you don't know how to tell, you), in French, a language with a higher status than Arabic. Both Fortuna and Noro affirm that Thérèse herself told the story about falling in the well, but while Fortuna uses Arabic (line 4), Noro repeats it in Hebrew (line 5). For the most part, the narration is maintained in two parallel languages: Noro talks in Hebrew and Fortuna in Arabic. Yet, perhaps because the narrators are husband and wife, language shifts are less effective in gaining the floor than in other circumstances.

What If She Can Tell Her Story?

Women tell relatively few stories about their childhood. These stories are usually shared within the family circle, creating a family "small tradition" which women keep. Though the content reinforces the low value of childhood in women's lives, a point clearly made in the story about Thérèse's fall into the well, the topics women do talk about are significant in that they underscore the process of acquiring a voice of their own.

These stories juxtapose tradition and modernity: one theme leads to the "natural" female role while the other points to the potential of "culture." To become a traditional woman is the choice of the mothers and other elderly women who help the girls move from childhood to womanhood, "as smoothly as oil." However, education opens another venue: literacy provided the girls with a third option, one beyond "man" or "grave." The women chose, or were forced to choose, the traditional route. Though school days stories are, in fact, failure stories—none of the women realized her scholastic potential—they are nevertheless repeated over and over again, more frequently and more voluntarily than those about the onset of menarche. Repeating the stories to their daughters is perhaps an implicit suggestion to explore this route and not immediately fall into the grave/man schema. The prestige brought to the family by education, be it a father (Odette) or the husband (Biya), is a proof of the value of this particular route.

CHAPTER 2

Marriage

To raise your spirit, remember your wedding night
illi yeḥab yezahi nafshu, yetfakar lilet ʿarshu

The elderly Tunisian women I studied believe that a girl needs one
thing in her life—*shaʿad* (luck) or *maktub* (what is written, fate)—
in other words, a husband. A man, however, needs seven kinds of
luck in his life, only one of which is a good wife. Tunisian folktales,
Jewish and Muslim alike, support this attitude by telling stories
about poor girls who are chaste and good, and who, while they
may suffer, are finally rewarded by finding their *shaʿad,* marrying
well and living happily ever after. The importance of a woman's luck
is evident in the saying *edʿei əl bintak beshaʿad u-rmiha fəl bir* (wish
your daughter luck, and throw her into a well), almost replicated
in the story about Thérèse falling into a well.

These women know that in Israel young women are not confined to the private sphere as they were in Tunisia, and that their
daughters and granddaughters may meet prospective husbands in
the course of everyday activities. Nevertheless, they continue to
tell the traditional stories and to use proverbs that reinforce the
importance of *maktub* and *shaʿad*. Moreover, they tell stories about
their own lives that exemplify and stress the central role of marriage
in their culture. These stories become a resource for their sense of
self as culturally defined—mature married women (Linde 1993,
119; Rosenwald and Ochberg 1992, 1). Since maturity and social
self are achieved only through marriage, it is not surprising that

51

stories about courting and marriage are part of a woman's everyday discourse. Women compare the way weddings were celebrated in Tunisia with the present, but more frequently they talk about the importance of finding the right match, the one prescribed (*maktub*) for them. These women have been married for forty years or more, mostly to men chosen by their families. They are aware of the conflict between the idea of romantic love and personal choice of their daughters and the norms and decisions of their own youth. In their wedding stories, told so many years later, they trace their lives as lived, reconciling them with the lives they perhaps would have chosen. The choice of themes and organization of the narratives demonstrate how narrators position themselves to create a coherent life story within changing cultural norms and personal ambivalence (Bamberg 1997, 336; Gergen and Gergen 1988; Rosenthal 1993; van Langenhove and Harre 1993).

This chapter begins with a description of weddings and the norms of marriage in the middle of the twentieth century among Tunisian Jews. This is followed by an analysis of the wedding stories of Biya and Odette, bringing to the fore the tension between traditional norms and romantic love. Finally, the chapter examines narrative events themselves as setting social boundaries and as mode of socialization.

Judeo-Tunisian Weddings

Marriage is the most significant event in the life of women in the Judeo-Muslim cultural world; unmarried women are socially invisible (Delaney 1987; Zamiti-Horchani 1986, 111). It is to be expected that stories about marriage, as the only significant (and public) rite of passage women experience, be told with a profusion of details (Valensi 1989, 66). Special attention is paid to the circumstances of the marriages—the suitors, financial arrangements, courting, and various ceremonies. As the proverb goes, *illi yehab yezahi nafshu, yetfakar lilet ʿarshu* (those who want to raise their spirits should remember their wedding night).

Though weddings are a favorite topic of conversation, women do not give full accounts of the many rituals involved unless asked to do so. They may mention some of the ceremonies performed during their own wedding in Tunisia (*ḥenna, shabbat lᵊ bnat,* or *qussan el ḥuta* [see following]), mainly in comparison to the paucity of rituals in Israel, but these do not seem to be a central aspect of the marriage. The issue they enthusiastically turn to, at any opportunity, is how and why they married their spouse. I recently asked Raymonde, born in Tunis in 1944, if her father paid a cash dowry when she married in Tunis (see following). She answered with a story about her two suitors, the one who asked for a dowry and was rejected, and the other, whom she married.[1] The important aspect of weddings thus seems to be the course of events leading to a particular husband, and thus shaping the woman's life, rather than the variety of rituals per se.

The following description of the Jewish wedding cycle in Tunisia is based both on written sources and on data provided in conversations with Tunisian women. Wedding ceremonies derive from different sources, many of them similar to local Muslim traditions, with an added Jewish meaning (Goldberg 1990; Valensi 1989). For example, the beautification of the bride includes feeding her, removing her body hair, and painting her with *henna,* all of which are practiced among Jews and Muslims in the Middle East. The Jerban Jewish beautification ceremony, however, has an additional element: the mother-in-law tears a sleeve from the bride's gown. This is explained as an act of commemorating and mourning the destruction of the Temple in Jerusalem (Valensi 1989, 76).[2] Geographical variations are particularly apparent in the ethnographic descriptions of weddings on the island of Jerba in the late 1970s (Valensi 1989) and in the city of Tunis in the mid-1950s (Cohen 1964). In Jerba, most ceremonies were conducted separately for the men and for the women, and the bride and groom did not see each other until the official religious blessing had taken place under the *ḥuppa* (bridal canopy). In Tunis, on the other hand, the period between engagement and wedding was a time when the betrothed couple could be doing *amuri* (courting, from the French *amour*). The wedding took place when the agreed upon goods and money could be accumulated. Geography also influenced the code of dress: in Jerba and Gabes (southern Tunisia) brides wore traditional garments, while in the larger towns the European white wedding gown was adopted.

The religious marriage ceremony, the *ḥuppa,* was but one of the events in the wedding cycle, which began a week before and

Marriage of Fortuna and Noro, Sfax, March 1941

ended seven days after the couple had been married. Most rituals prior to the wedding took place in the bride's home, and included feeding the bride, painting her with *henna,* removing her body hair, and bathing and dressing her. The mother-in-law played a central role during this stage of preparation, literally "molding" the bride into her new status (Valensi 1989, 75). Because no contact between the groom and bride was allowed, the mother-in-law served as her son's proxy, supervising the correctness of ceremonies (Sered, Kaplan, and Cooper 1999; Wasserfall 1999a). In these female-only rites the groom's role was not significant; mostly he was absent, or, as in Libya, he was a member of the male crowd watching some events as a spectator (Goldberg 1990, 63). In "modern" weddings in the larger northern cities the *henna* ceremony evolved into a party in which the groom shared the seat of honor with the bride, although decoration with *henna* was applied mainly to the bride.[3]

Festivities began eight days before the religious ceremony, with the evening of *otiyya,* the groom sending a basket with *henna* and presents including jewelry and traditional garments.[4] The *otiyya* was seen as binding; once the basket of *henna* was sent to the bride, the match was final. One of the signs of recognition of the importance of the *otiyya* was the inclusion of shoes in the basket. The women explained that sending shoes before the *otiyya* brought bad luck and would cause the match to be annulled.[5]

The Saturday preceding the religious ceremony was dedicated to the bride in two separate customs that gave the day special names. It was called *shabbat ə-dzaza* (the Sabbath of the chicken) because the bride's family prepared a stuffed chicken which was shared among all the relatives, the wings given to unmarried women to facilitate their "flying away" from their fathers' houses.[6] Young men frequently tried to steal the chicken, and the ensuing chase was another joyous occasion (Cohen 1964, 43). The second ceremony, *shabbat lə-bnat* (maiden's Sabbath), took place during the same afternoon. The bride's girlfriends and female relatives gathered in the house to keep her company on her last Shabbat in her parents' home. The songs sang on this occasion emphasized the sadness of separation from the mother and praised love and the qualities of the groom and bride; sexual innuendoes and irreverent talk about men were also common.[7] Frequently, this was also an occasion for displaying the bride's dowry.

An eleven-year-old girl dressed in Jerban marriage garb, Israel
1965. *Courtesy of Government Press Office.*

The most opulent prewedding ceremony was the "big *henna*," celebrated two or three days before the religious ceremony. *Henna,* a green herbal powder that turns into a red dye when mixed with liquid, is associated with celebrations, particularly weddings. *Henna* is believed to have power to ward against the evil eye, according to the women, but the red color of the paste may also symbolize blood. Furthermore, the changes in the color and consistency offer another level of symbolic interpretation—that of transformation of the bride from girl to woman (Wasserfall 1999a, 194).[8] *Henna* is applied on parts of the bride's body, particularly the hands (frequently the only visible part of the bride's body), sometimes in elaborate decorations that require the help of a specialist and may take long hours to perform (Valensi 1989, 78). For North African Jews this ceremony became one of the most important prenuptial events, ranging from being highly ritualistic, as in Jerba and Libya, to being a festive meal for family and friends, accompanied by music. The opulence of this and other ceremonies depended on the economic situations of the families.

A religiously important ritual preceding the *huppa* is the bride's immersion in the ritual bath, the *mikvah.* Jewish conjugal life is guided by the rules of *niddah*—time of physical separation for a couple—determined by the woman's menstruation. The state of *niddah* ends when the woman immerses herself in the *mikvah.* The rules of "family purity" stated in religious literature are relevant only to married women, and the bride is introduced to them by her first ritual immersion prior to consummating the marriage.[9] As noted by Wasserfall (1992, 1999a), menstruation transforms a girl into a woman, but the rules of the *mikvah* make her a Jewish woman. Unlike the regular visits of married women to the *mikvah,* which are done almost clandestinely (see following chapter), the bride was escorted there by female relatives, and a celebration, sometimes accompanied by music, would take place in the *mikvah* itself. The transformation of the young woman to a "bride"—decorating, depilating and bathing her—was done under the supervision of the groom's mother, who could inspect her daughter-in-law physically and test her conformity with tradition (see Sered, Kaplan, and Cooper 1999; Wasserfall 1999a).[10]

Succeeding these premarital rituals, the *huppa,* the religious marriage ceremony under the canopy, and the breaking of a glass vessel took place, followed by a meal. At this point, when all rituals had been performed and the man and woman were recognized as a couple, conjugation could take place. The stained sheet, proof of the bride's virginity, was not always displayed; it was nevertheless kept by the bride's mother as evidence of her daughter's honor. If the groom or both were French citizens, a civil ceremony was also required to ensure legal status for the wife and future children; this was carried out at the city hall, without festivities or guests.

The week following the marriage was a time for quieter celebrations, a time set off from work and other worldly concerns. On the Shabbat following the *huppa, shabbat sheba' braxot* (the Sabbath of seven blessings) was celebrated in the synagogue; an additional Torah scroll was read from in honor of the groom, and the biblical portion recounting Abraham's search for a bride for his son Isaac was read (Genesis chapter 24). Refreshments were offered in the synagogue and a festive meal was served in the groom's parents' house; the seven blessings recited under the *huppa* were also repeated.[11] According to Jewish law, sexual relations are suspended for seven days after defloration, due to coital bleeding. Following the period of abstinence, the bride would again immerse herself in the ritual bath, *mikvah,* this time without a bridal party, in order to be able to resume sexual relations. The final ceremony of the cycle occurred on the seventh day, in *qussan el huta* (cutting the fish). Here, the couple was given a large fish and knives to cut it, each from a different end, symbolic of "testing" to determine who would be master of the house. It was customary to give the husband a dull knife, and sometimes a piece of wood was inserted into the fish on the groom's side: the ritualistic reversal of roles was a source of great delight for the family and friends (Cohen 1964, 44–45). The fish was fried and served to all present, and the fishtail was cut, dried, and hung in the couple's residence as an amulet against the evil eye. With this event the couple returned to their daily routines.

During the entire marriage cycle the bride was passive; things were done to her and for her, and she was led from one place to the other without much time to reflect. In hindsight, Raymonde offers an emic explanation for this constant occupation: she says that young girls were not prepared for or aware of what marriage entailed; they were anxious and apprehensive, and festivities helped them through the crucial stages into the routine of conjugal life.

From an etic point of view, the entire cycle is an elaborate rite of passage, leading the bride (and groom) from one role and stage into the next. At the liminal stage, betwixt and between, during these two weeks, the bride and groom needed to be watched and were never left alone because they were susceptible to great danger. The dangers were perceived as resulting from the envy of others, be it humans who might cast an evil eye on them or other creatures, mainly the *jnoun,* residing in an alternate world and behaving in a similar way to humans. The liminal state of the bride begins at the moment she is officially a bride—when the basket of *ḥenna* is sent to her—and ends when she goes to the ritual bath for the second time, seven days after consummation of the marriage.

The two weeks of wedding cycle are a liminal period for the couple, but the danger—to the bride herself and emitted from her— is particularly grave during the time following her premarital ritual immersion. Married women immerse in the *mikvah* in the evening, and the couple is expected to have intercourse that same night (see following chapter), but in the case of a bride, there is an entire day separating immersion and intercourse. The bride is ritually cleansed and available for intercourse but additional ceremonies need to be completed before actualization (Wasserfall 1999a, 192). She is not yet a wife, but she has already been introduced to the Jewish wives' status by the ritual immersion and the sacred blessing. At this point she is a sacred object, waiting to be "used" for a religious commandment. She is like a Torah scroll, say some women in Gilat. Failure to complete the process—that is, not performing the marriage—is sacrilegious because the immersion and blessing have been in vain. Such an act may have grave repercussions, as the following story shows. A couple from Gilat was about to be married (in 1955), and the bride had already immersed herself in the *mikvah,* but the groom changed his mind and abandoned her. The rabbi predicted that misfortune would come to the community as a result of the sacrilegious act and, indeed, that same night a man from the community opened fire on two sentries whom he mistakenly took for Arab border crossers.[12] Perhaps because marriage is not an individual affair but involves the entire community, the punishment was not individual. The victims of the shooting were not related to the couple, but nevertheless were part of the community that witnessed (perhaps allowed) such sacrilegious behavior.

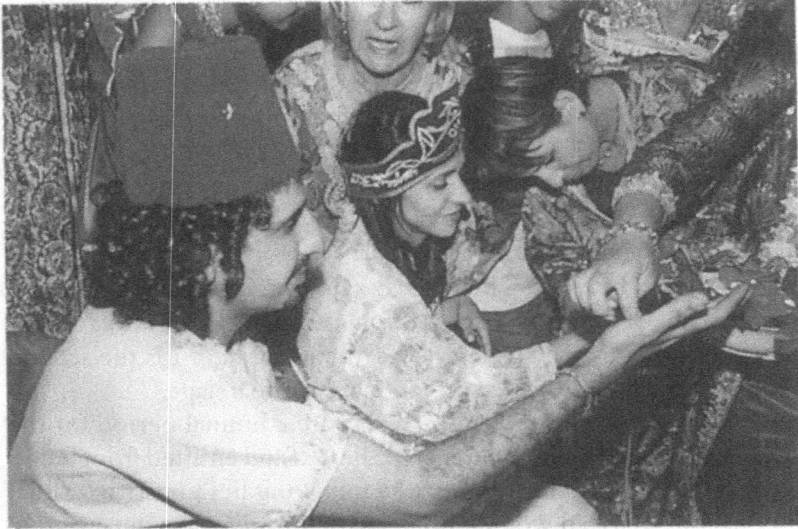

Female relatives apply *ḥenna* paste on Tsili and Moshe's hands, Jerusalem, June 1999. Traditional Tunisian outfits were brought from France by one of Tsili's relatives.

The number of festive rituals in weddings has been greatly reduced in Israel: only the religious blessing (*ḥuppa*) is regularly celebrated. The rabbinical authorities require the ritual immersion, and the bride is asked to provide a formal notification from the *mikvah* attendant. However, rituals continue to exist and are even gaining popularity. The *ḥenna,* for example, is an opportunity to celebrate one's ethnicity, an occasion to display traditional garb and serve a traditional feast. The Israeli *ḥenna* of the 1990s is a prenuptial party for families and friends, for men and women alike.[13] The couple may hire a professional team specializing in producing such events and providing traditional food and garb according to the customs of the group, whether Yemenite, Moroccan, or Tunisian. The tradition followed is that of the bride's ethnic group, and is only celebrated if *ḥenna* is part of her tradition.

Other rituals also continue to exist, though with less popularity than the *ḥenna*. The beautification has been replaced by a

Ronit and Dani wearing traditional Moroccan dress at their *ḥenna* celebration, Jerusalem, March 1989. Dani's parents are European Jews (Ashkenazim); Ronit's mother was born in Tunisia and her father in Morocco.

lengthy visit to a professional beauty salon, in which not only the bride but her female relatives as well are treated. In communities with a large population of Tunisians (for example, Gilat), *shabbat lᵊ bnat* (girls' Shabbat) is observed. It is an occasion for women to gather together, sing Judeo-Arabic love songs, tell risqué jokes, and eat the traditional stuffed chicken. Men are not excluded, but neither are they encouraged to participate. Even the visit to the *mikvah*, seen by many young (and secular) women as infringing on their privacy, is still being celebrated among some North African groups. This event is changing—the number of women participating in the *mikvah* party has been reduced to immediate relatives and friends, and the bride is not exhibited nude in front of the entire group—however, the mother-in-law sometimes insists on her right, and duty, to supervise the bride's fulfillment of the required *mitzvah* (Sered, Kaplan, and Cooper 1999).

Finding One's Luck

Marriage, with all its luxuriant festivities, was the dream of every girl; *sha'ad* and *maktub* are referred to constantly in women's discourse about Tunisia. In reality, a girl and her family needed more than luck to be able to marry. The emphasis on chastity resulted in early marriages; Ghaliya's marriage to a cousin at the age of fourteen was not exceptional, although other women married in their twenties. According to a Moroccan woman, it was considered shameful to marry off a girl after she had begun to menstruate.[14] Odette, on the other hand, said menstruation was a prerequisite for marriage, a proof of the woman's childbearing ability; her own marriage was delayed for three years for that reason. Odette's mother explained that since the groom did not have a mother to inquire for him, she felt responsible for ensuring that her daughter was capable of being a mother.[15] Even rumors of unchaste behavior could ruin a woman's chances of marrying a desirable man. In Gilat in the mid-1950s a young woman was married off to a non-Tunisian man from a neighboring community; no Tunisian would marry her because of her unsavory reputation.[16] A recent story tells of a rich family giving the aggrieved groom an apartment as compensation for his bride's prior loss of her virginity.[17] Another story indicates the peril of unchaste behavior in a more traditional setting, Yemen in the 1940s: "A rich Muslim married off his daughter to a man in another village. When the groom's family learned that she was not a virgin, they sent her father the traditional gourd filled with honey, but made a hole in its bottom. The father, who understood the message, waited for his daughter's visit a year later and killed her. The husband's protests and love for his wife were of no avail."[18]

The audience of Yemenite, Moroccan, and Algerian women disapproved of this extreme response, particularly since the husband had been happy with his wife, but they understood the father's insistence on protecting his family's reputation and honor. Telling me for the second time about her father not letting her leave home to study in France, Odette expanded the conversation that took place between her father and the French principal (see chapter 1, p. 35). In this more recent version, her father threatened to shoot his daughter if she did not do honor to him on her wedding night. The importance of chastity and virginity in the Judeo-Arab tradition is given as the reason for his not letting Odette out of his sight.[19]

While female chastity was de rigueur in all Judeo-Muslim societies, Tunisian Jewish families had another concern: the dowry. It was rare for a woman to be married "with only her shirt on" to a young bachelor. Stories about agreements broken off because the bride's family could not provide the promised dowry, and about last-minute rescues are common.[20] Wealthy men married poor girls for their exceptional beauty and youth or because of their own misconduct. My father's grandmother was an orphan who, dressed in men's clothing, would meet a certain man in a café. When word reached the chief rabbi, he sentenced the man to prison for taking advantage of the poor girl. He was released only when he sent her the *henna* basket for the *ottiya,* a binding act before the marriage.

During the twentieth century the bride's family in Tunisia was required to pay a sum of money, called a *dotta,* as dowry. The need for cash and the increase in the amounts demanded made it more difficult for poor families: "Even the worst of young men will not marry the daughter of the *grand rabbin* without a dowry" (Cohen 1964, 39). "Marrying up" in status became almost impossible, and poor girls had to settle for widowers with children, disabled men, or a position as a second wife. In the words of Cohen's informant (1964, 39), "only a woodcutter with torn pants is left for a person without a fortune." Or, as Odette (married in 1943) explains, "Now what do we do? The parents spent money, sent him to France to be a doctor, so when he returns he must marry [someone] with a big *dotta* to repay the expenses. It was customary for a bride to pay millions at that time."[21] The increasing use of money as a dowry is probably a result of changes in living conditions and occupations requiring the use of cash. The dowry was given to the groom, not to his family, an indication of weakening kin ties (Glazer 1981, 299). Daughters traditionally did not inherit; however, they received a share of the family wealth upon marriage. Sons received *dotta* when they married but had to pay in turn when they married off their own daughters (Glazer 1981, 308). The custom of paying *dotta* continued in Tunisia well into the 1960s, according to Raymonde, whose father refused "to give a prize for getting rid of her." Instead, she married in 1963 a man she herself met and liked, without a *dotta.*

The stories of my informants' marriages all stress the need for money. Even Raymonde mentioned the expenses her father incurred in furnishing the new couple's home, despite the lack of a financial agreement. Each woman has her own story about how she came to marry her particular husband, in the face of slim chances. My parents' marriage is an example of *maktub*, fate in action. In 1940 Kuka was telling her family about the match she was arranging for a relative, Fortuna, whose family had agreed to pay fifteen thousand francs for her to marry a young man, a friend of the family. Noro, who was just out of the army, asked why this match had not been offered to him, and Kuka immediately rearranged the affair, asking twenty thousand francs. The financial negotiations were brief and the wedding took place soon after.

Others drove harder bargains. Mamush, returning from the "Great War" needed money to open a metalsmith shop; the *dotta* he asked for was three hundred thousand francs. Yvonne, a good-looking seamstress from a poor family, was not deterred by the large cost and worked days and nights to collect the amount. She was a fine and fast worker and had a good reputation among the "bad women" who commissioned special outfits from her. Yvonne's mother kept her company, serving her strong tea in order to keep her awake and working. Mamush and Yvonne were happily married for over forty years.

Getting Married

Stories about getting married allow women to reconcile differences between social norms and personal preferences. They help women explain (to themselves as well as to others) their current situation within the larger tradition (Rosenwald and Ochberg 1992, 2). The stories of Biya and Odette, told as parts of conversations about their lives, allow for an examination of the way stories are structured and create a coherent perception of self.

BIYA: "I WAS NOT SUPPOSED TO MARRY HIM"

Biya's story about her marriage to Shimon was not new to me—it is part of her repertoire. Following Biya's story about her school-days, described in the previous chapter, Shimon talked about his worry-free youth; and his father told about some mischievous event, at which point I commented, in Arabic: "And then you married Biya?" Biya answered for him: "No, the story of my wedding, I was not supposed to marry him."[22] Biya explained that Shimon had typhoid fever and needed special treatment. Ḥayim mentioned the problem to a niece, and at her suggestion her sister Biya quit her factory job in order to take care of Shimon.[23] Once Shimon got better he immediately ate fried ribs, which caused a relapse. This is when destiny intervened, as can be seen from the text (full text appears in appendix 3).

1. Biya: It was like in the stories
2. When I heard about it [the relapse] I came running
3. Because I was in love with him
4. Esther: That is why he was ill again? He missed you?
5. Biya: No, he did not love me
6. He loved me as a cousin, but it was not love
7. But for me it was the other way around.

Biya, Shimon, and Ḥayim repeat how the word got to Biya about the relapse, since there were no telephones. Biya went back to Moknine to take care of Shimon, and this time he fully recovered. Many people came to visit Shimon during this time, among them Ḥayim's sister, Biya's aunt.

37. She told Ḥayim, "So, what present are you going to give my niece?"
38. She is the one who struggled on my behalf,
39. God helping from above and she down below.
40. She loved [him, Ḥayim] and he too loved her very much
41. My uncle [Ḥayim] told her, "All the stores are waiting for her.
42. She can go into any one and get what she wants."
43. She told him, "No, she does not need things.
44. She has the whole world.
45. My niece needs nothing.
46. Her trousseau is ready.
47. She fought for him; he will take [marry] her."
48. Like that.
    [Biya laughs, and adds in French]

49. I was glad. [pause]
50. He did not want to,
51. but he was embarrassed, so he said nothing.

Overlapping remarks by Ḥayim, who begins another story, but Biya continues:

65. Biya: Yes, the world is but stories, Rachel, I swear to you
66. And when he kissed me for the first time, oh, oh [laughter]
67. But he—no. He did not love me
68. Rachel: How long was it before you got married?
69. Biya: I did not want [to get married] we stayed [engaged] at least a year, a year and a half
70. I didn't want to.
71. I said maybe he was mocking me?
72. Maybe I would remain like this?
73. Until finally . . .
74. Shimon [comments in French]: It is destiny.

ODETTE: "FORGET ABOUT LOVE"

Odette's life story was told in the course of two taped interviews conducted in Hebrew at her home, with my assistant present.[24] Odette said she met her husband, Gabriel, when he arrived from Tripoli and opened a shoe store in her neighborhood: "He was good-looking and elegant. He loved someone else, a neighbor of his brother. His brother objected, told him, 'This family is not for you. If you are looking for marriage there is no one better than Leon's daughter, Odette. She is educated and quiet. There is no one like her in the neighborhood.'" Odette, however, did not continue to talk about Gabriel in this segment of the narrative. Instead, she told about her achievements in school (see previous chapter), about being very sick, and about the doctor who treated her:

> He was good-looking. From a great family, very rich. He was treating poor people and made house calls. At the time his brother died of typhoid, you know what it is. He was devastated, the poor man. So he came. My mother cried. My father was the doctor's tailor, so he liked him. He said to him, "This is my only daughter, Odette. Do you know what grades she has? Look at her! Can she recover from this?" And he [the doctor] said to him, "I just lost my brother,

less than a month ago. I will do whatever possible to save her. Everything." He [the doctor] fought for me, fought, until, with the grace
of God, I stood on my feet. Then he asked me, "What do you want
to do? You are finished with school. Your father doesn't agree to
send you abroad [to study in France]." I told him, "I'd love to be
a nurse." So he said, "Fine, just be well. Here is my address. You'll
come to me, and I'll teach you how to be a nurse." I went. It was
far, he had a house in the center of Tunis. What a house, a dream.
I went to him. Registering patients, receiving phone calls. I was so
impressed by the house; I would go down to shine the [doctor's]
shingle.

Odette continued to talk about the doctor, her work with him,
and how she learned and helped. She spoke about her father's objection to her work and about the doctor's marriage. She ended
this segment, which lasted about twenty minutes, by telling how
her father forced her to quit her work at the doctor's and how she
started working in a factory. Only at this point did she resume the
story of her marriage. "Look, it is a question of my honor. From
a nurse to go work in a factory? I was angry. I worked and earned
twice as much then [short pause]. Well, my husband had a shoe
store in front of our alley. His brother told him, 'That girl you had
your eyes on, she has no father. They are not genteel.' "

Gabriel's brother convinced him to pay attention to Odette:
Gabriel would send his servant to help her carry water from the
well. Odette knew him from the neighborhood, and also received a
magic sign that he was her intended spouse. Dreams play an important role in Odette's life (see also chapter 4), and therefore it is not
surprising that dreams also were a factor in her wedding. Like other
young girls, Odette admitted, she was curious about her "fate," so
she performed an act of divination all her friends used to do: she
put a pin under her pillow and chanted: *xlal ya xlal warini maktubi fəl
mnam* (pin, oh pin, show me my fate in a dream). In Judeo-Arabic
the word *"xlal"* is used to designate both a pin (straight or safety)
and a brooch women used for decoration and for fastening the
traditional garment (a colorful sheet of material wrapped around
the body and attached by the *xlal* to the woman's blouse). The *xlal*
thus may represent both male and female symbols: its pricking point
is phallic, but women use it for work or decoration. Furthermore,
the *xlal* connects; it brings together different things and holds them

together, a symbol for the act of marriage itself as merging different entities into one new unit.

In her dream Odette saw a man offering her a cup to drink from and saying *mazal tov* (good luck, Hebrew blessing in festive occasions). The following day was the wedding of Odette's aunt, and during the ceremony Gabriel offered Odette a drink from the cup of wine blessed during the nuptial ceremony. For Odette this was a clear indication of her fate: "and I said to myself, 'Alas, this one is going to be my husband.' He was good-looking, he was rich, but I didn't love him. I was working with a doctor, good-looking, green eyes, a dimple here, such a smile, and such a good heart. I was surrounded by doctors. He did not talk about me [to strangers?], and I loved. But, in short, if not for the money, he would have married only me. If he had not had to repay his parents." Odette talked about Gabriel's attempts to woo her, by giving her many presents and buying things for her. She continued,

> But I swear to you, three months I cried after he asked to marry me. He brought me a suit, took me to the hairdresser, made me shoes and suits. What would I tell you, Sandriella. From being so poor that I had to wear my aunt's dress, alter it, and shoes too large for me . . . I never found a story like mine in all the books I read. Nowhere could I find such a story.
>
> That's how I was. He made a Sandriella of me. I cried for three months. My father asked me, "Why are you crying?" I said, "I don't love him." He took me out to movies, not one but three a day. We'd walk by a store, I'd look, I never went to the main street, who'd take me there? We'd pass near a window, dresses. I'd look, just look. He'd take me inside, say, "Which one did you like?"

Odette further elaborated on how Gabriel did things for her but repeated her objection:

> I did not ask for anything because I did not love him. Three months I cried. Father came in with a knife, saying, "I'll be done with you." He said, "I am poor. You are educated, you are good-looking, you are gentle, and people love your steps in the street. But I am poor. If not [him] . . . no one, you'll remain like your two aunts, an old maid. All your beauty will not bring you a husband. All your education will not bring a husband. This one wants you, he is good-looking, he has plenty of money, gives you whatever you wish for. Everything—forget about love."

Odette married Gabriel and lived in great comfort. The fact that he was not her first choice is evident from her explicit statements about her lack of love, and even more from her selection of the events in her narrative (Rosenthal 1993, 69–70). The marriage story was told only in the second interview I conducted with her, of which twenty minutes were devoted to her work with the doctor. The rest of the time, she spoke of Gabriel, of her children, again about the doctor, and finally about her life in Israel.

Another absentee is Odette's mother, who is not mentioned even once in the marriage story. Though it is the father's role to give his daughter in marriage, the absence of Odette's mother is of special interest. In Fortuna's story, for example, she tells in detail how Hanna was involved in every step of the way, convincing her husband to pay the increased amount of *dotta,* and guiding Fortuna through the rituals. While in Biya's story both parents are absent, her maternal aunt responds to her plight and convinces Hayim to give his son Shimon to Biya. Yet Odette's mother is nowhere to be found. Only on another occasion, when Odette told me about her onset of menarche, did she mention her mother in relation to the marriage. Even then, when the mother was mentioned she was not acting on behalf of Odette, but rather feeling responsible for the future son-in-law, Gabriel, protecting his interest in absence of his own mother, by making sure the bride was in fact ready to be wed. The mother reappears in Odette's life story in the migration segment, at the end of the second interview. It is interesting to note that even though Odette's father represents the traditional position ("forget about love"), she continues to see him (and other males) as her role models. This is consistent with her position as the self-reliant decision maker she becomes in her migration story (see chapter 4).

Fighting or Accepting?

Given that our relationships are lived out in narrative form (Gergen and Gergen 1988, 18), these stories reveal a great deal, not only about ways of finding a spouse in Tunisia but also about the self-perceptions of the narrators and the significance of spouses in women's lives. The stories express the concerns and anguish of young women who needed to resolve conflicts between their feelings and cultural norms both at the time the events took place and at the time of narration (Linde 1993, 121). For them, as for other women of their age group, marriage was the norm and choices of spouses were made by the families in accordance with cultural norms, particularly social status. Women may have objected to an offer or even initiated a match, but the final decision was based more on financial agreements drawn up by the fathers than on personal choice. [25]

Biya and Odette grew up in poor families who could not afford to pay the required *dotta* for a desired match; their choices of a spouse were limited. They had to fight—a verb that appears repeatedly in their narratives—for their choices. Both stories are about struggle with life and death and love, but they differ in the "master narrative" chosen, in the type of narrative and in the outcome.

Biya's story follows the "persecuted heroine" model, the tale of a woman who suffers for no reason, or is falsely accused, and who must overcome obstacles until her innocence is proven and she marries or is reunited with her true spouse. The theme of suffering is central in her childhood story, summarized in French, *moi j'ai trop souffert* ("I did suffer a lot," appendix 1, line 56). The difficult life she lived in fact forged her character and made her able to face death itself. Biya's life imitates tales; her story follows the model set by folktales of the woman saving her husband or lover from death by her devotion (e.g., "Beauty and the Beast"). Saving Shimon gave her entitlement to his life; he became her reward. Cultural constraints, however, prevented her from claiming her trophy, and she needed a proxy (her aunt) to speak for her, to declare to Shimon's father: *hiyya ʿarket ʿali, huwa yaxudha* (Arabic, "She fought for him, he will marry her," appendix 3, line 47). The legitimation for Biya's claim to Shimon comes from tradition (the aunt) and from the universal order, God almighty himself: *hiyya ʿarket ʿaliya. rabbi mən fok wa hiyya məluta* (also in Arabic, "She is the one who struggled on my behalf, God helping from above and she down below," lines 38–39). Yet saving Shimon's life was just one part of her battle. She needed to win his heart as well, a common setback in romantic stories. It took almost a year and a half for Shimon to accept what was written (*maktub*) and admit (line 74): *ç'est le destin* (French: it is destiny).

Note the choice of language: Biya reports in Arabic the conversations between her aunt and Ḥayim, and her struggle over Shimon's body—a traditional theme in tales, which is consistent with women's role as caretakers. Yet the feelings she develops toward Shimon, and her struggle to win his love—the romantic entanglement of the story—is reported in French, the appropriate modern language, capable of speaking about love (cf. Djebar 1993). Her summary about suffering, also in French, may give the experience a general validity; her suffering was both in terms of traditional experiences, her having to fight for a husband, and "modern" values, her going to school and having to work for wages in a factory.

Biya's narrative is of a progressive type, ending with an implied stability-narrative (Gergen and Gergen 1988, 26). We, the audience, know that Biya and Shimon have been happily married for over thirty-five years. The fact that their lives in Israel have not been easy ones is not even mentioned in this conversation. For Biya, marrying Shimon was a peak in her life story, at least as told on this specific occasion: the poor suffering girl saved her lover from death, and they lived happily ever after.

If marriage is the happy ending for Biya's story, it is the beginning of a new and different life for Odette. As smart, beautiful, and generous as Odette was, she was unable to marry the man of her (day)dreams; instead she was destined to marry another man, whom she saw in a (night)dream. While Biya fought to win Shimon's body and heart, two men fight in Odette's tale: the doctor for her body, and Gabriel for her heart. Ironically, while the doctor fought for her body, in doing so he won her heart, and while Gabriel fought for her heart, he succeeded only in winning her body—he dressed her in modern outfits, took her to the hairdresser, and, in short, remade her. Odette blames cultural norms and demands for not allowing her to marry the doctor: "If it was not for the money, he would have married only me. If he had not had to repay his parents." Odette nevertheless sees Gabriel as a prince in a Cinderella story, and is grateful, "The man I married, I fell in good hands. Everything was fine for me."

Yet the explicit claim of a happy ending is not consistent with the story as told. The selection and sequence of events in Odette's story suggest that the role marriage plays in her perception of self is less central than it is the in the lives of Biya, Fortuna, and other women (Rosenthal 1993, 69–70). Marriage is required of the traditional woman, but Odette may perceive her identity not in relation to her husband but to other men, like her father and the doctor (Shotter 1993, 6). Therefore while the story of Odette's marriage may be a regressive narrative, her life story as a whole has a progressive structure (Gergen and Gergen 1988). Like Cinderella, she is living happily ever after, but this happiness is not the result of her marriage, but of a different perception of self. Odette's claim about the uniqueness of her story is substantiated: she is a new Cinderella, a mixture of traditional passivity and activity, a Sandriella.[26]

Marriage is an important event in the lives of both women, but while for Biya winning Shimon was a climax, for Odette, Gabriel was the means of fulfilling her potential of becoming a mother (see next chapter). The fact that Gabriel initially courted another woman may serve to alleviate her guilt over preferring someone else; or perhaps this information is included in her story in order to legitimize her behavior. Odette's ordeal did not end with marriage, but was deferred until a later crucial junction in her life, the meeting with Rabbi Ḥuri and immigration to Israel; Odette's trials and tribulations, as well as happiness, are found elsewhere, in her spiritual activities (see chapter 4; Schely-Newman 1999a).

Performance as Boundary Setting

Stories about marriage may be told at any time, though they occur most frequently around the weddings of children, relatives, or neighbors. These occasions present an opportunity for the women to evaluate traditions and to reaffirm or reject current social norms (Valensi 1989, 66). The introduction of a new person into the family, a bride or a groom, is also a time to examine family relations and group boundaries.

Sharing one's experiences may occur in the kitchen, the living room, or the yard, and before or after taking the bride to the beautician, while waiting for guests to arrive, or while preparing food for guests. Performances on these occasions are informal: almost everyone present may tell a story, and the others willingly assume the role of an audience, rarely challenging the right to the floor (Pelias and VanOosting 1987, 221–27). These proactive per-

Biya prepares couscous while her sisters tell stories, Gilat, July 1987. Her youngest daughter and grandchildren are part of the audience.

formances provide participants with opportunities to interpret their own stories and behavior and thus reexamine the social boundaries set by the particular wedding they are attending and the current norms of forming alliances vis-à-vis the traditional ways. Though informal and open to outsiders, these gatherings require a certain degree of intimacy—they are a family affair. Performance may in itself be a mode of exclusion and inclusion, an implicit way of redrawing social boundaries, parallel to what actually occurs at the weddings.

A fieldwork experience I had in the summer of 1987 demonstrates this assertion (Schely-Newman 1999b). I noticed a gathering at Biya's house and went over to congratulate the party on the marriage of a niece the next day. The guests were three of Biya's sisters, who live elsewhere in Israel, and other family members. When Biya introduced me and said that I collected stories, one of the sisters offered to tell me one. I asked permission to bring my tape recorder and camera and recorded what turned out to be an exciting narrative event. The promised story, however, was not immediately told.

Before I was accepted into the group as a researcher, with a camera and tape recorder, the sisters put me through an interrogation. They wanted to know about me in traditional terms: where I lived, to whom I was married, and what relations I had with my parents—the three basic aspects of identity common in North Africa, *aṣl* (ancestry), *nsb* (marital relations), and *bld* (location) (L.Rosen 1984). Biya served as my advocate, my "talking chief." She not only answered for me but also vouched for my adherence to common values. She reassured her sisters of my loyalties—"She does not like to live in America"; "She calls her parents frequently"—and praised the character of my husband—"He is such a good man." Only after this interrogation did the storytelling round begin. Following the narration I became once again the target of interrogation, this time about my intended use of the data collected.

The first story told was a novella about a woman seducing her neighbor, followed by three others about Arab men and Jewish women, and kernel stories about similar inter-religious alliances. All the stories were about improper sexual relations, a common topic at prenuptial gatherings. Yet, viewing the entire interaction as a single text, considering the participants as well as the content of stories, reveals further meanings: I was the only nonfamily member in the interaction, and thus I was an outsider at the event. Furthermore, the groom in the wedding to be celebrated was also an outsider; he was not part of the traditional pool of spouses for this family.[27] Given these two factors and the interrogation I was subjected to before and after the stories were told, it seems that the main issue of the interaction was not only fear of inter-religious relations (Jewish-Arab), or of the male as "the other," but negotiating identities and recognizing pretenders. Different aspects of personal identity were at the core of the interaction, beginning and ending with my own. The issue of false identity became more obvious as the interaction evolved. Each story, comment, and kernel aggregated into a warning message about outsiders, and the stories themselves progressed from the fictive and amusing novella about a woman tricking a man to events which might occur in Israel; the last story was about a friend of the family being "saved" by Biya's nephew from a romantic involvement with an Arab man. The way to escape potential traps is for young women to follow the traditional rules, not to act on their own desires but to rely on family experience, wisdom, and approval. The socialization process of learning how to distinguish friend from foe, insider from outsider, was carried out both on an explicit level—telling stories about assumed identities—and on an implicit level—in their interaction with me, which framed the entire event.

The particular narratives given were concerned with male-female relations, but the interaction as a whole broadened the issue of negotiating identities: being a neighbors' daughter did not automatically make me part of the intimate circle. Thus, while the explicit topic of the interaction was wrong choices made by Israeli women when not following traditional rules for choosing a husband, the implicit topic could be seen as being about learning to recognize and be wary of outsiders who pretend to be part of the group. I myself was first required to prove that being married to an outsider (a non-Tunisian), living away from the community (in Chicago at the time), and leading a different life (as a university researcher), and the effects of modernity (married but childless) did not change me as a Jewish-Israeli-Tunisian woman. Using their narrative competence, the elderly women acted according to a traditional Tunisian discourse strategy of avoiding passionate arguments while exploring sensitive issues by storytelling rounds (Webber 1991, 118). The narrative event reveals boundaries on several levels, including gender, ethnicity, and family. I was not allowed into the group until my commitment to the group's values had been satisfactorily validated.

Tales of Love, Tales of Fate

Stories of childhood and marriage are connected, one leading to the other. The parents' role was to ensure that their daughters followed the requirements of their culture: the only ways out of parental home were marriage or death. The women, however, may have had other desires or expectations (Rosenwald 1992, 267–69). This gap is mediated by stories that led narrators to evaluate their lives in relation to norms and also to reconcile personal wishes with group demands (Rosenwald and Ochberg 1992, 2). In telling about the events that led to their marriages, the women create a plot of their lives, a plot that better explains their current situation and helps them bridge expectations and actual experience (Ochs and Capps

1996, 27, 37). These stories are formulated according to traditional narrative structures, explicitly or implicitly: Biya implicitly followed the story of the persecuted maiden, for example, and Odette explicitly referred to her life as a Cinderella story. These stories are shared with the audience, forming and maintaining social relationships and a collective identity, reproducing gender differences and influencing self perception (Hollway and Jefferson 1999, 135). As such, the stories function as projective narratives, mapping out future actions for the individuals (Tölölyan 1989, 101). Women enjoy telling about their marriage at all times, but when unmarried women are present, they are a primary target, enhancing the socialization function of narrative (Alexander, 1993: Bascom [1954] 1965, 293–95; Peacock and Holland 1993, 372). As an unmarried student of folklore in my late twenties, I became aware that most of the folktales I was told as part of my fieldwork were about women actively pursuing a mate. The heroines did not hesitate to cross the boundaries of the private sphere to rescue their husbands. Cinderella, Sleeping Beauty, and other maidens waiting to be rescued by Prince Charming were absent from their repertoire at the time. The implicit message might have been to encourage me to change my "tactics" and actively seek a mate.

Marriage stories help us to understand the place husband and family play in the lives of the women who tell them. Marriage is essential in women's lives, a necessary step toward self-fulfillment. At the same time, the women are aware of the changes in norms, of the greater freedom that women today have in choosing their mate. They are wary, fearing wrong choices, but nevertheless recognize the new possibilities for their daughters and granddaughters. The existing tension between traditional cultural norms and the needs of the individual is mediated through the narratives (Rosenthal 1993, 268). Choices made for the women are presented in the best possible light (as with Fortuna and Odette), and difficulties endured in youth are turned into triumphant victories (as with Biya). The more important the wedding is for the individual woman, the greater will be the position of the event in her life story. Although women's lives and identities are no longer defined by marriage alone, weddings continue to present older women with an opportunity to talk about their own marriages and evaluate their lives by comparing traditional norms with modern ways.

CHAPTER 3

Motherhood

Too many is too much, none is a disgrace

ktartu mshum, u-ḥasrtu ʿara

Marriage gave women social recognition and a means of self-fulfillment through motherhood, a universally major aspect of female identity (cf. Dwyer 1978; Gilad 1989; Keddie 1991; Mernissi [1975] 1987; Ortner 1974; Sered 2000:5; Zamiti-Horchani 1986: 111). "Be fruitful and multiply, replenish the earth and subdue it" was the first commandment given to Adam and Eve (Genesis 1:28). As in other societies in the Judeo-Muslim world, Jewish women in Tunisia were valued mainly for their ability to reproduce. Failure to conceive immediately after the wedding was viewed negatively, the new bride compared to soaked fava beans (*kif el ful li tzer*), which rot if not cooked immediately. As described by Raphael Uzan, "A young woman who failed to become pregnant right away was not to be envied. . . . If the wretched girl remained childless over the years, then her husband's family would treat her as an outcast: 'Look at you . . . an empty, useless belly and still primping. What is wrong with you anyhow? Don't you like babies?'" (Awret 1984, 158)

Concern about reproduction was not limited to the husband and in-laws; women, too, see fertility and children as basic elements of their identity and feel that the relationship with their children is the most important one in a woman's life (Sered 1992, 23; Wasserfall 1999a, 190). Therefore, reproduction and the effort expended to become a mother are common topics in women's everyday discourse (Abu-Lughod 1993, 133–41; Wasserfall 1995,259). No special time or place is necessary for such talk, but the audience make-up may affect the treatment of the subject or even cause its avoidance (as will be discussed later in this chapter). As guardians of communal norms, and seeing infertility as a feminine "decease," the older women inquire and offer advice for producing children, preferably males (Sered 2000, 63). They frequently share stories about pilgrimage sites, miracle workers, and successful fertility clinics, and they also pray for childless women, whether kin or not, and perform pious deeds like lighting candles and giving charity.

The women of this study were girls and brides in their youth, but now that they have children they will always remain mothers. Thus, the discourse of motherhood is about what they are: Jewish mothers. Their identity is construed and constructed by religious practices and beliefs, and therefore this chapter begins with a discussion of the interaction between procreation and other Jewish female responsibilities. This is followed by an examination of the discourse of procreation from two perspectives: the exclusion of men and the emergence of meaning in conversational narratives.

Being a Jewish Woman

Throughout Jewish history women have been excluded from the public sphere. Their primary responsibilities are caring for their home and children (cf. Azmon 1995). This exclusion may be seen as a way of ensuring the good of the community (the proper socialization of future generations) or in terms of power relations (women take care of men's property, including children). The Jewish perspective is supported by the Tunisian-Muslim culture, which associates women with the risk of shame and dishonor, and emphasizes space and gender segregation. North African Jewish and Muslim women are seen—and see themselves—as belonging to the private sphere, their behavior controlled by the laws and customs of chastity and moral behavior (Dwyer 1978; Mernissi [1975] 1987; Sered 1992, 71; Zamiti-Horchani 1986). The identification of women with the private sphere is reinforced in oral tradition and metaphoric representations. The relationship between the house and the outside, the private and the public, are basic spatial oppositions frequently represented in proverbs, and are equivalent to the female-male dichotomy (Alexander and Hasan-Rokem 1989, 112). The house, doorway, edible items (honey, fava beans), and kitchenware are all used as euphemisms for women (Fernandez 1986; Schely-Newman 1996b).

Women's religiosity is defined differently than men's. Women are exempt from *mitzvot* (positive religious commandments), which are bound by time (e.g., daily prayers). Unlike men, women are not required to read Scriptures or to study religious texts, and traditionally did not learn Hebrew. In everyday practice women relied on oral traditions transmitted from generation to generation and reaffirmed by stories attached to textual traditions. Women's religiosity was based on activities in the private sphere; cooking according to dietary rules and raising children were endowed with an aura of sacredness, which might be equivalent to men's textual religion (Bahloul 1983; Elor 1994; Sered 1992; Weissler 1998).

Domestic roles and duties in procreation, food preparation, and the observance of sacred periods, mainly the Shabbat, are the basis for women's Jewish identity. The connection between women and these areas is substantiated by a passage in the Jewish code of law, the *Mishnah,* read by men on Friday night: "For three transgressions do women die in childbirth: because they have not been heedful in regard to their menstruation (*niddah*), in the separation of the priest's share of the dough (*hallah*), and in lighting the (*Shabbat*) lamp."[1]

These laws affect women's everyday behavior. The rules of menstruation regulate a couple's conjugal life; therefore, *niddah* affects procreation (Wasserfall 1992). The meaning of *hallah*—the burning of a small piece of bread dough in commemoration of the priest's share of sacrificial offerings—can be extended to include women's nurturing role. Food preparation is controlled by religious dietary laws: this implies keeping different sets of dishes for dairy and meat, inspecting the food brought home, and special ways of preparing food.[2] Candles are lit at sunset on Friday to signal the beginning of the Shabbat, a spiritually sacred day stressing the gastronomical and the sensual.[3] Furthermore, Shabbat establishes the schedule for the entire week. As it is forbidden to cook or kindle fire on Shabbat, women begin their preparations as early as Tuesday or Wednesday, shopping, cleaning, and cooking in order to ensure that the entire house and household are ready for Shabbat.

All work must end before sunset on Friday, when women light candles, marking the temporal boundary and creating the holy day (Sered 1992, 102).

Though these Tunisian women are not familiar with the *Mishnaic* text, their stories indicate that they perceive the three areas of activity referred to as central to their self-identity. Written texts thus play a role not only in maintaining rules but also in establishing the underlying assumptions of what constitutes female (and communal) Jewish identity (Goldberg 1990, 9). Women's stories underline the interrelationship between motherhood, nurturing, and Shabbat, so that failure in one area predicts or even causes failure in others. One example is the story about a pregnant woman who, like other women, baked her Shabbat bread at the public oven. She suffered an instant miscarriage when the bread did not rise properly (this will be discussed in more detail in the following text). Another story, about a woman who was accidentally shot by a sentry in Gilat, stresses these connections: the woman, who was carrying a flashlight on Friday night, was suspected of being an Arab infiltrator. She was shot and injured, miscarried a child she was bearing, and was divorced by her husband (see chapter 4; Schely-Newman 1993).

A third example of the connection between the three areas of women's identity is a story told by Biya to Jeani about the lack of religiosity among younger people in Gilat. On a Friday night, after lighting candles, Daniella (a neighbor) went to Biya's home to borrow some peppers for cooking dinner. Daniella's son was sick that week, and the mother was worried about the forthcoming test results. Biya assured Daniella that if she avoided cooking on Shabbat her son would be found to have nothing wrong with him. Concerned, Daniella vowed to change her habits and prepare the Shabbat food in advance. The medical tests showed that her son had no serious problems.[4]

While praising her own faith and guiding capabilities, Biya was also reaffirming the interrelation between the three laws for women. The ability of a woman to safeguard her children is related to the extent to which she observes the Shabbat laws, particularly those related to her nurturing role. Cooking on Shabbat is not simply a breach of a religious law; it is a breach of a major woman's law, and therefore it affects the very essence of her being a woman, the welfare of her children. Women's concerns seem to underscore the importance of maintaining a Jewish household, not just literally following the prescribed women's *mitzvot*.

Discourse of Procreation

While nurturing and Shabbat are fundamental to the identity of Jewish women of all ages, the rules of *niddah* relate only to married women of childbearing age. According to Jewish law, men are obligated to fulfill their wives' needs, both material (the provision of food and clothing) and sexual. The laws of *niddah* regulate conjugation; physical interactions between husband and wife are forbidden while she is in an impure cultic state. Vaginal bleeding causes impurity; after bleeding ceases and a specified number of "clean" days have passed, a woman must repurify herself through immersion in the ritual bath, *mikvah*. Only then can contact between husband and wife resume.[5] In this way fertility and sexuality are maintained within the boundaries of Jewish law. In North Africa it was the responsibility of elder female kin to introduce the bride to her new role and instruct her in the Jewish ways, but in Israel this role has been taken over by representatives of the rabbinical authority (Sered 2000; Wasserfall 1999b).[6] To ensure proper separation between husband and wife, couples have special sleeping arrangements for the time when the woman is *niddah*, the trousseau of a bride includes sheets for separate beds, and each couple has its own set of signals to indicate when physical contact between husband and wife is to be abstained from and when it may resume. The connection between women's *mitzvot* and wedding was emphasized by an older Moroccan rabbi who explained that the *henna* used in the wedding is an acronym for *hallah, niddah,* and *hadlaka* (candle lighting) (Sered, Kaplan and Cooper 1999, 158). *Mikvah* thus defines Jewish women's identity and differentiates them from women of other religions, and these topics are at the heart of the discourse of Jewish female identity (R. Rosen 1981, Wasserfall 1992, 1995, 1999a).

Rules of *niddah* are directed by women's bodily cycles: a woman is expected to check herself in order to establish her cultic state, giving women a measure of control over reproductive resources (Deshen 1989, 112). However, although the women themselves decided the proper time, the women in Tunisia would not attend the *mikvah* without their husbands' consent, since going to the *mikvah* on their own initiative might have been interpreted as being overtly lascivious.[7] Women say that men, too, kept track of the calendar; however, it was the woman who decided the proper time for immersion and thus, intercourse. Even if the husband was impatient, he, too, had to adhere to the religious commandment and wait for his wife to proclaim herself pure again by going to the *mikvah*.[8]

"Family purity" rules regulate the intimate life of Jewish couples; however, going to the *mikvah* is a proclamation of sexual availability, because the ritual bath is a public institution. The visits expose a woman's private life to the community: proper immersion is done in the presence of the bath attendant, and sexual intercourse is expected to occur following the immersion. Women's fertility thus comes under community control, since visits to the bath can be monitored (Wasserfall 1999a). The heightened sexuality is expressed in stories about assaults women have suffered during or immediately after immersion (Schely-Newman 1999b).[9] A married woman who does not go to the ritual bath is either pregnant, menopausal, having domestic problems, or breaching a basic law.

Because everyone knew what followed the immersion, much effort was put into keeping the visit secret, even from the family. The public "proclamation" of sexual readiness was the basis for many suggestive remarks; a woman with a basket at dusk was frequently greeted by men with "*mashya l'el ḥammam?*" (going to the *mikvah?*). Alice remembers how in order to perform her religious duties (in Tunisia) she used to take her two young children along with her across town; she was too embarrassed to ask her mother-in-law to watch them. Anxieties, shyness, and a sense of modesty continued to exist in Israel: Fortuna jokingly talks about a time when she pretended to be carrying away kittens in order to explain to her father-in-law why she had to leave the house with a basket. In a small community like the *moshav,* where everyone could discern the trip to the *mikvah,* women sometimes chose to go to another community rather than be seen and be subject to comments.

In their stories women voice concerns about being observed by men or about fears of assault, but other issues are also indicated in the repeated accounts. The elderly women see immersion in the ritual bath not only as an act allowing intercourse, but as necessary to ensure the birth of purely Jewish children and therefore, visits to the *mikvah* involve concerns about conception (Schely-Newman 1999a). This belief continues to be held and women know that the entire community, particularly the husband's family, is expecting them to have children. Women know that the mothers-in-law also count the days following each visit to the *mikvah,* watching for signs of pregnancy, be it *ziyada* (an addition, delay in menstruation) or changes in the behavior of the woman. However, women do not perceive menstruation as a punishment, nor do they immerse in the *mikvah* for fear of death in childbirth. They do so because they care for their families and wish for healthy children, shifting the focus from penance to fertility (Weissler 1998, 68, 71).[10]

Women are expected and wish to have children, yet they may also be ambivalent or fearful of miscarriage or of difficult pregnancies, and they are also aware of the difficulties of caring for many children. The situation is not different in modern Israel, where the secular establishment as well as religious authorities encourages procreation, seeing motherhood as a national mission (Sered 2000, 5).[11] It was expected that a woman would conceive following the ritual bath and intercourse; failure to conceive, along with difficult pregnancies or miscarriages, were major concerns.[12] Yet, the older women are also aware of the difficulties in raising a large family in modern Israel. Talking about people in Gilat, Biya commented that, *ktartu mshum, u-ḥasrtu ʿara* (too many is bad, its lack is shameful). Though the proverb is generally used to stress the need for moderation (Yetive 1987, 87), Biya was talking about her daughters, one struggling to raise eight children and the other having difficulties conceiving (she eventually had two boys, after several years of anxiety).

While the *mikvah* discourse recognizes men's central role in domestic and conjugal life, stories women tell minimize man's contribution to procreation. Once the woman conceives, pregnancy, childbearing, and childrearing are female responsibilities in which the man's role is negligible. When asked about their experiences as mothers, women rarely talk about their husbands. They confide in other women about pregnancies, miscarriages, bleeding, and other issues. Telling other women about her youngest child, whom she tried to abort, Greena proclaims several times, *rabbi yᵊshamaḥni* (may God forgive me), with no mention of her husband. A man's role in procreation is reduced to intercourse—planting children in a

woman's womb. He is not expected to take any further responsibility or to participate in the discourse of reproduction. Just as
reproduction belongs to the adult-female sphere of activities, so
too does the discourse connected with it. The presence of the male
in either is seen as interfering rather than as helpful.

Male Exclusion

Women, of course, know that children are born following intercourse and that men play a role, though limited, in parenting. Only
when specifically asked, however, did women refer to the actions
of men in these areas. Most of the women I interviewed about
childbearing customs had delivered their children at home in their
countries of origin; in Israel, they were assisted by neighbors at
home, or gave birth in the hospital. [13] Women always enjoyed comparing the customs of their own time with the present, but fieldwork I conducted in 1993 was especially relevant because I was
noticeably pregnant at the time. This gave them an opportunity to
discuss practical aspects and share their knowledge with me (Schely-
Newman 1995b). I was collecting data relating to childbirth and
asked about the practice of the husband being present and helping
his wife during delivery. The women drew a clear distinction between the past, their own time and experience, and the present, in
relation to their daughters and granddaughters. In their opinion,
it now is a good practice, because the husband "can see what she
goes through." Yet they were appalled by the mere idea in regard
to themselves and their own times, seeing it as unchaste and against
the rules of *niddah*. Not only would a man's presence at the scene
of birth be a disgrace, but also it could cause serious problems, as
in the following story (a synopsis):

> A woman was assisted during delivery by both her mother-in-law
> and husband. The mother-in-law noticed that even though time
> had passed since the delivery, the woman had not gone to the *mik-
> vah,* explaining that her husband had not left her money to do so.
> Suspecting that her son was in some shock following the birth of
> his child, she asked him to buy her some honey. The mother then
> poured the honey in a plate and attempted to cut through it, but the
> honey settled back. When the son inquired about the meaning of his
> mother's actions, she explained that the woman is like honey, "This

is the gate of God. During labor it opens so that the baby can come out, and then it closes back again, as in every normal woman."[14]

This story was retold on other occasions. In a Moroccan version (told a week later in the same *mo'adon*) the husband's fear prevented him from intercourse. He explained to his mother that he was afraid to go into his wife's abdomen. In another context the story was not even told: the woman talking about conjugal problems resulting from the presence of a man during delivery simply mentioned the word honey and made a cutting sign with her finger.

What is common to all versions is men's ignorance of and inability to handle their wives' anatomy and reproductive systems. Even a gynecologist is said to have divorced his wife shortly after he assisted her during delivery; the story clearly indicated that this was the cause for divorce (see Schely-Newman 1995b). The connection between honey and sex is also found in the pierced gourd story mentioned in the previous chapter, and the use of edible items, particularly sweets, as metaphors for women is universal (Hines 1999). In Hebrew honey has special feminine meaning: the numerical value of the letters in the word *devash* (honey) is the same as that of the word *ishah* (woman), linking them in traditional Jewish modes of interpretation.[15] All versions of the honey plate story condemn the involvement of a man in the process of delivering his children.

Procreation is expropriated from men. They father offspring, name them, provide for them, and take pride in them, but in everyday care, from the moment of conception, children are a women's concern. Progeny is an important measure of a man's worth: wife and children are the property of the husband and he is their legal representative in the Judeo-Islamic world (cf. Keddie 1991; Deshen 1989; Katzir 1976). Nevertheless, conception and the well-being of children are women's responsibility: bearing children and raising them belong to the female domestic sphere and are accomplished with the help of God and the social network women cultivate (Sered 1992, 106; Sered 2000, 5). When a woman gave birth and was impure for a period of time, unable to care for her family, female relatives and neighbors would take charge, an act of reciprocity defined by Yemenite women as a "loan" extended to one another. Expectant mothers shared their anxieties, worries, and joys with other women, including the mother-in-law, who in the honey plate story had a crucial role in solving the domestic problem by instructing her son as to women's "mystery." The mother-in-law served as a proxy for her son, but also as a surrogate mother for the bride, particularly when women married at a very young age (Katzir 1976, 75). Mothers did not discuss sexuality with their daughters, nor did they carry out the initiation of a bride into marital life. Mothers explained to their daughters what to do when they menstruated, and made a connection between menstruation and childbearing, but sexuality itself was left to another female, frequently the mother-in-law. The transformation from a girl to a Jewish woman and the "handing over" of the responsibility for the sexual life of the new bride was symbolically carried out in wedding ceremonies. [16] This double socialization is found in life stories of Yemeni-Israeli women (Gilad 1989, 12), and in a study of Moroccan women in Israeli *moshavim* (Wasserfall 1992), as well as in an analysis of Jerban (Tunisian) Jewish wedding ceremonies (Valensi 1989). [17]

The marginal role of the husband in the domestic-sexual sphere is expressed by the content of the honey plate story. When the husband was not willing (or able) to perform his conjugal duty, his mother had to symbolically perform a sexual act on his behalf, showing him what must be done by cutting and re-cutting the honey, using her finger or a knife. This marginality of men is reinforced by their exclusion from the telling of these stories. None of the versions of the honey plate story and no conversation about birth or intercourse took place in the presence of men. This particular story was told only after a careful check to determine if a man was within hearing range. [18] My colleague Zivia, who heard a presentation in which I analyzed this story, asked her mother about it. The mother, from the town of Gabes (Tunisia), was appalled that it had been told to a mixed audience. Her shock and anger may have resulted not only from a feeling of indecency, but also from her sense that making it public was a transgression of a private code, compromising the female autonomy in reproduction. Childbirth is a subject about which women are the experts, and sharing this knowledge with men may endanger their relative superiority in their only indisputable area, motherhood (Martin 1990). Thus telling such stories in the presence of men, like allowing men to be present during labor, can be seen as divulging the secrets of womanhood, and endangering the intimacy of sisterhood.

How Stories Are Born: Conversational Narratives

Narration in conversation frequently occurs in response to comments made, to illustrate a point, attempt to alleviate tension, or pose a challenge to previous utterances. Narrative texts cannot be treated as entities separate from their verbal contexts (Peterson and Langellier 1997, 136; Sawin 1999, 254). The purposes or functions of conversation and embedded narratives do not always coincide; meaning emerges in negotiating between the content of tales, the different levels of contexts, and the social identities of the participants (Blum-Kulka 1997, 101–4; Langellier and Peterson 1993, 56). The stories discussed in this chapter were not narrated randomly; they emphasize the importance of observing Shabbat for the sake of children (Biya about Daniella) or the perils for conjugal life resulting from man's involvement in childbearing. A story that might be titled "Bread, Shabbat, and Miscarriage" demonstrates the disruptive effect of men's participation in domestic-female discourse (the entire story appears in appendix 4): "Esther, Shushan's pregnant wife, put her bread for Shabbat to bake in the public oven, as all the women in Moknine (and other places) do. When she saw that the bread did not bake properly, she was so aggravated and distressed that she had an immediate miscarriage." Jeani, the narrator, concludes her story by adding that whenever she went to bake bread she was told, "This is where Esther, Shushan's wife, miscarried her child."

The referential meaning of this story emphasizes the homology between the three aspects in Jewish-female identity: procreation, nurturing, and Shabbat. Failure in one area may predict failure in the others (Schely-Newman 1993, 1996b, 2001). Furthermore, the *kusha* (oven) is a public institution, just like the *mikvah;* women's actions in their private sphere are put on display, be it their adherence to "family purity" laws or to the communal norms of what is considered "good" bread, appropriate for Shabbat consumption. Older women are the ones who point out to the younger ones the pitfalls of not conforming with rules; as a young woman in Moknine Jeani was told about the event, and now, as a grandmother—who just celebrated the birth of another

Jeani, Miḥa and the pot, Gilat, July 1988

grandson—she is transmitting the message to a younger woman, me. Yet contextualizing the story and examining the development of the conversation in which it was embedded disclose other, potentially subversive, meanings.

The story was told when, during a scheduled and taped interview I conducted with Miḥa and her husband Fradji about their life in Gilat, Jeani, their next-door neighbor, arrived to return a pot she had borrowed for the celebration of the birth of a grandchild. Talk about the celebration for the newborn led to recalling the words of their elders and joyful narrative occasions in Tunisia—mainly on Thursday nights, when women prepared the bread for Shabbat. Childbearing and women's identity remain at the heart of the interaction, "cooked" in the returned pot (Schely-Newman 2001).

Talk about baking bread for Shabbat was embedded in a nostalgic discourse about life in a more traditional society, the Jewish community of Tunisia (see chapter 5). The relatively long story—a two-minute narration—includes many additional details, locating events and people in the proper place and time. These details help construct a representation of a bygone life—part of Jeani's heritage, as well as Miḥa and Fradji's. The conversation includes several perspectives. The three adults offer me, a younger woman raised in Israel, a glimpse of the "good life" they had in Tunisia, while, on another level, Jeani tells the three of us about particular events of which she had firsthand knowledge (Shuman 1993b, 136). At the same time, the miscarriage story represents experiences shared by the older women, the grandmothers, who succeeded where poor Shushan's wife failed. I wish to argue that the inclusion of this sad story, which stands in contrast to the harmonious discourse of the rest of the conversation, was a result of Fradji's too-active participation in a conversation about Jewish-female core values.

The conversation about life in Tunisia and the wise words of the elders was blended in a nostalgic tone. The shift into a more critical perspective occurred when the topic of baking bread for Shabbat was raised. After describing storytelling events in general, they then narrowed the description to a specific time and activity: bread baking for Shabbat on Thursday nights (lines corresponding to Appendix 4).

42. Jeani: My brother would sit and read to us, and we would wait for the story
43. Fradji: Every night, every night.
44. Jeani: A little bit every night so he wouldn't get tired and the story would continue
45. Esther: Like "A Thousand and One Nights."
46. Miḥa: During winter, my uncle would read to us every night
47. Jeani: Roasting chestnuts on the fire . . .
48. Fradji: [overlap] and peanuts
49. Jeani: We had nuts and roasted chickpeas.
50. Peanuts were very expensive in our area
51. Peanuts came from Tripoli, Devora's town. Only chickpeas and nuts.
52. We'd all be sitting in bed, wrapped in a heavy blanket, but only one night [a week]
53. Miḥa: Exactly. In our town too, just one night.
54. Esther: Friday night?
55. Jeani: No, Thursday night.

56. Thursday nights when we prepare bread at home and took it to bake in the *kusha*
57. Everyone did it.
58. From two A.M. until the morning, and we . . .
59. Fradji [laughing, overlap]: They had no time, had no time.
60. Jeani: We'd knead until the grains of salt put on the dough fell off
61. And we'd shape the loaves or mark them,
62. and my mother would take them on her head to the *kusha*
63. The *kusha* was not far from us.
64. She would open the oven and put in the bread.
65. Later they'd put in peanuts for sale.
66. She'd put in the bread and wait.
67. She could figure out the time when it would be ready.
68. If it came out nice and shiny, she'd return happy
69. Miḥa: They'd say to her, happy Shabbat
70. Jeani: Tell her, blessed Shabbat.
71. But if it came out yellow or ugly [claps hand] she'd beat her heart
72. Esther: What would come of her?
73. Jeani [singsong]: Woe to the Shabbat, woe to the Shabbat.
74. Miḥa: They'd say, "If the bread comes out well the entire Shabbat will be a good day."
75. Fradji: Bread is essential, bread is essential
76. Jeani: She'd say, "Oh Father God, isn't it enough that I'm working all night?
77. Aren't you satisfied?"
78. All that worry about a bit of bread we don't even need.
79. Fradji: Right.

The main narrator was Jeani, but each member of the audience contributed to the flow of conversation. In lines 42–47, each of us harmoniously echoed Jeani's description of the narrative events, including my comparison to "A Thousand and One Nights." Fradji's addition "and peanuts" (48) was an interruption, however, as it forced Jeani to digress to explain why she omitted peanuts from her story. Yet when the specific time of the narrative was recalled, the focus of the conversation shifted from the pleasures of storytelling to the hardship of the work: "From two A.M. until the morning and we . . ." (58). Fradji's laughing comment, "They had no time, had no time" (59), was left without response and Jeani completed her sentence and continued with talk about her mother, but the pleasant experience shared by men and women alike was replaced by exclusively female worries. Miḥa supported Jeani by repeating the common belief about the homology between "nice bread" and a good Shabbat (69, 74). Fradji's comment (75) "Bread is essential" might require a response, but it was ignored, as Jeani continued to describe her mother's reaction to an ugly, yellow loaf. She summarized her mother's plea to God by commenting, "All that worry about a bit of bread we don't even need" (78). Who is this *we*? Is Jeani still quoting her mother's words, or giving her own opinion? Or, is she serving as the voice—an animator—for generations of Jewish women (Duranti 1997, 274)? This utterance presupposes a second voice whose identity is not easily identified, allowing Jeani to manipulate the distance between herself and the object of criticism, the patriarchal order or God himself (Irvine 1996, 136; Shuman 1993b, 151). Interpreting this utterance as a reproach, rather than a lament or cry of desperation, transforms it into a covert reply to Fradji's claim: it is possible that *bread is essential* for men, but for women it is *a bit of bread we don't even need*. Jeani did not ignore Fradji's comments, but gave him an indirect answer, an answer that is further elaborated in her story about Shushan's wife.

The effect of Fradji's interference—his mocking male perspective in the midst of domestic-female discourse—is noticed in the next segments of conversation. Miḥa attempts to avert the confrontational exchange with a harmonious story about Fradji's parents amusing the children on Saturday mornings by pulling nuts from under the blanket, as if they came out of the *kusha* (lines 80–84). The three elements of female Jewish identity are again present: Shabbat, food, and children. Miḥa's claim for the floor is not challenged, but Jeani returns to the hardship of women as soon as Miḥa's story is over. There is no pause between the two:

85. Jeani: Nice.
86. Fradji: Yeah.
87. Miḥa: Every Saturday they woke up early and went there.
88. Jeani: Remember Shushan Damri, who lived with us over there [in the *moshav*]?

The miscarriage story is an expanded reply to Fradji, in that it confronts and challenges men's position about the importance of bread by stating the price women sometimes pay for being unable to fulfill their roles of nurturing, procreation, and Shabbat.

Jeani calls our attention to Shushan, but in fact the story is about his wife. Throughout the story we know only her social roles as wife and mother; more accurately, we learn of her failure in fulfilling these roles.

88. Jeani: Remember Shushan Damri, who lived with us over there [in the community]?
89. Miḥa: Yes
90. Jeani: She, may we hear only good tidings, had many children, and they died.
91. Miḥa: Oh, Levitil's mother.
92. Jeani: Yes, Levitil's mother.
93. Until she was able to keep the boy and girl alive, God knows.
94. She bore many, many and they died.

Once identified, and her motherly status explained, the orientation is complete and the scene is set for the complication (Labov and Waletzky 1967). The woman was pregnant and the bread she prepared for Shabbat was not satisfactory. The woman's distress at the sight of the bread coming out of the *kusha* is echoed in the prosody of the narration, slow and rhythmic:

120. *hiya madetula wa hiya kisha'ṭ fi*
     (A) she gave it to her and she looked at it
121. *wa hiya ḥabla xamsha* ‖ <*ḥodashim*>
     (A) and she pregnant five (H) months
     "The attendant gave the bread to Esther, who looked at it, and she was five months pregnant."

Miḥa overlaps the last word by exclaiming "wau!" and Jeani continues in a rhythmic voice:

123. *wa bdat qalek tindab 'ala wuzha*
     (A) and started they say she wails on her face
124. *tiḍrab 'ala kulba tiḍrab 'ala wuzha*
     (A) she hits on her heart she hits on her face

125. *tidrab 'ala kubla ḥata rmat e-ẓrir ṛadik*
    (A) she hits on her heart until she miscarried the child there
    "They say that she started scratching her face, and hitting her heart, till she miscarried the child on the spot."

The climax of the story, the miscarriage, is then repeated, as is the progress of the pregnancy, thus emphasizing the loss and suffering of the woman:

126. She miscarried it, five months old.

The story is about an individual woman, Shushan's wife, Esther, yet she is like all other women. She "kneaded the bread *like we do* until two A.M." (line 104), and she reacted to the outcome exactly as did Jeani's mother. Both women hit their hearts in despair, but while Jeani's mother addresses her outrage to Father God— "Aren't you satisfied?" (line 77)—Shushan's wife, described as *nerwuza* (hysterical?) and fearful of her husband, has an anxiety attack which ends in a miscarriage. The similarity between Shushan's wife and other women is further expanded at the end of the story (lines 134–36): "They feared their husbands a lot because of the bread. If it did not come out nice they'd tell them 'It's your fault.' Not the fault of the oven attendant." The accusation, "your fault" is uttered in the language of religious authority, in Hebrew, thus potentially reinforcing the distinction between the male sphere of literate religion and women's religiosity based on domestic activity and oral traditions (Sered 1992, 90–101).

The similarity between the actions of the two women underlines Esther's tragedy: she is someone's wife and mother, as are all women, and serves as an illustration of gender relations in past days. However, despite the similarities, the miscarriage is an individual tragedy of a specific woman: Only at this point in the story do we learn her first name:

130. *uni ester mert shushan rmat e-ẓrir*
    here Esther, wife of Shushan, miscarried the child
    "This is where Esther, Shushan's wife, miscarried her child."

Reading the story as subversive, as challenging the patriarchal order, rather than as supporting gender construction, raises

93

additional questions (Abu-Lughod 1990, 47). Jeani and Miḥa are part of the same culture; they believe in the sacredness of Shabbat and view their role primarily in terms of nurturing and mother-hood. Like the Bedouin women studied by Abu-Lughod, the older Tunisian Israeli women support the patriarchal system and abhor modern attempts to stray from it (as seen earlier in this conver-sation). Jeani and Miḥa are proud of their fertility, proud of the festive meals they prepare for families and friends. Nevertheless, while accepting the social order, they do object to and resist the demands of individual men who, like Shushan, can drive their wives to extreme distress.[19]

What Is the Text?

The miscarriage story can be analyzed independently of its sur-rounding utterances. The cultural context supports an interpreta-tion of the story as mirroring gender construction: Tunisian Jewish women perceived food preparation as fulfilling a sacred religious requirement (see Sered 1992). Yet the empathy shown toward Es-ther, and the utterances surrounding this story, lead to a different interpretation, one based on the conversation that preceded the story. This suggests that textual coherence cannot be judged in terms of content alone. Coherence is not an absolute property of a text, but depends on temporal ordering and sequentiality (Linde 1993, 13–16). The story of Esther is coherent, though it includes several digressions; but so is the entire segment of the conversation about bread baking, which may be seen as *the text*. The sequence of utterances by Jeani, Miḥa, and Fradji imply a causal relationship; the miscarriage story may be seen to be a result of previous utterances, mainly Fradji's interference.

Every time we segment data, each decontextualization and entextualization produces a different text, with potential additional meanings (Peterson and Langellier 1997, 144; Silverstein and Ur-ban 1996, 12–13). An analysis of the miscarriage story as it emerges from the interaction between the participants, setting, cultural val-ues, *and* previous utterances supports the interpretation of the story as subversive (Blum–Kulka 1997, 2; Bauman 1986, 5–6). The two interpretations may coexist, revealing the potential of resistance and polysemy inherent in oral texts. In both readings Shushan's wife is the heroine. Either she is a tragic figure who is unable to cope with the constant vigilant eyes of the community and collapses under the pressure and miscarries, or she is resisting the patriarchal order, going beyond verbal reproach to the original Patriarch, Father God (as did Jeani's mother) by actually rejecting her fetus, the physical mark of her relations with her husband. The Judeo-Arabic word for miscarriage and abortion is the same, *rmat,* meaning *threw.* In both interpretations Esther's personal story serves as an opportunity for us, a mixed audience—another old woman, an older man, and a younger woman—to examine moral values in a spatiotemporal perspective. The story of Esther's miscarriage becomes an indexical marker around which gender relations and specific events occurred and are evaluated. The radial nature of the *kusha* as communal nexus is highlighted both by referential indices, such as temporal and spatial shifters (deictics), and by nonreferential indices, such as language shifts (Silverstein 1976, 1985). When considering the entire interaction and the subversive reading, the events can be seen as reflective of each other. The deflated bread reflects the inability of the wife to remain "inflated"—pregnant; and the rejection of the fetus, the miscarriage, reflects the rejection of improper inter-ference of a male in the female discourse of reproduction, similar to the more explicit rejection of male interference in women's re-production that the story of the honey plate indicates.

Reading the story as subversive suggests that a male's partic-ipation in the female discourse is the key for the escalation. This interpretation may also be supported by the way Jeani navigated the conversation back into harmony by calling the younger generation into the conversation (139) "And when I tell that to my daughters-in-law, they die of laughter." The gender-based tension is replaced by a generation gap, the young who are unable to understand what the older people went through. The here and now can be compared with then and there, and Fradji may now rejoin the conversation as an equal partner. Indeed, the continuing conversation returns to a harmonious nostalgic discourse about life in Tunisia (see chapter 5).

Once a Mother, Always a Mother

Stories about childhood and marriage are about the past even though they bear relevance to the present context of narration. The discourse of motherhood, on the other hand, is about the present. Stories discussed in this chapter tell about past events, but these are not only sources of ethnographic data; they are not just about baking bread or co-habitation with in-laws; they are about timeless motherhood and reproduction, and thus represent self-explanatory models for alliances and socio-moral behavior.

The stories the women tell about motherhood reconstruct female identity within a Jewish holy context (Sered 1992; Wasserfall 1999a; Weissler 1998). The women have created and sanctified a "Small Tradition" of their own, in which reproduction plays an essential part (Sered 1992, 71, 87). This tradition has its exclusively female discourse, which sometimes defies and resists male dominance. The older women do not attempt to change power relations between genders or to redefine their sphere of activity (Abu-Lughod 1990). Instead, they use narration as a way of preserving their autonomy in matters of procreation. Women, they believe, are responsible for reproduction (knowledge of men's infertility is a recent phenomenon) and prefer the company and help of other experienced women, who can be trusted in such critical matters. Men are portrayed as ignorant and helpless regarding women's sexuality; regardless of age or expertise (whether newly married, a father, or even a gynecologist), the man is turned once again into a child who needs to be taught the basic facts of life. Men's attempts to take an active part in this sphere are doomed to fail: men may become "impotent," cause miscarriages, or provoke confrontation and disharmony by interfering in female discourse.

Stories like the honey plate episode may be understood as ridiculing men's ignorance while reassuring females of their autonomy in matters of reproduction, but sexually irreverent talk does not contradict the fact that women respect and sometimes even fear men (Abu-Lughod 1990, 45). Nevertheless, in the areas of childbearing and childrearing, women continue to protect their autonomy by excluding men from participating in either the events, the scene of birth, or the discourse thereof. Female exclusivity may be the result of gender segregation imposed by male domination, but in the stories it is presented as women's choice. Entitlement for participation excludes those who lack the experience of motherhood, particularly those who can never be part of it—that is, men (Schely-Newman 1995b).

CHAPTER 4

Immigration

Real stories are the best stories
xrayef taʿ əl ḥaq xir məl xrayef el kul

Prior to the establishment of the State of Israel, Jerusalem was a spiritual focal point, the object of religious aspirations and hopes for a Messianic age for the majority of Jews living in Diaspora. Emissaries from the Holy Land were treated deferentially, and people living in Jerusalem were endowed with a certain aura of piety.

Rachel, Fortuna's great-grandmother moved from Jerusalem to Tunisia with her brother following a dream about an impending catastrophe that was about to beset the city. The chief rabbi of Sfax offered them his home and eventually married Rachel. Together they had several children, among them Fortuna's grandfather. Throughout her life Rachel remained distraught about living so far from her beloved Jerusalem, and she frequently shared her recollections of the Holy City with her granddaughter Leah, Fortuna's mother. According to Fortuna's story, Rachel's wish to return to Jerusalem was finally fulfilled:

> Leah was young, twelve or thirteen, when poor Rachel died. And she, Rachel, her heart was in Jerusalem. You would really feel sorry for her (*ça fait de la peine*). They say my mother had a dream. Leah dreamt that angels came and took Rachel along with them to Jerusalem. She told her father [about her dream] and he said, "Go tell it to your grandfather, he'll be pleased." Look at the tears streaming from my eyes. He told her "Go tell your grandfather."

97

She went to him and told him her dream. He said, "She [Rachel] really went back to Jerusalem."[1]

The shared dream of "returning to Jerusalem" was realized by all of the women in my study. What they encountered in the Holy Land, however, was not the biblical Jerusalem of their imagination, but a series of farming communities being built on barren land. The new lives they were to assume in these *moshavim* required rapid, radical, and unexpected changes in their traditional roles. Married women in Tunisia rarely worked for wages. Unmarried women sometimes worked to build up their trousseaux or to help their families, but always under the strict supervision of their father or siblings. During the early stages of the *moshav* development, however, when pressing financial circumstances forced men to seek employment away from home, women were left to tend the family farms or even to look for outside work to help provide for the family. This all-important situation led to unprecedented changes in the division of labor and of family roles, giving women greater responsibilities (Andezian and Streiff-Fenart 1986; Shokeid 1971). The expansion of women's responsibilities was the implicit result of the structure of the *moshav* as a collection of independent farming units based on nuclear families for the most part. Women were now seen as part of the workforce; they were partners with their husbands in the ownership of the family farm and had the right to vote or be elected to official positions within the *moshav*, although this right was rarely invoked.

Stories told about the experience of immigrating to Israel— why, when, and what changes occurred in women's lives—are seen as factual. Their content and the dialogue between individual and master narratives are examined in an attempt to explain the interaction between life and narrative in the process of becoming self-reliant.

Women's Stories: Truth and Genre

In their stories women express their apprehensions about abandoning familiar customs and modes of behavior. Some of the stories follow what became the master narrative of immigration to Israel: they are tales of success in overcoming numerous initial difficulties.

Emphasis is placed upon the changes people underwent as they positioned themselves as either active or passive actors in the process. The tellers' choice depends on individual factors, such as participation in Zionist activities prior to migration and familiarity with the master narrative. Content and style of narration also depend on gender: for instance, while men tell about pioneering activities, stressing physical changes in the locale, women concentrate on the welfare of the family and tend to emphasize personal aspects of change. Migration, however, changed gender relations and responsibilities, and these changes, in turn, affect narration.

For both practical and theoretical reasons, truth and falsehood criteria cannot be applied to these stories. This is due to the very nature of the events, and the fact that it is almost impossible to ascertain "what really happened" forty or more years ago. Some information is documented in the *Te'udat 'oleh* (immigrant card), an official record given to each household by the government to include the date of arrival in Israel, initial housing arrangements, financial and other assistance, and so on. Additional data can be found in the official archives of the *Sochnut* (the Jewish Agency), the immigrant camps, and the *moshavim*. Newspapers are also a source of information about the general state of affairs in the camps and about unusual or tragic events that occurred at the time. However, the everyday struggles of adjustment are of less concern in public records than the need to accommodate hundreds of thousands of people in the new environment (Chafets 1986; Segev 1986). The ideological position of the Establishment was that the country would serve as a "melting pot" in the formation of a new "Israeli" culture and identity which would be acquired by all immigrants after they had shed their old cultures (Bar Yosef 1968). This official attitude was certainly not conducive to paying attention to comparatively mundane and personal problems, particularly in light of the commonly held conception that the culture of non-European immigrants was nonexistent and was therefore unworthy of preservation or documentation (Shohat 1997). Volunteers working with the immigrants frequently lacked a common language with them, and despite their dedication and eagerness to help teach "the right ways" of doing things, there was not among them much understanding of the immigrant's personal identity, culture, or needs.[2] For the women, this marginalization was even intensified, because

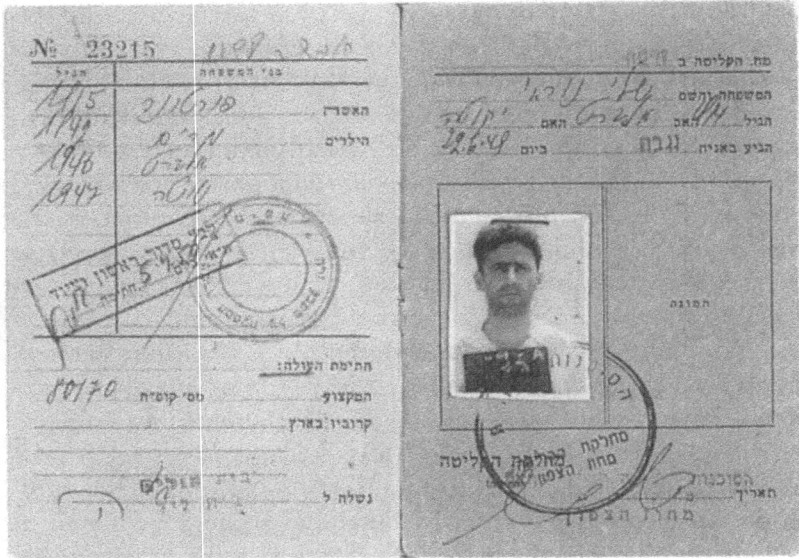

Noro's *Teʿudat ʿoleh* (immigrant's card) with personal data and official information

their sphere of activity—the private and personal—is not perceived as significant. When women are mentioned in "objective" sources they frequently remain nameless, rendering the study of women's lives even harder (S. Reinharz 1994).

Lack of "objective" sources for confirming truth is secondary to the theoretical approach. The stories analyzed in this book are the tellers' reconstruction of experiences from the perspective of the time and place of the narrative event, not the narrated events themselves (Bauman 1986, 7). Like all personal narratives, the stories represent the truth of experience manipulating the "truth" to a certain degree (Langellier 1989, 251; Stahl 1989, 18; *Interpreting Women's Lives* 1989, 261). Their value is measured by the creativity of the narrator in performance, and by his or her entitlement to retell the stories; factuality has little to do with acceptance (Jackson 1988, 282; Oring 1990; Shuman 1993b, 136). More important than a clear memory or the amount of forgotten details is the question of why particular events are chosen for telling in a given situation (van Langenhove and Harre 1993, 96). Their stories and memories, nevertheless, are set within the framework of the collective memories of the large migration waves of the 1950s (Weissberg 1999). The stories about immigration presented in this chapter are, therefore, a reflection of actual changes and their implications for the distribution of familial power. Such changes have other added significance in terms of entitlement to narrative genres, that is, when and in what contexts narrators are expected to use a particular genre.

Genres are not neutral classification systems but part of the politics of interpretation (Shuman 1993a, 71). Since genre is a cultural construct (like gender), definition and entitlement are a point of contention and challenge; they are an arena for the discursive reconstruction of identity (Kapchan 1996, 4; Shuman 1993a, 83). In Tunisia men were the public storytellers; female storytelling took place in private, before an audience of women, children, and occasionally grandfathers (Hejaiej 1996, 11). In a study of historical narratives in a Tunisian village, Webber (1985, 1991) notes that men told *hikayah,* or stories about experiences "worth" telling, drawn from the recent and distant past, and real or legendary adventures. Women, who spent their time in the private sphere, told fictional narratives, or *xurafah,* which were metaphoric representations of their world and concerns (Hejaiej 1996, 60; Webber 1985, 310).[3]

Choosing to Immigrate

The decision to immigrate to Israel was based on a combination of factors, including Messianic-religious aspirations, Zionist ideology, post-1948 exultation about having an independent Jewish state, and the growing sense of unwelcomeness in Arab countries that had recently gained independence from colonial rule (in 1956 in Tunisia). In the Arab world, animosity between Jews and Muslims increased in almost direct correlation to the escalation of the Israeli-Palestinian conflict.

The religious meaning of living in the Holy Land led the rabbinical authorities to allow and even mandate a divorce in cases where one spouse refused to join the other in what was seen as a sacred decision. As noted in previous chapters, women generally accepted decisions made for them by the males in the family— about education, going to school, whom to marry, and where to live. Nevertheless, it was sometimes the women who used the threat

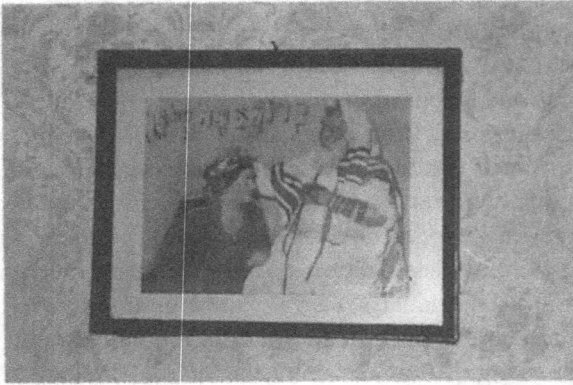

Picture hanging on
the wall in Odette's
living room: Rabbi
Ḥuri blessing her
before he left
Tunisia for Israel

of divorce to convince their husbands to migrate, as can be seen in
Odette's story.

In 1955 Odette was married and living in La Goulette, a suburb of Tunis. They were wealthy, living comfortably in a large house
with servants. The Jewish Agency had erected a camp nearby where
Tunisian Jews were processed and cared for on their way to Israel,
and Odette used her nursing skills to help people in the camp. One
of the people she aided was Rabbi Ḥayim Ḥuri, a religious leader of
Southern Tunisia.[4] Asked to supply household items for the elderly
rabbi, Odette offered to host him in her own home. Furthermore,
she helped gather an audience for a sermon he preached, and when
the rabbi fell ill she cared for him and help him recover. According
to Odette, the rabbi acknowledged her help in fulfilling his dream
of immigrating to Israel by blessing her; a picture of the rabbi con-
ferring his hands on Odette's head is displayed in her living room.
Meeting the rabbi, healing him, and being blessed by him affected
Odette's life. This is a pivotal point that shapes her life and stories, as
Rabbi Ḥuri became her mentor (Schely-Newman 1999a). At this
point, the comfortable life in Tunisia was no longer satisfactory for
her and she wished to follow the rabbi to the Holy Land even against
her husband's wishes. Soon after Rabbi Ḥuri left for Israel, Odette
decided that her family should migrate as well. In her own words,[5]

> I had no reason to come to Israel. I had no reason. My husband had
> a very good position. . . . I had no reason to come. . . . I told my

husband that I want to immigrate to Israel. So he said, "No, you
have no reason to." He said in Arabic, "Israel is for everyone. Let all
the [other] Jews gather there. This is not the time, Odette. We have
it very good, we lack nothing. We help smuggle the poor people
[out of Tunisia]. We'll immigrate later, what are you missing here?
Why do that?" [addressing me] Do you know, Esther, what I did? I
went to the *rabbanut* [religious authority, in charge of marriage and
divorce].

Esther: Is that so?

Odette swears: By the life of—by the *hillulah* [the religious celebration marking the day of a rabbi's death]. I went to the *rabbanut* and
told them I wanted to go to Israel. They said, "And your husband,
my child? You have children, you need your husband's signature." I
said, "No, he doesn't want to go." . . . And I am not a woman who
likes the *rabbanut* or divorces. But for Israel I told him [her husband],
"Look, if you don't want [to immigrate] I'll leave you, but I'll take
my children and go. I am no better than Rabbi Ḥayim."[6]

Odette's ardent wish to follow Rabbi Ḥuri convinced her husband,
but did not spare them from the shock of arrival at a new *moshav* near
Jerusalem. Choosing to migrate despite her husband's objection, she
felt a need to compensate him by relieving him from the rigors of
immigration, as far as she could: "I did not work all my life. But I
had to—to work, to help my husband. I did not want anything to
be missing, so he could blame me, tell me, 'You wanted this. From
the good, from Heaven, you brought me to Hell.' " Aware of the
contrast between the glorified image of the desired Holy Land and
the reality she encountered, Odette was able to find consolation
in her condition: "But I say to myself this is not true. God, how
big Israel is. Millions of generations wept for Jerusalem and did not
reach it, and I, Yehudit,[7] will reach Jerusalem, *prozdor yerushalaym*
[the Jerusalem's Corridor, where the *moshav* is located]. Why did
I merit this grace? Because of his [Rabbi Ḥuri's] prayers." Odette's
ambivalence about immigration and her resolution to face the difficulties are expressed in a description of her initial encounter with
the *moshav*, told in a weeping voice.

How many nights I dreamt of my house, how many nights! I came
from a resort town, God threw me—God put me here. I don't want
to say, "threw." He put me here for the best. I said, *Aminadav* is the
name of the place? They said yes. I hadn't seen it yet, but I said,

"I hear from people who read Torah that Aminadav was the first to
throw himself into the Red Sea—I mean the courage I received—he
threw himself." I saw cities, I saw this. I said to myself, "What? Am
I better than Aminadav?"

Odette chooses to link her personal story to the master narrative of Jewish immigration, that of the Exodus led by Moses, by
referring to a Talmudic legend. According to the Talmud, when
the Israelites escaped Pharaoh they found themselves at the shores
of the Red Sea with the Egyptian army rapidly closing in behind
them. Nahshon, son of Aminadav, leaped into the water, causing
the sea to part.[8] Odette, who like other traditional North African
women, is not versed in Scriptures (Goldberg 1996, 34), confuses
Nahshon with his father, Aminadav. Nevertheless, by quoting a
sacred text in her story Odette frames her daring threat (divorce) in
an acceptable mode. The intertextuality creates additional meaning
and enables her to find consolation and pride in what she has done
(Briggs and Bauman 1992, 147). This story, as well as the "call" of
Rabbi Ḥuri, allows her to mitigate her nontraditional position of
taking the active role against her husband's wishes, and initiating
the immigration (Schely-Newman 1999a).

Encountering Reality: A Nightly Arrival

Immigration, the first step toward a new life, was followed by an
encounter with the bleak reality, the "Hell," into which the immigrants were thrown. I asked Ghaliya why they went to Gilat; a
lengthy answer followed:

People said, "Let's go to *moshav*," and my husband joined them. . . .
They said, "Let's go to *moshav* we will live there and work." . . . I
didn't know what a *moshav* was, I thought like Tunis, the name of a
city: Sfax, Maḥras, Souse. I didn't know what a *moshav* is [audience
laughter]. . . .
      We were told, "Come to *moshav*." What's a *moshav*? We
thought, a town called *Moshav. Yallah* [Arabic: let's go, hurry up]
quickly quickly. When we said to a *moshav* they were happy, the
Sochnut. "To a *moshav*? To a *moshav*? Great great, quickly." They
brought a large truck and put some blankets and beds and children
[in it] and we all got on. "To a *moshav*? *Yallah,* go." And we rode and
we rode and we rode. We arrived at Tel Aviv, and the driver stopped

in the middle of Tel Aviv. . . . We sat there and they brought us cookies and sweets. "Why?" "Because you are going to a *moshav*." [laughter] *tah mezallu* [Arabic: damn], is it a jail? [laughter]. I was scared. . . . After half an hour or an hour the truck went on. It was all sand. No road. We would soon get to Gaza. He [the driver] didn't know the road, and now it was dark, dark. The border police came, stopped us, "Where are you going, to Gaza?"[9] "No, we are going to *Moshav Gilat.*" "Not this way. Go back, go back the other way." Then he turned and we went, went, went, the truck hardly moved. By the time we got to the *moshav* it was pitch dark. Where, where, where? My husband's cousin was there. They said, "Go into his tent and we'll see tomorrow." . . . We got there. Dark, couldn't see anything until morning.

[In the morning] I raised the rag, that thing from the tent, and thought, *hashakum smallah* [Arabic: oh my God] only piles of sand up to the sky. Not even a green branch! Nothing! Nothing! . . . No bird, no green, no truck, no road, no houses, nothing! What is this, where, what is this? And there were maybe eight tents, maybe ten. I don't remember exactly.

[Later on] I had nothing to do, I sat near a shack. And sat and cried and cried and cried. "What's wrong?" I told him [her husband], "Where, where did they bring us? No! No! No! No! I want to go back, I don't want to stay here. No people, no road. Where is the road? Where is the town? Where are the stores? No, no, no, no, I want to go to the house, where I was, where I was." He said, "No, this is a new town. It will be built and be nice. That one is not a new town. Stay here and you'll see, we'll stay here together." All right. I said nothing. I could do nothing.[10]

Ghaliya is not the only one who remembers arriving at the new *moshav* at night, only to discover desolation the next morning. Alice describes her arrival at Gilat in similar terms: "We came at night, arrived at night. We got off the trucks and they told me my brother was here, so we got off. We got off at night. At night we did not see anything. How would we know what [there was]? In the morning we got up, Gamra and Nana and Fortuna screaming, 'Oh, oh, what is this place they brought us into?' "[11] The arrival story is not limited to Gilat or to women. The narrator of the following was a man in his fifties. "We arrived from Morocco in 1956 and asked for Jerusalem. They put us on trucks and brought us at night, to *Moshav Matta*. When we descended, the trucks left and we stayed here. In the morning—we are urban people; we know nothing about farming—in the morning we saw mountains, thorns, rocks. A total shock."[12]

The motifs of lengthy journey and night arrival seem to be fundamental to many migration stories set during the early years of Israeli statehood.[13] Former foreign minister David Levi, who immigrated from Morocco and lives in Bet Shean, a development town in the Jordan Valley, includes a similar story in his autobiography, contrasting the excitement of arrival in Israel with the reality of the place: "We did not sleep a wink all that night. The reality we found the next day was even worse" (Avneri, 1983, 30). Night arrival became part of the master narrative of immigrants, emphasizing the feelings of deception many Sephardi immigrants of the 1950s felt. Indeed, the trip from the immigrant camps, which were generally located in the center of the country, to the remote *moshavim* and development towns was lengthy. During the early 1950s there was no comfortable transportation nor were there highways, and transferring immigrants from one part of the country to the other involved an enormous amount of bureaucracy. However, the stories about night arrival told so many years after the actual trip suggest that the night is not simply a temporal reference but holds a personal meaning. The trope of the night emphasizes the shock, the feeling of dependence and vulnerability. Not surprisingly, arrival accounts give the immigrants a passive role throughout: "They brought us"; "We were taken"; "They drove us"; "Told us to stay." This allocation is obvious in Ghaliya's narrative: her only response is to complain and cry. The transformation from passive to active roles occurs when narrators are able to connect the nightly experience to their actions on the following days (Schely-Newman 1996a).

Taking Charge: Life Changes

The transition to a rural community changed people's lives drastically. Merchants and craftsmen learned how to become farmers, and to build homes and roads, and were trained in the use of arms. Men continued to earn a living for their families by working outside the community, either part time or full time, while women were left to tend the farm, with its chickens, a cow, and an acre or two of irrigated land. These new responsibilities coincided with a decrease in traditional kin-related help. Immigration to Israel frequently broke apart extended families; some of the young were eager to join the new state, while older members had to first sell their property or were held back for medical or financial reasons. Even in cases where whole communities were moved to Israel by the *Sochnut*— especially when the continued existence of a Jewish community was in danger—the traditional division of labor had to be altered. Shokeid (1971), who studied a *moshav* whose population was transplanted from the Atlas mountains in Morocco and resettled in Israel, notes that the structure of the *moshav*, with its individual farms and small, separate homes, required women to be more involved in supporting the family. In this new setting women began to form social networks with other women within the immigrant community, networks that were based on needs rather than kinship. Relationships and networking with the nonimmigrant society made the women primary agents of modernization and change within the community itself (Andezian and Streiff-Fenart 1986; Katzir 1984).

The participation of women in the workforce and their contribution to family income revised marital relations (Shokeid 1971, 194). Women became the representatives of the family, as Odette sadly notes when talking about the hospitalization of one of her sons: "People in the hospital did not know who the father was. In school they did not know who the father was. . . . At the children's wedding they would ask, 'Who is the father?' I was a mother and a father, and that will continue until I die." Education became another domain of woman's responsibility, even though traditionally men were responsible for their sons' education.[14] This role shift is evident in Ghaliya's story:

> Yair was a very, very good boy. He went to high school in Beersheba. . . . Every day I gave him money for the bus and a sandwich to eat. Leave him hungry? Well, when he would start eating, some other kid took his lunch. Every day he came home hungry. "What is it, my son?" He says to me, "Mom, there is a kid who takes it from me." "Where?" "Near the bus." Oh, God, I must go. Once I went with him. I found him. [He was] a tall guy. They said he was from *Moshav Sharsheret*. I told him, "Aren't you ashamed? A little kid who goes to study, the whole day left by himself. We do not live in Beersheba, and you take it and leave him hungry? I swear to you, if you do it again I will call the police." And he never took my son's lunch again.[15]

The husbands of Ghaliya and Odette left all family affairs in the hands of their wives. Like most men, busy with work, they were frequently absent from family celebrations, leading to complaints such as "My husband goes nowhere. I always go alone." The absence of men due to work was not restricted to festive occasions; work away from home forced women to take an active part in protecting both their household—as Ghaliya did with Yair—and the community itself.

Armed Women: Active Protection

The impact of frontier life is a central theme in the historical discourse in Gilat (Schely-Newman 1993, 1997). Like Aminadav and many other *moshavim,* Gilat was purposely located near the Israeli borders and thus subject to infiltration by Arabs, a fact that required sentries to guard the community every night. Shlomo, one of Gilat's founders, explained that women had to participate in guard duty because there were not enough men. Women were taught to use guns to protect their homes and families, and this often resulted in "heroic" and amusing stories: a teenaged woman once shot at stockings hanging on a clothesline, mistaking them for an Arab infiltrator. Yet the use of firearms for self-protection also resulted in accidental shootings in which people were maimed and even killed.

Vaguely recollecting a story I once heard as a child in which a woman shot and killed her husband, I asked my parents what happened (the full text appears in *Appendix 5*).

1. Esther: [Tell me] the one who shot out of the window, or something . . .
2. Fortuna: Noro may know it.
3. Noro: What is it?
4. Fortuna: Do you know it?
5. Esther: You said something about someone shooting her husband . . .
6. Fortuna: One day a man went on guard duty. He told his wife.
7. She said, "I'm afraid to stay [home] alone."
8. He told her, "If someone comes and makes noises or something, shoot, it's okay."

9. Noro: Yeh.
10. Fortuna: She told him, "No, no." He said, "It's okay. Shoot."
11. Yeh. That same night, as it happened, her husband unexpectedly came back.
12. She heard steps.
13. She quickly took the Sten gun and shot.
14. It turned out to be her husband.
15. Esther: Oh, oh, was she on bad terms with her husband?
16. Fortuna: No, no, she wasn't.
17. Esther: Father, wasn't she on bad terms with her husband, this woman?
18. Noro: I don't know. I don't remember the story exactly
19. Esther: In what *moshav?* But what do you remember exactly?
20. Noro: Nothing, I don't remember anything of this case.
21. Fortuna: No, I heard people, like that.
22. Esther: And in what *moshav* did it happen, do you know?
23. Noro: In Gilat, in Gilat, that woman who was shot in the legs . . .[16]

Noro began to tell another story, about a woman who went to the outhouse at night, carrying a flashlight. It was Friday night and the sentry was sure that the figure he saw was an enemy, not a Jew, because a Jew is forbidden to turn on or carry lights on Shabbat (appendix 5, lines 42–53). The sentry, therefore, shot and wounded the woman. Note the polyphonic style of my parents' narration, similar to the story about Thérèse falling into the well (chapter 1). Though Fortuna admits Noro's entitlement to tell stories about guns (lines 2, 39), she nevertheless tells the story herself. I, too, acknowledged the male entitlement to these stories by referring back to Noro to expand (lines 17, 19).

Two years later I interviewed my parents again, this time in the presence of my older sister Miriam and her daughter. We were talking about shooting events in Gilat and Fortuna retold the story of the woman who was shot, followed by other stories. Because of Noro's stroke he was not able to participate actively in the narration, and the floor was given to Fortuna. Noro's contribution was a mere confirmation of facts (line 14, following), the same facts he had previously denied (preceding, lines 18,20). Both Miriam and

Fortuna telling stories about guarding the home, Kibbutz Lavie, April 1989

I participated in the narration in a joking manner, recalling our childhood memories and acknowledging Fortuna's experience and entitlement (full text in appendix 6).

1. Fortuna: There was one woman, wait. On another *moshav*, listen.
2. Esther: Yes.
3. Fortuna: In Brosh in a *moshav* like that.
4. Her husband told her, if you hear a noise, shoot. If you hear noise, shoot.
5. Esther: Yes. [to Miriam] Listen and tell me if you know this one.
6. Fortuna: If you hear a noise, shoot
7. and he went, to guard duty or something like that.
8. Then he came back, understand?
9. She heard a noise—he knocked on the door I think and she shot him.
10. Miriam: Who was it?

11. Fortuna: Her husband.
12. Esther: Which *moshav* was it?
13. Fortuna: On another *moshav,* say Brosh. Put Brosh.
14. Noro: It's true, it's true
15. Fortuna: She shot him.
16. Thought he was an Arab, she shot him, *sham'u-ᵊl-xir* (Arabic: God forbid), it turned out to be her
17. Esther: Oh oh, did she kill him or just injure his legs? [Joking remarks about shooting]
20. Esther: Did you shoot too?
21. Fortuna [laughs]: No, listen to this.
22. I . . . Once . . . Noro went on guard duty.
23. You understand, went to the other side [of the *moshav*].
24. He was late. Baḥla my sister was with me, and I said, "Oh [claps hands], Noro is not back yet."
25. It was almost 1:00 A.M., and I had a gun.
26. I told her, "I am going to shoot."
27. Baḥla my sister said, "No, no, don't shoot, who knows who's walking by?"
28. I told her, "Who can be walking by at 1:00 A.M.?"
29. No, I'm going to shoot so Noro will hear me from the other side" [and return home].
30. Miriam: Yeh, with Margo. With Rachel [Baḥla, Fortuna's sister, who lived with us for some time].
31. Fortuna: Rachel. She says to me, "No," and I say . . .
32. I climbed to the window on a bed, because we had a bed.
33. Esther: Right, she had to climb onto the window.
34. Fortuna: From the window, and put the gun out, and wanted to shoot. I was ready.
35. She tells me, "Don't shoot there must be . . . ."
36. I told her, "At one after midnight? Who is going to pass by after midnight?"
37. Finally I say, "Yes," and she says, "No."
38. In the end I did not shoot. I did not shoot [all laugh].
39. After fifteen minutes Noro came home.
40. Esther: He heard, how did you know?
41. Miriam: How did you know how to shoot? Who taught you to shoot?

42. Fortuna: Noro taught me to shoot. Before he went on guard duty. I shot two or three times.
43. Miriam: Training, there were trainings.
    [all laugh]
44. Esther: You were training mother?
45. Fortuna: No, I knew.
46. No, but Noro was on guard duty every night, and you were little, sleeping.
47. He told me, "If you hear a noise . . ."
48. He tells me, "You hear a noise or scratching on the door, or something, shoot!"
49. I learned to shoot! I would put the gun near my head, upright like that.
50. Esther: Loaded?
51. Fortuna: You understand, and I stayed awake, when I heard some scratching, I'd get up.
52. No, I sleep very lightly.
53. I lay on the bed sleeping, like this, and the kids sleeping here, and I stood near the window.
54. No, lying or standing.
55. When I hear scratching, I shoot. What! the truth, I never shot.
56. Esther: Since then she's learned to lock the door.
57. Fortuna: I didn't shoot. [17]

These three stories connect women with a quintessential male symbol, the gun. The story of the woman who was shot was also told by other people in Gilat, with the addition of various details. The woman was pregnant, and her husband, a doctor, was on guard duty. He suggested that she sleep at the house of a relative, but she preferred to remain at home. She then went out at night, perhaps to the outhouse, or because she was scared, or to meet someone. The sentry, who saw an unidentified person between the houses, fired. The woman was wounded and apparently miscarried; her husband divorced her and she left the community. Obviously, injuring a woman is a serious matter, but the stories blame the woman for breaching communal norms, for not keeping the laws of Shabbat, for not remaining in the protection of her home. This event did occur, as it was reported in a newspaper at the time, but the reasons for continuing to tell the story (and for others wanting to listen to it) have more to do with the construction of the story as a synthesis of issues of morality and communal boundaries than with the unfortunate woman herself. The details, even the identity of the woman, are far less important than the social drama of crime and punishment reenacted in the story (Schely-Newman 1993).

The two other stories tell of women using guns, rather than being a target. Fortuna threatens to use the gun, but does not do so. Furthermore, it is Noro, her husband, who entrusts her with the weapon and who teaches her how to use it (line 42). Guns are used to safeguard the home (lines 46, 53) and now are within the female sphere of responsibilities. Chaperoned by her sister, Fortuna stood guard inside the house to protect her family. The third story, of the woman who shot and killed her husband, may be an urban legend born from the fertile ground of fears and anxieties in a rapidly changing world (Fine 1980, 236–37). Other versions claim that the husband instructed his wife to shoot, then tested her: She did exactly as she was told, and unfortunately for the husband, she passed the test (cf. Brunvand 1984, 28–31). The intertextual connection—the dialogue—between the three stories is reinforced by the fact that they were told in one cluster. This dialogue is further enhanced by the similarities between the actions and words used by the narrator. Both were instructed in the same manner. In line 4 Fortuna says of the other woman: "Her husband told her, 'If you hear noise, shoot. If you hear noise, shoot.'" About her own experience she says (line 48): "He tells me: 'You hear a noise or scratching on the door or something, shoot.'" It is interesting that Fortuna removes the destructive potential of the gun in a woman's hand from Gilat into another *moshav.* Her insistence on locating the events elsewhere—say "Brosh"—serves to distance them from the here and now and to release herself from any responsibility for its accuracy (Shuman 1993b, 150). Transferring the event away from "us"—Brosh is not far from Gilat, and is settled by Moroccan-Israelis—may also be in deference to Noro, who denied that such an event could occur in "our" community.

Tension between male role as protector of women and children and the reality of women carrying guns still exists in the Israeli discourse on gender role and place (Sered 2000, 76–77). In the context of migration and cultural changes, these tensions are more pronounced and are fertile ground for stories that indirectly emphasize the potential of danger and conflict. Guns were given to women because of a real need to protect the community, but at the same time, when a woman takes on the male role of protecting the family from external threats the traditional responsibilities of the male are truncated. Giving up or sharing his protector role casts the man in the role of an outsider. In this new situation the woman is not only mistress of the private sphere but guardian of its boundaries too. The interpretation of these three stories as an arena of struggle over control and power is supported by the identity of the narrators. Both men and women told the story about the woman who was shot by the sentry, though women gave more details (Schely-Newman 1993), but only women narrated the story of the woman shooting her husband. As a subversive story it threatened Noro's position, and he, therefore, did not remember it. However, he told the story about the woman who was shot in her legs, since it restored communal order by punishing the woman as she stepped (literally) out of bounds. Fortuna's initial hesitation to tell the story of the woman who shot her husband in the 1987 interview may be understood as deference to her husband, at least formally. No such hesitation exists in the second version, told in 1989; after Noro was silenced by a stroke, Fortuna assumed the role of the family narrator. Moreover, the audience now included a granddaughter who was to be married that same week, and this was a time to elaborate on stories about gender role and power (Schely-Newman 1999b).

"Instant" Transformation

The changes taking place in women's lives—their taking charge of their children's education, making decisions in everyday matters—did not occur suddenly. In all likelihood, the process of taking on additional roles and responsibilities was gradual, forced by changing realities. Necessity, rather than ideological commitment to personal freedom and choice, hastened the process of "liberation." The changes in women's roles took place within the framework of traditional culture, and attempts to stray too far from tradition could result in severe consequences, as the shooting stories indicate.

While the actual changes were gradual, some women created an "emancipation" narrative in which the gradual changes collapsed into one event, as evidenced by Odette likening her life story to the act of jumping into the sea ("Am I better than Aminadav?"). With this intertextuality Odette claims personal responsibility for emigration and settling in her *moshav*. Her husband plays a minor part; in fact, he is an obstruction in her life story. She needed his permission to immigrate to Israel, but the decisions are presented as her own. From this point on in her life story, Odette is an independent woman.

Odette is not the only woman with an "emancipatory" story. One of Ghaliya's narratives seems to demonstrate in a poetic manner the instant transformation from passive to active. The story of her arrival at the *moshav* from the immigrant camp has been quoted above: the family arrived at night, not knowing what to expect, was confronted the next morning by a barren desert, and her only response was to sit and cry. However, Ghaliya did not end her story at this point. Rather, she continued on to tell how she and other pregnant women were taken to the nearby town of Beersheba for a medical checkup, a modern practice never before experienced. As she left the clinic she saw an abandoned house, with a courtyard and a lemon tree, the same kind of house she remembered from Tunisia:

> I told my husband, "I am not going back to the tent. I want to live here. Everyone is Jewish here, there is no fear, even without doors, even without windows. I'll stay here. I am not budging from this house." So he told me, "No, what are you talking about? This town is in ruins. It's all falling apart. It's all ruined. It's ruined, and our town is new, will be new and will be nice. This one will never recover, this Beersheba [laughs]. All ruins, all falling. Now go home."
>
> I had Roni, no, Avner, little at the time. I told him [her husband] "Let's go and buy him clothes." We went to the department store, or I don't know which store. I forgot. A top and a bottom, so nice. So we got on the tractor [to return to the *moshav*]. I took out the outfit to show Buba, "Look!" and the wind took it away! [all laugh] "Hey Kiki [the driver], hey Kiki, stop!" We just hardly bought it, just hardly. We had only a little money. "Hey Kiki stop!" "What is it, Ghaliya, did you fall off?" "No, Avner's outfit, the wind blew it away." So he started going back, going back, until we found and retrieved it. And then we continued back to the *moshav*.

This story of the return journey to Gilat mirrors the story of the initial journey to the *moshav*. The *moshav* was far away from the immigrant camp, a distance that is iconically mirrored by the lengthy narrative; the second trip is much shorter and so is its account. Leaving the immigrant camp was a happy occasion; the immigrants did not know what a *moshav* was but were glad to leave the camp for their own homes. Ghaliya returned to the *moshav* from Beersheba only reluctantly, however, wanting to remain in a house that reminded her of what she had left behind in the town of Gabes. This was no longer a nighttime trip into the unknown; she knew exactly what was waiting for her—a small tent in the middle of nowhere—but she still accepted her husband's order: "Now go home." Furthermore, Ghaliya herself was silent during the first journey. Other people spoke, "Let's go to *moshav.*" *Sochnut* officials did not give them time to reflect, rushing them, "To a *moshav?* To a *moshav?* Great, great, quickly." The answer given to the border patrol, "We are going to *moshav Gilat,*" is a collective answer, not Ghaliya's. Ghaliya's only response when she is faced with the fait accompli on the morning after is to cry and complain.

However, in this section of the narrative (which immediately follows the night arrival story) Ghaliya gains a voice. She asserts herself, telling her husband, "I am not going back to the tent." Even when she follows her husband's order ("Now go home"), she mitigates the direct order by initiating an action, "Let's go and buy him [the son] clothes." Yet Ghaliya does more than initiate an action; she also takes action to keep what she has gained, to prevent anybody or anything (even the wind) from depriving her of it. The parallel structure of the two arrival stories supports the interpretation of this segment as an emancipatory tale, which marks Ghaliya's transformation from a passive to an active player in her life. Both trips include two stops, one involving getting goods, the other involving a physical return. On the first trip the family is *given* candies; on the second, Ghaliya and her husband *buy* a garment. On the first trip the driver is *turned back* by the border police after he takes the wrong turn; on the second, it is Ghaliya who *orders* the driver to go back to retrieve the garment. The reasons for changing course—fear of Arabs in Gaza in the first case, and the desert wind in the second—continue to be the two main obstacles that the settlers had to cope with in their early years (Schely-Newman 1996a, 1997). In a variety of ways, then, this story encapsulates Ghaliya's transformation from passive immigrant to active individual.

Gaining a Voice: Entitlement to an Audience

The actual experiences and the increase of women's responsibilities come together with the appropriation of the male genre *ḥikayah,* stories about real events. Men are the main narrators of public events and the official history of the community in terms of economic changes and governance. However, other experiences, such as raising children, working in the fields, and the procurement of food, are told by women to mixed audiences. Real-life events from the domestic sphere are seen as worthy of becoming "stories," and may even be considered the best type of stories. *Beemet a-torah, xrayef taʿ əl ḥaq xir ml xrayef el kel* (I swear to you, real stories are better than all other stories), claims Alice when talking about everyday events.[18] Sabra Webber's distinction between the terms *ḥikayah* (male real stories) and *xurafah* (fictive female tales) has not been maintained in Israel, where men and women use the terms interchangeably. However, when we consider the content of stories, we find that women are, in fact, expanding the genre of "real" stories to include their own experiences. Furthermore, women do not limit their stories to events from the domestic sphere, but include in their repertoire events concerning their husbands, neighbors, and other males. Having been there during the years when the community was being built entitles women to tell about local events from that time not only in exclusively female settings but in mixed groups as well. When I interviewed couples, the wives frequently took an active part in narration; they showed little hesitation (framed within acceptable norms) about interrupting or correcting their husbands. The joint narrations of my parents are an example. On one occasion, when a mixed group discussed the state of research and knowledge about Tunisian Jews in Israel, a young man blamed the older generation for being "ashamed of their heritage." Ghaliya responded: "Why didn't they come to me? I would have told them everything!"[19] Clearly, she sees herself as competent, and as entitled as others to instruct in Tunisian mores and traditions. Perhaps she is criticizing the younger generation for not acknowledging women as a potential and authoritative source.

The use of a male genre of speech is particularly evident in Odette's story; quoting a sacred discourse helps to create additional modes of interpretation and implies positive evaluation of her own

"Why didn't they come to ask me?" Ghaliya asks her audience, Gilat, July 1988

pioneering act (Briggs and Bauman 1992, 147). Odette interprets the community's name in a Midrashic mode, a traditional male Jewish way of reading into sacred texts frequently used in rabbinic homilies. Her assumption of the male role in making the decision to immigrate is enhanced by her usurpation of a traditional male genre, even though she admits that she is not familiar with Scriptures, and actually misquotes the Talmudic source. [20] The fact that the story was told to a female audience notwithstanding, Odette asserts herself in her authoritative role not only in the content but also in the manner of telling her story (see Schely-Newman 1999a).

A New Woman?

"Immigration brings a new situation which, at the same time as it weakens family bonds, increases the number of alternatives and hence the uncertainty about decisions to be taken in all areas of social activities," conclude Andezian and Streiff-Fenart (1986, 165). These changes are explored and elaborated in the stories women tell about emigration experiences. Their focus of activities remains the home and family, but the division of labor and responsibility has been altered, giving women a stronger say in family matters (cf. Shokeid 1971). The new roles women took are expressed in the way women position themselves as active, claiming responsibility for

118

their own behavior (van Langenhove and Harre 1993, 84). Moreover, we hear women using their own voices rather than simply reporting inner speech or other people's words. The more active they become, the less we hear of their husband's words or deeds. Changes have also affected the role models women use; this is particularly evident in Odette's life story, in which the mother is absent. Odette's life in Israel was shaped and influenced by the encounter with Rabbi Ḥuri: she was blessed by him, and her life took a different turn after that point, as he replaced other significant people in her life, including her father and the doctor. The model set by her mother was ineffectual, and the silent plea of the mother—kissing her toes on the last night before embarking on the long voyage to Israel—was to no avail: it was too late for Odette to change her life. [21]

CHAPTER 5

Everyone's Grandmother

Now that we are old, one should not be bashful.
Tuwa kif waḥed kber ma kᵊqas yaḥshem

The socially invisible girls became women: wives, mothers, and grandmothers, engaged in raising families and adjusting to the new life in Israel. Now, as elderly women, they are able to view their lives in retrospect and to compare, confront, and reflect on customs and values in Tunisia and in Israel. Older women have had liberties denied to younger women. Describing the lives of Algerian women Djebar says, "Only speak of what conforms, my grandmother would reprove me: to deviate is dangerous." And, "How could a woman speak aloud, even in Arabic, unless on the threshold of extreme age?" (Djebar [1985] 1993, 256). The Tunisian-Israeli women in their seventies and eighties have acquired entitlement to an independent voice and are now capable of discussing almost any topic. During an interview with Alice and her daughter I asked about visits to the *mikvah*. Alice now became more aware of the presence of her son-in-law who criticized the need for the ritual bath in modern days. She continued to relate her taxing experiences of going to the bath, hedging the topic with, *tuwa kif waḥed kber ma kᵊqas yaḥshem* (literally: "now, that one has grown older, he is no longer bashful"). Perhaps she was criticizing us, the younger mixed audience, for taking the liberty to discuss the *mikvah* openly. Or, she may have been expressing the tension that still exists between the freedoms of old age and traditional attitudes towards the female sphere of experience.[1]

Opportunities for reflection on their lives are endless: any setting may be suitable and any person may qualify as audience, provided a rapport is established first. Simple acts, such as helping to carry packages, inquiring about health, or assisting in bureaucratic processes, are frequently sufficient to initiate extended conversation and storytelling. For example, my chance encounter with an elderly Israeli woman who needed assistance with paperwork at an airport led to a short conversation and additional insights into the lives of Tunisian-Israeli old women. Reḥana explained that her husband "hates to travel" but she wants to see her children, therefore she travels on her own to visit them, even to Los Angeles.[2]

The women talk about issues that concern them, issues perceived as central to their identity, such as stories about their relations with relatives and neighbors, stories representing their moral duties as caregivers (Gergen 1992, 139; Paoletti 1998, 79–80). They talk about their own lives, but also share with each other the stories of other women, friends and elders. Following traditions learned by generations of silent women, the stories they share bear witness to the drama of their own lives (cf. Djebar [1985] 1993, 154). Hearing the same stories over and over again gives women entitlement to incorporate other women's stories into their own discourse about womanhood.

This web of female relationships is examined in the first part of this chapter, which describes what being an older woman entails in everyday Israeli life in the 1990s. The second part of the chapter treats the discourse of nostalgia and the poetic structure of oral narratives (Hill 1992; Hymes 1998; Silverstein 1985).

Being an Older Woman

The Center

Odette, Fortuna, Ghaliya, Alice, and others spend three to five mornings each week at a *mo'adon kshishim* (community center for elderly people), where a variety of activities are offered to them for a minimal fee. Such centers vary in size and in the types of activities offered, depending on the number of participants (cf. Sered 1992). For example, the elders of Gilat visit a *mo'adon* located in a regional community center, which operates five days a week,

Odette and friends in the *mo'adon*, Aminadav, July 1988

Sunday through Thursday, until 2:00 P.M., and serves ten different *moshavim*. It is wheelchair-accessible, with bathing facilities and a staff that includes professional social workers and physiotherapists. The visitors receive a morning snack and full lunch and are offered a variety of activities and adult courses. The small center visited by Odette is located in the library of *moshav* Aminadav. It is open on Sundays, Mondays, and Wednesdays from 8:30 to 11:00 A.M., and serves three *moshavim*. Despite a lack of facilities, smaller centers like this one have an important advantage: they are usually located in the middle of the *moshav*, near the grocery store and clinic. The elderly are able to visit the doctor or do some shopping while attending the center.[3] Traveling to the larger centers with better facilities limits the mobility of the elderly, as they frequently need to rely on others to help with errands or to take them to the medical clinic. In some communities, such as Aminadav, the elderly have decided to forgo the amenities of the larger centers and remain in the small local facility, with limited activities and a nonprofessional staff.

The elderly are encouraged to take part in deciding on the activities offered, within budgetary limits. For example, during March

Odette, Sara, and Tamu catch the winter sun while waiting for the bus, Aminadav, December 1992.

1999 the Aminadav group took an excursion to the south of Israel, as part of an ecological learning program. The planned trip included a visit to a waste-disposal site and a visit to Sde Boker, where Israel's first prime minister, David Ben-Gurion, is buried. Led by Odette, the group insisted on an additional stop, at the grave of Rabbi Ḥuri in Beersheba, located on the excursion route. The trip was satisfactory and fulfilling, giving the women the opportunity to perform pilgrimages to the graves of two revered persons: the father of the State of Israel and a venerated saint.[4] Visitations to graves are an important aspect of saint veneration but lack of funds often prevents group pilgrimages. The members of the *mo'adon*, however, find ways to use existing funded programs to perform what is seen as a religious duty.

Most members of the smaller centers are women; the men who attend tend to sit at different tables, joining the women only when food is served. The number of men in the larger centers is higher, but they remain a minority compared to women and engage in limited types of activities.[5] Some activities, though, such as excursions, attract nonregular members, including men. The centers are perceived as a place for old people, and are called *dar l-ʿazawez* (house of the old), a term bearing negative connotations. Gabay, a Moroccan who lives across the road from the Aminadav center, told me that he knows that he is old, but that going to the center would constitute admission of the fact (cf. Paoletti 1998, 24–25). Men in Gilat gave similar responses: "Only old people go to the center." Women, too, are aware of their ages. For example, the women I photographed during regular activities said that they disliked the photos because they revealed their wrinkles. Odette and Biya offered to trade them for "better" pictures, from their youth. However, despite sensitivity to physical appearance, women are more ready than men to acknowledge their current stage in life, perhaps because being grandmothers is a confirmation of their having lived a good and useful life. Or perhaps their ability to continue performing traditional duties of nurturing and caring reduces the need to deny old age as a sign of uselessness or redundancy. For men, going to the center may be perceived as an inability to perform one's duty to work and to earn money; the level of denial of being old is therefore more pronounced. Men would rather be associated with less "idle" activities—helping their children at work, shopping at the neighborhood grocery, going to the open-air market, or spending time at the synagogue.

Family Relations

The fact that they are now seventy or eighty years old and have spent the last forty or fifty years in difficult conditions has not benefitted the health of these women, and increasingly illness becomes a constitutive part of their normal experiences. The most frequently visited institution in the community is the clinic, and every woman carries with her a variety of pills for treating pain, hypertension, heart conditions, diabetes, and other ailments common to the elderly.[6] Initial encounters with women usually included complaints about health, and in each recurring visit I learned more about specific medical problems. Still, although their children are grown and usually living in their own homes, the women continue to prepare large meals, mainly for Shabbat and holidays. On such occasions children are expected to eat with their parents in the parents' homes, or at least have a taste of their mothers' dishes. Each of the women swears that she alone knows how to cook the "real" traditional dishes appreciated by her children and would never deny them these pleasures. Even if a woman is expected to spend a particular holiday with only one of her children, she will prepare traditional dishes for the others.[7] Women's schedules, therefore, including visits to the center, are always subject to special family events, as well as to the Jewish calendar.[8] My interviews with the women at their homes were frequently conducted against a background of preparations for some family event or unexpected guests.

Family and children are a favorite subject of conversation. In the center, women share their joys and sorrows, so that personal histories become common knowledge and may be retold by other women. The center also serves as a "referral service": the women advise each other on remedies, names of doctors, prayers, or sources of help in finding a match for marriage. The social ties between women exceed the boundaries of the *mo'adon;* they sometimes collect money for a small gift to celebrate an event in another woman's family, or when death occurs in the family of a member of the community they go as a group to offer condolences during the *shiva* (seven days of mourning).

CHILDREN

The elderly women continue to be involved in the everyday life of their families, and their responsibility toward their "dependents" is not negotiable, regardless of age or physical condition. They are expected to care for their grandchildren, allowing the parents to work. When Thérèse exclaimed once that she would not care for her grandchildren because it was the responsibility of the parents, she was accused of being selfish. Unconditional care is extended to the husband; even women abused by their husbands do not refuse to care for them when they are sick. The women complain about mistreatment by their husbands and commiserate about their lot, but no "decent" woman will turn away from helping her husband when he needs her. A Moroccan woman from Aminadav told me about how her children had convinced her to agree to take care of her sick husband after he left her for another woman. Another woman, who was physically abused during her marriage, nursed

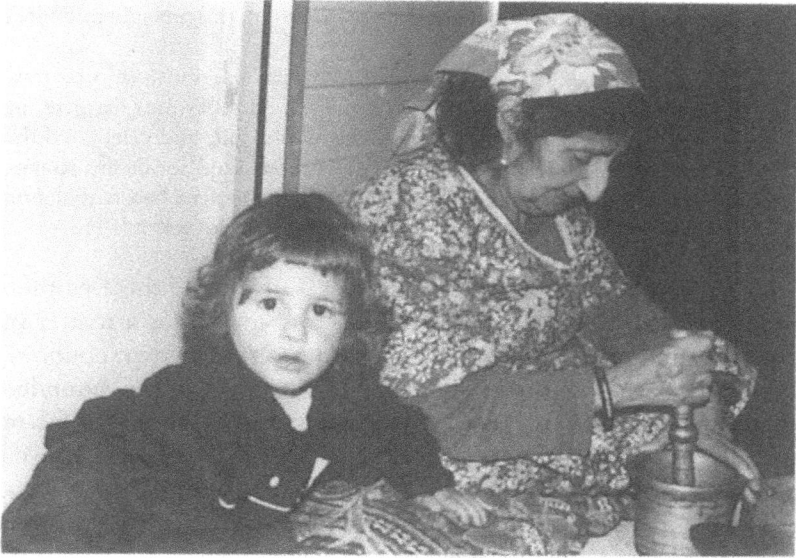

Generation to generation: Fortuna tells her grandson stories and proverbs while watching him as part of her grandmother's job, Gilat, December 1990.

her husband for several years when he suffered a stroke; after his death she was reluctant to talk about her unhappy life with him.

Total commitment to children assumes a certain reciprocity—that is, it is assumed that children will care for their elderly parents when necessary. Yet not all children are equally reliable. Women are expected to be more strongly connected to their families. Hence, in a reversal of earlier attitudes toward gender, in old age it is not the sons who are favored but the daughters. This reversal is demonstrated in the following folktale:

> On a cold and rainy day a maid looking out the window saw her master's father in the street. The mistress ordered her to bring him into the house until the rain ceased. Later the wife's father was seen in the street, but in his case he was also given dry clothing and a hot meal. The husband's father told his son of the differential treatment, but asked him not to punish his wife.
>
> When the woman gave birth to their first son, the midwife joyfully went to inform her master, but instead of the expected reward for the good news, she got a slap in the face. The ceremonies for the birth were conducted as minimally as possible. Some time

127

passed, and the wife gave birth to another son; this time the midwife's "reward" was two slaps.

When the wife gave birth to a girl, a servant, who by now feared his reaction, informed the father. To everyone's surprise, he gave the servant money, bought his wife a gift, and celebrated the birth of the girl with great fanfare. When asked about this strange practice, he explained that the rainy-day incident had taught him that only a girl would take care of him when he was in need.[9]

Israel in the 1990s, however, is not Tunisia, and these women who took care of their elderly parents and in-laws as a matter of course cannot expect the same treatment from their own children. Not only have patterns of residence changed, from the extended to the nuclear family, but distant residences may also be a factor in preventing or limiting help. Furthermore, daughters, as well as sons, usually work. Concerns about being old and dependent have become more acute and are expressed in frequent discussions and stories about the disrespect or neglect from children, especially daughters-in-law.

Families with dependent elderly members now require different solutions. However, even when a parent is in poor health, placing him or her in a nursing home is seen as abandonment. It is felt that a person should die in his own home or in the hospital while being treated for illness. Nursing homes are not seen as a place where elderly people receive better treatment or improve their health, but rather as a solution for children who "throw out" their parents instead of caring for them. The mere thought of a home is enough to kill a person, as in the case of Ḥayim, who, it is told, died in the hospital on the day his son signed the papers transferring him to a nursing home.

Reality, nevertheless, requires children to find solutions for elderly parents in need of constant care. One response is to hire live-in helpers, a workforce that comes mainly from the Philippines, in a procedure that involves bureaucratic effort at high cost.[10] The presence of a nurse in the house, however, causes problems, not the least of which is xenophobia. Many women, though frail and sickly, refuse to take "a strange woman" into the sanctity of their homes: the presence of a foreigner, it is feared, may be interpreted as an indication of the failure to fulfill one's roles. When a woman is ill or when a man is a widower and outside help is necessary, other problems emerge, resulting from ethnocentrism over cultural differences. Serious questions need to be considered, including how to communicate, what types of food to use and how they should be cooked, and whether the rules of *kashrut* are being kept properly. I heard of families looking to employ Muslim women from Arab countries, such as Morocco, because these families felt that a common cultural background and language increased the possibility of harmony and success.

THE HUSBAND

Most marriages were traditionally arranged by the families, and for many couples marriage functions mainly as a means of connection for raising a family. When the woman reaches menopause she is relieved of sexual requirements and is free to a significant degree to lead a life separate from her husband, without fear of social sanction. Old age thus allows women to devote more time to spiritual endeavors, especially pilgrimages, and in fact old women visit the synagogue more frequently than do young women (Bilu and Hasan-Rokem 1989; Schely-Newman 1999a; Sered 1992, 49–50). In Israel the women also attend religious classes, where they learn formal rules for observing the holidays, or learn about the Bible. They are proud of their achievements, exhibiting the commendations and awards they have earned.[11]

Freedom from sexual obligations decreases a woman's responsibilities toward the husband. According to Reḥana, "Now that the children are all married, I do not have to listen to him or stay home with him." Ghaliya and Odette were less explicit, but they, too, feel no need to confer with their husbands when making plans. In fact, spousal relations are overturned: in old age women are not as vulnerable as they were when younger, and they have their adult children and their female network to which to turn. Furthermore, their experiences and those of other women have taught them that men are not always reliable. A story told by Ghaliya about my grandparents, Braham and Kuka, is an example of the changes in status (see appendix 7 for the complete narrative):

45. in Sfax he [Braham] left her [Kuka] for five years and went to France
48. and left her with three children

50. and then when his daughter got married she sent a message
    to him saying
51. just come just come
52. so people won't say she has no father
53. don't bring anything
54. well
55. that was then
56. that's what he did in his youth
57. and later when he got older
58. he was peeling bananas for her
59. because now he'd turned old
60. he was good for nothing.

This story of abandonment is part of a larger story (to be expanded later in this chapter) that expresses a woman's view of a man's life cycle. Not many men left their wives for another woman in a foreign country and repented later, but other types of neglect and abuse were well known. Fortuna's childless maternal aunt, who raised her, accepted two successive co-wives out of fear that her husband would divorce her. Anxiety about not fulfilling the husband's expectations may itself cause harm, as in the case of Shushan's wife's miscarriage. A husband who follows his mother's advice and in doing so neglects his own wife considers his behavior only a minor infraction. In old age the roles seem to be reversed, as the wife's obligations toward her husband diminish but he still needs her to cook and care for him.

The independence women gain with old age is enhanced by the Israeli socioeconomic situation. Although most women did not work outside their homes, their work on the farms was recognized by the government for social security eligibility. At the age of sixty they began to receive a small income in their own names. For some women this was the first money they had ever earned. The money is often used to pay fees to the center, to pay for small purchases, and even to support adult children, with or without the knowledge of their husbands.

Mores and Values

Feminine identity is bound to moral duties (Paoletti 1998, 79), duties that increasingly encompass people other than one's own offspring (cf. Sered 1992). As "everyone's grandmother," these women are concerned with the well-being of the young and their proper behavior in general. In criticizing the behavior of the young, they are examining and formulating their own values and opinions about the present and the past. Almost every conversation about the present raises the issue of the loose morals of the times, as witnessed daily and represented in the media. These elderly women are appalled by the way young women, frequently their own granddaughters, dress and behave. The values of their youth in other countries are compared with those of the present, as stated by women in the center: "We had good education there. They used to punish [people] for moral breaches. A fornicating woman [the word said in a whisper] would be tied to a horse's tail." Referring to the laxity in adhering to menstrual abstinence, they comment: "That is why there are many accidents, many problems. People are like donkeys, they don't know. They keep saying these rules are nonsense [repeated loudly]."

The elderly women who criticize the behavior of younger Israelis nonetheless are also aware that in general women's status has improved in Israel. There is a minimum marriage age (some of the women interviewed were married before menarche), polygyny is illegal, fathers are required by law to support their children, and social agencies are available for help in many areas. The living conditions in nuclear households allow a woman a certain degree of independence in her own home, rather than being under the authority and constant scrutiny of a mother-in-law, and young women are not forced to marry men they did not choose. The ambivalence nevertheless exists, because the reputation of the woman may be tarnished, as the women in Aminadav claim: "It is good that a man and woman know each other before getting married; but, on the other hand, this may result in wickedness, because they may then leave each other [before marriage]."

Women's expectations of conjugal life have changed in Israel, and the elderly women are aware of both the benefits *and* the disadvantages of the new reality. For them, the husband was not perceived as partner in child rearing, but as a facilitator: without a husband, decent women could not be mothers (Schely-Newman 1995b). Still, today's reality offers other, less satisfactory, models of motherhood. The ambivalence among these women vis-à-vis gender roles and marital relations is evident in conversations about unmarried mothers. Having a child out of wedlock is clearly a breach of moral values, a result of improper moral behavior. Yet children are a woman's most important assets, so that given the choice between no children or a child out of wedlock, the latter can be acceptable. At least "she has somewhere to lay her head," Biya said of a forty-year-old single woman who bore a child. The mother will not have to "fall" on relatives when she gets old; her child will take care of her. This child (born in 1990) is considered by his mother's family and the community at large just another of the grandchildren. [12]

This is not to suggest that the older women approve of sex outside of marriage; on the contrary, they continually criticize it, along with the way women dress and act in public. Television shows and advertisements are used as a yardstick for moral evaluation; the trials and tribulations of the characters in the TV soap opera "The Bold and the Beautiful" are a regular topic of conversation and evaluation. Women frequently share tales with sexual innuendos, and tell off-color jokes even in the presence of men. Yet, some taboos exist, as when I suggested showing the Tunisian movie *Halfaouine: Child of the Terraces* (1995, directed by Ferid Boughedir) in the Aminadav *mo'adon*. The film tells the story of a Muslim boy coming of age who is torn between the women's sensual world and the adult male society. The movie depicts Tunisian women's domestic culture, which I recognized and therefore assumed women would enjoy reminiscing about. On my next visit I was very surprised to learn that Odette and Rachel had vetoed the showing as being immodest. Further questioning revealed that they feared the women would be offended by the nude scenes in the *hammam* (public bath) and other explicit sexual allusions. It seems that the boundary between proper and improper behavior is an acceptable subject of talk, but not of actual witnessing together, even if only in a televised fictional version of life and in a female-only group. Women judge the appropriateness of a topic for discussion according to their own expectations and perceptions of their audience, gender being one of several factors. There is a proper place and time for irreverent talk—for example, at the time of a wedding, when women mimic sexual acts and mock men's behavior (Sered, Kaplan, and Cooper 1999). Yet shared viewing of sexual behavior perhaps transgresses that amorphous boundary of modesty and impropriety.

Odette's objection to showing *Halfaouine* to her women friends from Morocco, Yemen, and Kurdistan resulted from different concerns about proper ethnic representation, as she explained when I inquired about her objection to showing the movie. When I argued that the women watch television with more explicit scenes, she explained that the movie did not properly represent Tunisia. Although the film described Muslim, not Jewish, society, she felt that the depiction of Tunisians as naked women, lascivious men, and "horny" boys might tarnish the "proper" image of what Tunisia is really like. That image, she, the only Tunisian in the group, felt the need to preserve and protect. Odette even chastised me when I told her that my husband (an American) enjoyed watching the movie with me, saying that I, as her daughter, should also be careful about what I was sharing with a "stranger."

Talking as Old Women

Life in Tunisia is a favorite topic in conversations among the elderly, men and women alike. Most of these conversations include a comparative dimension that favors the past over the present—that is, nostalgia.

Discourse of Nostalgia

The women frequently talk about their youth in Tunisia and the homes in which they lived. Ghaliya remembers the layout of her house, and Fortuna can name her childhood neighbors. Odette becomes very emotional when she talks about her house: she had to be hospitalized after a friend who visited Tunisia showed her a picture of the house in La Goulette—a case of true homesickness (Davis 1979, 8; Hertz 1994, 80). The actual house becomes a "site of memory" for many migrants, a juncture point for reliving and reevaluating the past and the present (Bahloul [1992] 1996).

The discontinuity typical of migration is heightened when the country of origin is made inaccessible for reasons beyond one's control. Jewish immigration to the United State and to Israel was generally considered permanent, and the past was left forever in the old country (Kugelmass 1993, viii–ix). Nevertheless, the global growth of tourism and political changes has made root-searching tours (as they are called in Israel) fashionable as well as feasible. Such tours partially mitigate the discontinuity of migration, while providing the migrants and their descendants with a sense of communal-ethnic identity resulting from participation in "tribal rites" (Levy 1997; Kugelmass 1993).

For many years Tunisian-Israelis were unable to visit Tunisia because of the general state of war between Israel and the Arab countries. Jewish emigration from Arab countries was mostly accomplished through a third country, and visits to the country of origin were not possible on Israeli passports.[13] Following the Oslo accords in 1993 between Israel and the Palestinian Authority, relations with Arab countries began to improve, and the Tunisian government opened its borders to Israeli tourists. Small and large groups, frequently composed of family members or neighborhood groups, began to conduct pilgrimages to Tunisia; Israeli-Tunisians were given a chance to visit their past, which for many was literally a foreign country (Lowenthal 1985). Israeli groups typically land in Tunis, the capital, visit the island of Jerba with its ancient synagogue (a traditional pilgrimage site), and continue on to other major cities, all of which once had large Jewish populations. Traditional tourist attractions—beaches, Roman excavations, or desert treks—are replaced by pilgrimages to sites bearing particular significance for the visitors (Deshen 1997). Visitors use free days to visit and investigate their old neighborhoods, the graves of their ancestors, and, if possible, the actual homes in which they once lived. Jeani speaks enthusiastically of the friendly people now residing in her old house, but mentions other houses where the current owners suggested they go back to Israel. Others tell about encounters with old neighbors, as well as the excitement and pride of being able to speak Arabic freely and be understood. Biya is waiting for an improvement in the political climate before she takes the trip; the stories her cousin Adrienne told about the old house on the brink of demolition have increased her motivation and desire. She does not want to witness a pile of rubble, as was the case of another neighbor, who apparently cried for hours as she watched bulldozers clearing the area of her home to make way for new construction.[14]

Even people who clearly indicated (in pre-1993 interviews) that they had no interest in visiting Tunisia because it was no longer "home," are now signing up for visits. The change in political climate alone cannot explain the change of mind about seeing Tunisia again. Perhaps formal relations with Tunisia have legitimized the yearnings for the past. Other explanations may be related to changes in Israeli society at large: tolerance toward public demonstration of ethnic pride and acceptance of hyphenated Israeli identities. The popularity and stated importance of visits to European concentration camps, as part of the high school curriculum, is another aspect of the revised thinking about Jewish life in exile as a source of identity. The Israeli today attempts to reconnect with the past as part of his or her understanding of the present, rather than striving to achieve a new identity disconnected from the past, as in the original Zionist vision (Katriel 1993; Katriel and Shenhar 1990). The legitimization of the Jewish past, and the feasibility of actually reconnecting with it, contributes to the curiosity about and the longings for one's past.

The tension created in meeting the remaining Jewish population of Tunisia and the inevitable comparison of the three main groups of Tunisian Jews (Israelis, French, and Tunisians) affords another opportunity to reflect on hyphenated identities (Deshen 1997; Levy 1997). The chance to take a second look at one's origins allows the Tunisian-Israeli tourists to reevaluate the wisdom of emigration. Visits, and even more, the videos, stories, and pictures shared with other Tunisian-Israelis about them, become opportunities to reconstruct memories, to halt the process of forgetting. Furthermore, these recollections are not only about the specific tour recorded on video or in still photographs, nor is the focus the particular house, neighbors, or open-air markets. The visual and oral recollections serve to generally explore the lost past and reinforce group identity through sights of memory (cf. Nora 1989). Visits to Tunisia and stories about them allow an additional perspective of comparison: not just between how things were in Tunisia and the Israeli present, but also between Tunisians in the past and at the present. For instance, Israeli visitors emphasize that side by side with modernization in the large cities ("there has been great progress") there are also signs of poverty. For North African Jews these trips emphasize the fact that the past, in fact, is no longer theirs; the feelings of loss or alienation are expressed in the report of encounters with the local Tunisian Muslims, both positive ("things have changed for the worse since you [Jews] have left Tunisia") and negative ("Why did you come here? Go back to your country").

In general, as Levy (1997:42) notes, these trips help the Maghrebi Jews find their Israeli identity.

Talk about the past usually means engaging in nostalgic discourse, comparing the past favorably with the present, even though, in fact, life now, particularly for women, is better than it used to be. What people actually yearn for is not necessarily the past as it was but the stability and understanding gained in hindsight, the "ordered clarity contrasting with the chaos or imprecision of our own time" (Lowenthal 1989, 29–30). Since such a comparison was not possible when the past was "the present," nostalgia can discount or ignore suffering and fear, allowing for a selective memory that emphasizes the positive (Vromen 1993, 76).

Nostalgic discourse is characterized by both propositional content, for example, stressing communal cohesiveness, and formal features, such as a "return" to the pure language of the "good old days," that is, an apparent increase in the use of Arabic in the discourse (cf. Hill 1992). When the older settlers in Gilat get together, they talk about Tunisia, emphasizing proper behavior, especially respect for one's elders; the strong ties and mutual responsibility of community members toward each other; and even the good relations with the Arab population ("more trustworthy than the local Palestinian Arabs").

However, the past was, in fact, not always better than the present, and for women it might have been worse. These elderly women, while not as well physically as they were in their youth, nevertheless enjoy better health care, a higher standard of living, and increased independence. Thus, the dialogue between past and present can easily slip into talk about darker aspects of the same past about which they are so nostalgic. When conversations focus on issues upon which people disagree, a tone of reflexive nostalgia, questioning the reasons for longing, and even counternostalgia, may be the result (Davis 1979; Hill 1992).

To Nostalgia and Back: A Second Look at Shushan's Wife

The conversation between Jeani, Miḥa, and Fradji emphasized these nostalgia-related aspects. As noted in chapter 3, Jeani joined my interview with Miḥa and Fradji when she returned a pot borrowed for a traditional celebration. The framing of the interaction itself was reminiscent of an older time, with emphasis on mutual help and traditional celebrations. The use of a proverb as implicit criticism of a younger woman introduced an additional crucial element of nostalgic discourse—the behavior of the young. The nostalgic shift to the "pure speech of yesteryear" was thus inevitable, and the shift was enhanced by Jeani's explicit comparison between past and present (appendix 4):

36. *tra tishmaʿ mᵊni tuwa kᵊlma*
    (A) see you hear from me now a word/story
37. *yequluli tesapri lanu safta*
    (A) they tell me (H) tell us grandmother
38. *nᵊqulm ya ḥasra*
    (A) I tell them *ya ḥasra*
    "See if now you can hear even a word from me now. They ask me, 'Tell us grandma' and I say '*ya ḥasra*.'"

Jeani laments the lost words, either the content of forgotten stories or literally the words that cannot be translated into Hebrew for the grandchildren to understand. It is not only the loss of wise words but also the loss of Arabic, the language of eloquence itself, which she misses.

In addition to switching between Arabic and Hebrew, which marks the generations, Jeani (and Miha) use a formal marker of nostalgic discourse, the term *ya ḥasra*. Deriving from the root *ḥsr* (missing, loss) the term is used to indicate sorrow about bygone, irreplaceable things (Cohen 1975, 262). In Israel *ya ḥasra* is an ethnic marker of Tunisians, who use it to modify positive past experiences either from their recent Israeli past or their remote past, as in Tunisia. As an ethnic marker the idiom may be used by the young to frame childhood memories even when they are speaking Hebrew with their peers, provided, of course, that their addressees, too, are of Tunisian origin.

The idyllic picture evoked by Jeani, Miha, and Fradji, of bygone days and nights in Tunisia, listening to enchanting stories in a warm family setting (wrapped in blankets) begins to tarnish when the gaze focuses on what actually happened at those times. Narration took place on Thursday nights while preparing Shabbat bread, but baking bread involved female anxiety about fulfilling one's roles properly. Furthermore, as I suggested in the story of Shushan's wife (p. 92–94), Fradji's comments could be interpreted as mocking male interference in gender-exclusive issues. His comments heightened gender tension and proved the inaccuracy of nostalgia: everyday Tunisian life had not benefited women as much as it might have benefited men (Hill 1992). Jeani's response is implicit criticism, expressed in a subversive and counternostalgic story about Shushan's wife, the pregnant woman whose inability to sustain the pressure and anxiety of her roles had caused her to miscarry. This story stands in contrast with the gentle dialogue between past and present, in which the difficulties, pains, and sufferings of that past were masked under the heavy blanket of positive collective memory (Vromen 1993, 76). The counternostalgic story regroups the participants: while during the nostalgic segment I, as a younger person raised in Israel, was marked as an outsider, the story of Shushan's wife allowed me, as a woman, to be considered an insider, but marked Fradji, the male, as the outsider.

The interlocutors did not dwell on this gender-based tension. Jeani's explicit criticism, that husbands blame their wives for the unsuccessful bread (lines 134–36 in appendix 4) is mitigated by shifting the issue from gender to generation:

139. *kif nahki l*əl knayen yemutu be dahk*
(A) when I tell to the daughters-in-law, they die of laughter
140. *qultlum hu*
(A) I told them oh
haya kashe kol davar sham
(H) it was difficult every thing there
141. *kashe kashe*
(H) difficult difficult
"When I tell my daughters-in-law they laugh.
I tell them everything there was very difficult."

Jeani's daughters-in-law mock the experiences of their elders, a common topic for nostalgia (Hill 1992, 264). The mocking is framed in Hebrew, the language of the present, a shift that forces Jeani to abandon the comfort and eloquence of Arabic for the formality of Hebrew. The uneasiness about the present and therefore the longing for better times are marked by the propositional content and by the language shift. With this reported encounter Jeani is able to praise the present as affording more comfort in everyday life, while at the same time she condemns the behavior of the young. This dual position allows the three adults to return to a more harmonious discourse, in which they discuss general aspects of the past, such as communal cohesiveness. It shifts the conversation away from the particular chronotop—the public oven, *kusha*—into a less focused, vague conversation. This distanced perspective makes it possible to ignore specific negative aspects of the past, as in the story of Shushan's wife. This shift was not abrupt, as the conversation slid from a positive evaluation of the present, with accommodations like washing machines and gas stoves that make life easier for women. These, however, cannot compensate for the loss of communal ties in the present, as compared with Tunisia in the past.

The shift back to harmonious discourse is also marked by a change in language: Jeani speaks Hebrew to her daughters-in-law (lines 139–141), and the inequalities of the present are criticized in the appropriate language. Jeani (in Hebrew):

And how do we feel today? We don't feel it. Whoever has [money] can enjoy life. Those who don't, have nothing (lines 146–49)

But in Tunisia, where the community cared for the unfortunate, things were different, as asserted in Arabic, by Fradji:

They were not worried about tomorrow, would not worry about a thing (line 152).
Miḥa: There were treasurers of the community. It was their responsibility (line 153).

Note that Jeani initiated both shifts in the conversation. While Fradji's comments might have irritated her as a woman, thus initiating the counternostalgic segment, she seems to be satisfied with voicing only an implicit challenge, not to the social order as a whole but to selected aspects of it.

Poetics of Narration

The conversation with Jeani, and other conversations quoted in this study, are typical of informal, unstructured interactions, including frequent topic shifts, friendly competition for the floor, personal narratives, and bits of gossip about others. A close analysis of its flow, however, indicates a structure in which even digressions function as building blocks, fitting together to create a complex architecture (Silverstein 1985). The entire conversation has some inner order, which provides meaning to almost every isolated utterance. The cohesiveness is additionally enhanced by poetic elements, such as parallelisms, and repetitions reinforce the universality of women's actions, underlining the existence of poetic elements even in mundane texts such as conversations and oral narratives.

Although oral narratives are not expected to be rhythmic, text segmentation may reveal underlying poetical features (Hymes 1998). Poetic narratives, even if they recount personal events (rather than heroic adventures), transform the simplest story into a memorable text, endowing the events with additional meaning. The following story demonstrates how Ghaliya's narrative competence allows her to redraw kinship lines, positioning herself as a "true" daughter and a mirror image of my grandmother. By doing so she is also able to implicitly instruct her audience in ways of resistance.

THE STORY OF KUKA

My father's parents, Mama (mother) Kuka and Baba (father) Braham, migrated to Israel from Tunisia in 1955 and lived in Gilat until they died (in 1964 and 1967, respectively), in a house located between Ghaliya's and my parents'. Being elderly and without means of transportation, their house soon became a social center for women, who liked to chat with Kuka, and also for men, who took advantage of Braham's experience as a barber.

The story is part of Ghaliya's repertoire, and I heard it from her on several other occasions. This particular rendition of events was narrated during an interview I conducted with Ghaliya about the history of the community; the audience included four of her children. Talk about people who currently live in the community reminded her of the "good old neighbors," my grandparents. The story, like the entire conversation, was narrated mainly in Arabic with a few Hebrew words. I have followed Hymes's (1998) suggestion regarding segmentation of prose narrative to enhance its poetic

Noro escorts his mother, mama Kuka, from her house to his. Noro in a typical outfit for desert farming and Kuka in traditional Tunisian garb, Gilat, 1960.

structure. Minimal responses appear in parentheses. See appendix 7 for the full text.

1. Your father and Lalu Uzan used to plant
2. they had in the field (yes) cucumbers
3. and bell peppers
4. and hot peppers
5. and tomatoes (yes, yes, right)
6. and they transport full carts
7. like this

After the introduction of the "rich" farmers—my father and his partner Lalu—the other element of the equation follows:

8. and we were a large family (right)
9. and my husband works in *Solel Boneh* [Israeli construction company]
10. we could hardly buy anything
11. just hardly (yea)

Once the men are introduced, it is time for the women to appear: the narrator, my own mother, and the main protagonist, Kuka, lauded in the extreme.

12. [in a low voice]: I say
13. oh God I wish I had a bit of that [crop]
14. to prepare dinner for my kids (yea)
15. your mother never gave us
16. and I never asked (yea)
17. and I cannot say "give me"
18. but *ummi* Kuka
19. may God lighten the heavy earth on her
20. that *ummi* Kuka how good she was

Kuka's character is further amplified when compared to Braham's:

21. her husband
22. God forgive them all
23. [was] a miser
24. may God forgive them all
25. only one's character remains (yea)
26. Yes

27. so when *ummi* Kuka
28. may God forgive her,
29. came [to Israel]
30. what a wonderful woman (yea, yea)
31. what sweet speech
32. and what eloquence
33. and what company

Kuka's exceptional qualities are summarized in what can be seen as the utmost compliment:

34. being with her was better than in a café.

Ghaliya continues to describe Kuka's everyday life—she did not spend all her time in idle chatter. She was industrious, as well as a coquette:

35. so your father used to give her bags and bags of peanuts [to sort out]
36. and when she had nothing to do in the afternoon
37. she dresses
38. makes herself pretty
39. combs her hair and makes coffee (yea)
40. she thought much of herself

The reference to Kuka's womanly behavior recalls Braham, who apparently was not as impressed by her charm:

41. and he
42. God forgive him
43. her husband
44. what he had done to her

Ghaliya now expands her digression from the initial story of the vegetables she longed for and tells of the mistreatment Kuka suffered from her husband.

45. in Sfax he left her for five years and went to France
46. Yudit [in Hebrew]: yes always [overlap]
47. Ghaliya: In France
48. and left her with three children
49. Yudit: [overlap, in Hebrew]: Noro always tells that

143

50. Ghaliya: and then when his daughter got married she sent a
    message to him saying
51. just come just come
52. so people won't say she has no father
53. don't bring anything

The abandonment story (mentioned previously) does not include
explanations. Both the narrator and the audience were familiar with
the story. We knew that in the mid-1930s Kuka had urged Braham
to go to France to bring back their older son, who did not return
home after his army service, and that Braham, like his son, had
met a Parisian woman and lived with her. In a coda for this mini-
narrative Ghaliya stresses the transformation in gender roles and
positions:

54. well,
55. that was then
56. that's what he did in his youth
57. and later when he got older
58. he was peeling bananas for her
59. because now he turned old
60. he is good for nothing.

What Ghaliya emphasizes is not just the reversal of gender roles,
but her own entitlement to the story:

68. yea she told me the poor woman
69. otherwise how would I know
70. she is from Sfax
71. and I am from Gabes [two towns in Tunisia]

Once Ghaliya established her special relationship with Kuka, the
vegetables were reintroduced.

73. so I would come [to see Kuka]
74. she knows the situation (yea)
75. may God forgive you oh *ummi* Kuka
76. she'd fill up a pillowcase
77. a pillow case
78. fill it up with everything
79. sweet peppers
80. hot peppers

81. tomatoes
82. and cucumbers

But Kuka could not dispose of the vegetables at her wish; she could not openly disobey her husband, the miser (line 23). Instead,

83. and she waits until her husband goes inside
84. and tells me
85. take my dear take
86. go my child go
87. go and prepare dinner for your children go
88. So that her husband wouldn't see her (yea)
89. he does not want [to give away the vegetables]

At this point we realize that the story has no digressions, that in fact all of the details about Baba Braham's behavior are essential because they explain the reason for Kuka's subversive behavior, while at the same time the special connection between the two women is reasserted, based on common experience:

99. because she tells me
100. tells me
101. I have suffered too
102. I also had children and have suffered
103. take my dear take
104. God forgive her
    [end of this story].

The linear development of text does not correspond to the progression of events. The story line includes temporal digressions into the future (now that the main characters are dead) and the past (the abandonment), and includes general comments on the narrative-time present (Kuka's daily behavior). This temporal structure is added to other binary oppositions: us/them; inside/outside; men/women; young/old; now/then; generous/miser; here/there. The surface level of the narrative, the repetitions, the parallelisms, the rhythm, and the audience's response, in turn, emphasizes these oppositions.

The story about Kuka demonstrates the dynamics of conjugal life and gender roles: men abandon their wives, but suffering women understand and help each other in many ways, sharing experiences and goods. Women know how to right a wrong, how to transfer the bountiful crop to its proper place, the kitchen of a needy family. Kuka is not a disobedient wife but a compassionate and understanding woman, who recognizes in Ghaliya a twin spirit with whom she is able to share secrets. Though they did not know each other in Tunisia, their fates brought them together and made Ghaliya a confidante of Kuka, much closer than was my mother, Kuka's daughter-in-law (lines 15–16, 68–71, 101–2).

Ghaliya's narrative posits "them" against "us," with Kuka as mediator, a role emphasized by the physical location of her house, between my parents and Ghaliya's family. Kuka is Noro's mother (and my grandmother), yet this relationship is not evident in the narrative itself. Ghaliya talks about *babak* (your father, lines 1, 35) and mentions *emak* (your mother, line 15), but calls my grandmother *ummi Kuka* (my mother Kuka), as opposed to *mama* (mother) Kuka, a term used in my family. Although this choice may not be intentional, the expropriation of Kuka from my family facilitates her role as a mediator between the rich (they, lines 2, 6) and the poor (we, lines 8, 10, 15, 17). A person who is not familiar with the characters might assume that Kuka is a member of Ghaliya's side of the family. This point is reinforced by the inquiry of the son:

93. Ariyeh: Who's that
94. Yudit: Esther's grandma
95. Ghaliya: mother—
96. Esther (overlap): my father's mother
97. Ghaliya: father's mother how she—
98. Esther (overlap) they used to live here

Note that Yudit and I, not Ghaliya, directly answer the question. This representation of characters allows Ghaliya to establish new kinship lines, to make Kuka part of her own family, *ummi Kuka*. Ghaliya becomes Kuka's coterie, if not her actual daughter: both women suffer, and Kuka confides in her and tells her about her life. The similarity is clear to Kuka, quoted as saying to Ghaliya, "I also had children and have suffered. Take, my dear, take" (lines 102–3). Fortuna, the daughter-in-law, is not part of this inner circle of suffering women: Noro is present and properly provides for his family. Is this the reason why Fortuna is unable to sympathize with Ghaliya and does not offer to share her bounty with the less fortunate?

Ghaliya's criticism is implied—"your mother never gave us [any-thing]" (line 15)—and she is too proud to ask for help from others (lines 16–17). Only a woman who has suffered in her own life, like Kuka, can be charitable. Ghaliya's criticism of Fortuna and her own special relations with Kuka appear shortly after, in another narrative, about the day Kuka died: It was a Friday morning, all women were busy cooking for Shabbat, when Braham called for help because Kuka had fallen down. Ghaliya was the first one to answer the call, running barefoot from her hot kitchen while Fortuna hesitated at first, needing to take a sweater lest she would catch a cold.

The similarity between Kuka and Ghaliya implies another ho-mology, that between the husbands. Braham represents the nega-tive, untrustworthy male who left his wife and children for a long period of time. This event from the remote past brings the binary oppositions in the story to a climax by implying potency (a Parisian mistress in the background) and old age impotence:

57. and later when he got older
58. he was peeling bananas for her
59. because now he turned old
60. he is good for nothing.

The final victory is women's; they keep their powers, while men, once they are old, become "good for nothing" and are reduced to having to cajole their wives in order to be treated right.

The men and women in this narrative collapse into stereotypi-cal behaviors: suffering women and neglectful, uncaring men. Men (Noro, Lalu) produce and bring sustenance into the private female sphere (the house), where Braham stands guard. Nevertheless, the women outsmart them. Kuka is the "great mother," and at the center of the plot. She is sedentary: people come to visit her, her husband leaves her and returns, her son brings her vegetables, and she helps transform them from raw to cooked food for the children (lines 35, 87). The uniqueness of Kuka is amplified by the repeated formulaic blessings conferred upon her by the narrator: "May God lighten the heavy earth on her" (line 19), "may God forgive them all, only one's character remains" (lines 24–25). Yet, she remains a flesh-and-blood woman, still concerned about her appearance despite her age, dressing up and making herself pretty (lines 37–40). Above all, she is presented as a model for all other women.

The repetitions, parallels, and formulaic expressions reinforce the intratextual connections in the narrative. Ghaliya puts Kuka on a pedestal. She is a good woman, and also a good mother, helping her son Noro (line 35) as she cared for her other children when Braham abandoned her. Ghaliya's entitlement to Kuka's story is stronger than the one claimed by Yudit, who overheard it (line 49, "Noro always tells that") and me, a member of the family. This firsthand knowledge gives Ghaliya the authority to revoice Kuka's words (Shuman 1993b, 151). Finally, the special relationship between the women is acknowledged by Kuka herself, quoted in a constructed dialogue, "I have suffered too." The use of other people's words reinforces Ghaliya's claim on Kuka's story, while at the same time it emphasizes the connection between the two women, a special relationship created by the parallel between the two, even though, "She is from Sfax, and I am from Gabes" (lines 70–71). Some of Kuka's aura is thus transferred to Ghaliya, rather than to Kuka's other female kin: a daughter living in France at the time, and her-daughter-in law living next door. Similarly, the homology between Baba Braham and her own husband is strengthened. Ghaliya becomes another abandoned wife who has to care for her family and does so successfully, as shown in her stories about life in Israel (as seen in the previous chapter).

Ghaliya, like the other women, uses the narratives to create and recreate her identity. Relationships with others, family and neighbors, are a major concern, and these are shaped and reshaped in narrative (Gergen 1992; Paoletti 1998). However, since each narration of events provides new—contextually sensitive—perspective, a close examination of the text offers two levels of meaning (M. Goodwin 1997). On the referential level, the story of Mama Kuka, as told in 1987 by Ghaliya, is a story about women taking charge when necessary, even when their action requires challenging traditional gender roles and relations. Yet, this particular setting provides the key for understanding Ghaliya's need for a mother figure, not only because she was orphaned at an early age. The story was told during a taped interview I initiated; however, the real addressees might have been Yudit and her sister Dina. The poetic structure of the story reinforces maternal bonds and implicitly suggests a model for resisting male dominance. For that purpose, perhaps, she appropriates my grandmother and her story to be her own, and while doing so, paints my own mother in a less than favorite light. On other occasions with a different audience, Ghaliya told of the same event with little mention of my mother.

Women of Valor

Both older men and women enjoy telling and listening to stories, particularly about their own lives; however, gender differences are evident in the contexts, the structure, and the content of narration (Gergen 1992; Sawin 1999; Schely-Newman 1997). This was made especially clear when I interviewed members of the same family in their own homes. I have observed that men and women prefer gender-exclusive settings. For example, when women visit each other and the conversation turns to female issues (gossip about other women, children, etc.), the man in the house tends to "fade" from the interaction by reading a newspaper, watching television, or leaving. In mixed settings there are clear "rules": even if the narrated events have been experienced by both, the women frequently defer to the men as main narrators, correcting and commenting when necessary. Yet entitlement to knowledge or experiences supersedes gender specifications, as seen in the case of Jeani telling about the shooting of a woman (chapter 4) or about Shushan's wife (chapters 3 and 5) in the presence of men.

The elderly Tunisian-Israeli women are not a homogeneous group; they differ in their physical conditions and in their interpretations of "being old." Some generalizations, however, may apply, particularly regarding their perceptions of their duties. All see their role as caring for the younger generation, and this is perceived as reciprocal. Just as they cared for their parents, so they expect their children to care for them. Husbands may not be reliable, and children are a woman's safeguards. This is why a woman's role as a mother is uppermost and unwed mothers are accepted. Women evaluate each other in terms of the extent to which they have fulfilled gender roles within the Jewish world; to be a good woman is to be modest, to have children, and to care for others. Their stories elaborate these values both in content and in poetic structures that reinforce notions of "good" and "bad."

Being older gives women permission to express their opinions in their own voice, and to be more critical of the social order.

Yet, they do not tell stories about everything in their lives; painful experiences are not related or are given alternative interpretations, turning the women to the real heroines, as with Shushan's wife or my grandmother. The abusive husbands are either neglected or ridiculed. The women's stories are thus not an account of what has happened, good or bad, but a metacomment on the social order. By voicing their concerns women set an example for their daughters about ways of resistance within the traditional setting itself.

CONCLUSION

Only the stories are left.
Ma ka ʿdu kan lə xrayef

The stories treated in this study were told mainly to other women
and are about women's concerns, lives, invisibility, and silence. As
such, these are gendered texts, defining and evaluating women's
role and responsibilities, shaped according to culturally accepted
modes (Paoletti 1998, 3). The women evaluate their past from the
perspective of the present, a present in which women's status has
greatly changed. Implicit resistance can be detected in stories about
childhood, marriage, motherhood, and emigration, and more so
in stories about old age. Even nostalgic discourse about life in
Tunisia may turn into counternostalgia when conversations focus
on women's lives. The challenges, and resistance, to the prescribed
traditional gender roles are expressed on the referential and contextual levels and through the definition of tellable experiences: events
from the daily lives of women have become worthy of narration.
These events, even mundane troubles, are, in fact, "the best stories
of all." They may not yet be a new genre, but a hybrid form, expanding the female realm of experience to be included in what has
traditionally been considered an exclusively male realm (cf. Webber
1985). The mere act of narrating about oneself allows women to
give their own version of their lives, thus empowering them; they
are the ones deciding which events in their lives are meaningful and
why (Kirshenblatt-Gimblett 1989). As a daughter of the group,
I participate in this talk; as native ethnographer, recording their
stories, I give the women a public voice, and offer my gendered
interpretations. I attempt to bridge the gap between the vanishing
and the emerging ways of speaking, the emic and etic explanations

151

that link their worlds and their stories. The result provides a better understanding of this particular culture (Philipsen 1992, 123).

The elderly Israeli-Tunisian women in this study are not all cut from the same cloth. Biya, Ghaliya, Fortuna, and Odette differ from each other in their levels of literacy, religiosity, health, and interest. Nevertheless, their narratives indicate significant similarities which allow us to consider the women as cohorts and to aggregate their stories to a case study. Their stories are shaped within a similar tradition, embedded in the collective memory of Jewish lives in a Muslim country and of voluntary displacement to a locale with a spiritual value. The intersection between the individual and the collective allows us to combine their personal narratives into one story of an elderly Jewish woman who is no longer (solely) Tunisian, but not yet a fully assimilated Israeli. The generalized protagonist of this story does not speak "proper" Hebrew, Tunisian-Arabic, or French. She ascribes to the moral values of her traditional world, but expresses (and enjoys) greater independence in her life. She accepted and learned to love the spouse chosen for her, but encourages her daughters to follow their hearts. She longs for the communal cohesiveness of Tunisian life but likes the amenities of Israeli life. She challenges the women's role, but does so in the traditional Tunisian way of storytelling, or in a Jewish way, by appropriating sacred genres of speech (Schely-Newman 1999a; Webber 1991, 118). The newly acquired access to sacred texts—through Hebrew and religion classes—creates a new religiosity; in addition to lighting candles at holy graves, our protagonist uses prayer books and reads sacred texts. Within these changes of language, mores, modes of behavior, and narratives, the elderly women attempt to transmit and hold on to their values while expressing resistance to some aspects of that life. The nostalgic and counternostalgic discourses are narratives of loss, an attempt to hold on to the past and transmit it to the next generations (Kapchan and Strong 1999, 243–44). The women are aware that their way of life and modes of speaking are vanishing. Their grandchildren do not speak Arabic, and adhere to the directness of Israeli style (cf. Katriel 1986). Yet, though these are narratives of loss, they are also narratives of gain, a response to changes and a way of preserving important values while acquiring newer ones. Thus, while the stories tell about the past, they are in fact stories about the present and about transmitting values and modes of resistance to their audience. The stories trace the route that Tunisian-female-Jewish-Israelis have gone through, acquiring an additional chord with which to weave their stories in each stage and constructing and reconstructing their identity— objectifying themselves, rather than being defined by the "others," whether non-Jews, men, non-Tunisians, or younger people. I wish to argue that within the context of migration the potential for social changes and adaptation is greater than in sedentary populations, and the study of life stories provides an important key to understanding the processes of adjustment.

The stories women shared with me show how childhood provided them with the basic needs for their lives: induction into the women's world and words. Childhood also provided these women with the new experiences of French schooling, an event that set them apart from their own mothers. Appreciation of French probably results from the fact that it was a language learned in childhood, while learning Hebrew as adults was much more difficult. It may also be suggested that since Hebrew is identified with the male domains of religion and official authority, French remains a language in which women can excel without competition. In a sense it is a language of liberation, of freedom to expand their imagination into the world of literature, and of the ability to keep their family ties through correspondence. Education was for the women a road toward modernity, and learning French was an asset that, even if not used for practical purposes, still gave them a starting point for developing their own voice.

The stories women craft are not about everyday jealousy, neighbors' quarrels, or current domestic problems. The events that are framed as stories and performed as such are elevated from the humdrum of everyday life. These stories are repeatedly told and thus may serve as a model for the audience, and a metacommentary on everyday life, rather than a report or discussion of current events. The women adhere to traditional values of modesty in their dress and behavior, and yet their stories are sensuous and full of implicit sexual meanings. These meanings, however, are not represented in never-never land and with fictional characters; these are stories about real people like themselves, stories filled with sexual symbols, hidden in cooking pots and jars of honey or evoked by bananas and pins.

Though the stories indicate changes in women's roles and ways of coping with the difficulties of immigration, it should be emphasized that the stories are not proclaiming emancipation from male authority; they express resistance, but from within tradition (cf. Gal 1991). In the telling of stories about the early years of the community, public events continue to be a male domain. Nevertheless, women are entitled to tell about these events from their own perspective. Without directly challenging male authority, women have appropriated a male genre and male words. Their actions gave them the right to be equal partners not only in working and owning the farms but also in telling their stories. The stories bear meanings both in their content—telling about women's lives—and in the performance itself, which challenges traditional modes of narration and definitions of audience, while expanding the scope of tellability and of experience itself. The mere narration to a mixed audience is a claim for reevaluating women's work and worth (Sawin 1999, 253). By their actions these women help ensure the physical survival of the family, but by telling the stories of their heroism they also ensure the survival of their ethnic and gender identity (Langellier 2000).

Narrators and Audience

The audience for the narratives is not fixed but elusive. Indeed, narrative can take place almost anytime and anywhere, to anyone ready to listen, and is a joint production of narrator and audience. As a native ethnographer, the field for me is not a foreign country in a distant place, but my home, and my identity is in itself a cultural factor that plays a part in creating and analyzing the tales (B. Tedlock 1991, 71). Throughout the work on this book, even while collecting data, I was concerned with how to best present the women. Anthropologists customarily respect the privacy of interviewees; however, this is not always the choice of the people themselves. When Barbara Meyerhoff published her study of the Jewish elderly community in Venice, California, using pseudonyms, the people were offended by the erasure of their identities: "Manya was incensed: 'you interviewed me for hours, I told you everything. Then you left me out of the movie.' . . . Then the film was shown on national TV. She was more annoyed and hurt than before. 'I still don't forgive. It wasn't enough you left me out of the film when it showed in Los Angeles. Now it showed in Detroit where my children live. You left me out also in Detroit.' " (Meyerhoff 1988, 273)

Adhering to anthropological custom, I used pseudonyms in previous publications, but when I informed the women about this practice they told me that they preferred to be known by their names because they were proud of their history and wanted to have their achievements known; in essence, they wanted to be visible. Both the men and women in the study were pleased to receive photographs of themselves and copies of the stories I had collected from them, and agreed to have their life stories and pictures made public.[1] The context of my fieldwork created more complex relationships between the "I" and the "them." The women's position caused me to realize that since the stories are my mother's stories, obscuring the women's identities affects mine, while using their real names establishes and reinforces my own sense of self.

Judeo-Arab society does not see women as detached from their families, but assigns them a role—daughters, sisters, wives, or mothers—definitions that determine the way they are treated (Abu-Lughod 1988, 152). In initial interactions, women wanted to establish my identity prior to, or concomitantly with, addressing the issues I raised. When I visited a *mo'adon* in Maoz Zion, a suburb of Jerusalem, for the first time, the elderly women (mostly from Kurdistan) expressed some hostility, immediately telling me how much we, younger Israeli women, are spoiled, and that we know nothing of their experiences: "We gave birth to babies crouched on the floor, while you lie on a bed, legs spread out, with your husband watching." My response that "I came to learn and share the knowledge I gained from my own mother," was sufficient for me to be invited to come as often as I wished and to be told that "you are like a daughter to us."[2] Even in Gilat, where my identity is established, professional gear marks me as the "other." When Biya's sisters offered to tell me a story, they hesitated when I reappeared as an ethnographer with my recorder and camera. Only following their interrogation and the support given by Biya, establishing my marital, parental, and residential identity, was I allowed to be part of the group (see chapter 2). Furthermore, I frequently encountered sympathy for my life course: some women felt the need to console me for having only one daughter, while others commented that "pity," I could have raised a larger family instead of "wasting" my time in years of study. Not that academic life, per se, is not recognized as worthwhile, but it is not perceived as women's priority. This was made clear to me while visiting friends with my mother in October 1998, when Jeani proudly mentioned a young man, born in Gilat, who now teaches at the university of Haifa. Even my mother did not mention that I, too, held an academic position. The women were more interested in hearing about the progress of my daughter, the possibility of my having more children, and the whereabouts of my husband. Being a native facilitated access to the field, but my approach to data and local wisdom made me different; to be a "halfie" means not to fit the common mode but to struggle for recognition of what we are by our different "tribes" (Abu-Lughod 1993; Narayan 1995). Straddling the invisible boundary of the women's community, I had access to knowledge but also responsibilities toward the image of the group. Yet this image itself is contested and differently held by the larger Israeli population and by members of the group, as demonstrated in Odette's objection to the showing of the movie *Halfaouine*. The women themselves were aware of my marginal position and perhaps saw me as a conduit through which the traditions might be transmitted, not only to the younger generations but to the outside world as well.

Though sometimes I interviewed women to gain insights and information about their lives, much of the data was volunteered. Women, particularly in Gilat, spoke to me the way mothers transmit family stories to their daughters. Like other narratives, family stories serve as an interface between individual experiences and the society, and therefore serve as a socialization medium to the way families function, a legitimization of social control of the family institution as well as an instruction about subversive strategies (Langellier and Peterson 1993, 50; Ochs and Capps 1996, 31).

The women present themselves (in their stories) as daughters, mothers, wives, sisters, grandmothers—and their stories emphasize this variety of roles and relationships. We women grow up to become mothers ourselves and struggle to create our own female identity from within the role model set by our mothers (Gergen 1992, 132). This struggle is most obvious in the life story of Odette, who presents herself as her father's daughter, minimizing her mother, a choice that may indicate traditional devaluation of women's role. The central role of the father in the life stories perhaps marks the

Fortuna and
Esther having a
chat, Gilat,
summer 1993

fact that the women realize their role in the new country requires
more than what their mothers provided. Thus, while they continue
to act the way their mothers did—being themselves mothers and
wives—they may also choose to see their fathers' lives as more significant. They may not fashion their life stories after their mothers',
but they present themselves as role models by emphasizing current
values, such as education and self-reliance. They stress the importance of women in guiding girls to womanhood, being at their sides
during crucial stages of their lives from the outset of menarche. In
particular, they stress the importance of other women as a resource
for emotional and practical support.[3]

Dialogic Interpretation : *"Les Cris de la Vie"*

The type of interactions I maintained with the women underlines
my role in the production of the texts: I was not an eavesdropper
but an addressee, a ratified audience (Goffman 1981). Furthermore,
family interactions and storytelling cannot be analyzed solely from

the point of view of content; gender and generational telling require multileveled analysis (Langellier and Peterson 1993, 63; Sawin 1999). I was an important part of the context that shapes the interactions. Therefore my own voice is intertwined with those of the elderly women, and my utterances are not deleted from the texts or the analysis. Ethnography and performance studies pay equal attention to both the audience and the narrators, as well as to the dynamics of interaction. The emerging texts are a dialogue between the parties, rather than a monologue delivered in the authoritative voice of the ethnographer. The dialogue sometimes was more explicit, when the roles changed and I was observed rather than being the observer. This dynamic prompted me to question my contribution to the development of the text; examining it not as "enduring object," but looking at its production, and at myself as a possible catalyst in the outcome (cf. Briggs and Bauman 1992, 146). This reversal of roles was particularly evident when Biya's sisters came together for the wedding of a niece (chapter 2; Schely-Newman 1999b). Not only did the sisters hesitate to narrate before they could place me in a familiar and acceptable role, but the group was aware of my shifting roles between participant and observer. The question about my use of data, "Now that you take the stories over there, what do you do with them? I want to know," was explicit and indicated wariness about the image of the group and perhaps even suspicion regarding my ability to represent it correctly. My response, at the time, explaining folklore collecting methods and narrating a story, appeared to be sufficient for the occasion. Yet questioning my positions inside and outside the community heightens the concerns of hybrid identity, that of a "halfie," an insider with the knowledge and power to take the words out (Narayan 1993). Giving the "natives" a voice and writing about them accurately I believe is an answer to such concerns.

The analysis and presentation of data are affected by concerns about identities, tending toward a dialogical approach, which gives the "natives" a voice similar—if not equal—to that of the ethnographer (D. Tedlock 1983). The emphasis on personal stories from a performance approach renders the interactions themselves, not only their referential content, into texts to be examined. Methods adopted from the ethnography of communication expand the interest beyond the immediate setting to include cultural norms as factors in the analysis (Hymes 1974, 1996; Saville-Troike 1989). The ethnographic endeavor itself is not just collecting information but a dialogic process between participants, in which the voice of the native is privileged as much as that of the ethnographer (Philipsen 1992, 182). What is studied are everyday intimate and dynamic interactions, grounded in their historical and ideological processes as occurring in their natural setting, rather than abstractions or reductions of encounters (Conquergood 1991, 187; Pelias and VanOosting 1987, 223). The outcome, the ethnographic work, must therefore give a voice to all participants and consider the variety of constraints existing in interactions.

The voice of these elderly women has not been silenced. In fact, they have always had a voice, albeit heard only in private, within the boundaries of their group and community. The women have acquired a voice and narrative competence from their childhoods, but their life experience have amplified it, allowing their voices to be heard by others. Their school experiences have had an impact on their daughters: despite criticism of other women in Gilat, Fortuna and Ghaliya sent their oldest daughters in 1956 to a co-ed boarding school to complete their education. The door to literacy, cracked open for the mothers, was further opened for their daughters with the help of Israeli counselors who advocated and supported the move. Ghaliya tells how a female counselor comforted her regarding the decision to send her eldest daughter to the boarding school, assuring her that "a good girl will remain chaste regardless of the conditions." My sister Miriam still praises the counselor who helped her find another high school after Noro removed her from the co-ed secular school she attended.[4] Since those early years in the history of Gilat, no girl has been kept out of school because of modesty concerns, and the *moshav* includes several professional native women.[5] These experiences indicate that while the older generation of immigrant women chose their fathers as role models, these same women today may serve as an example for their daughters to follow.

Dialogic Presentation: *"L'écrits de la Vie"*

The dialogic approach mentioned previously has implications on the manner of presentation and writing. A method of presenting narrative encounters allows the reader to identify the elements that shape the emergent text and contribute to the way I choose to interpret them (Conquergood 1992; Crawford 1996; B. Tedlock 1991). The particular genre of texts, life stories, is conducive to this approach of analysis and writing. Life stories result from collaboration with the native speaker, and the negotiations between narrator and researcher are an important element in the final product (Crapanzano 1980, 10). As an audience actively participating in the production of the texts to be analyzed, I cannot detach myself from the texts in the analysis. I was part of the texts, as much as the narrators, and the result is a hybrid form of writing, a pastich work of weaving my voice with that of the women, in a style that is possibly recognizable as "feminine" in Western tradition (Coates 1997).

Presentation of these life stories requires different levels of translation; providing the semantic equivalent of the Arabic, French, and Hebrew texts in English is not sufficient. What is needed is the process of "transduction"—bringing their experiences to life, not only allowing the stories to be understood by those who do not speak the languages, but also allowing others to understand the narrators' lives (Silverstein, in press). This process requires entextualization and contextualization—transferring the entire experience from its oral and gender-specific setting on the Israeli *moshav* into a written form addressed to a different audience.

In writing this book I am sometimes the author of the stories, but more frequently I am only an animator, repeating other people's words and serving as a "sound box" to my motherline (Goffman 1981). What is achieved in the process is more than just the women telling their stories and others understanding them. I am also gaining my own voice, as hybrid as it may be, combining my mother's experiences and stories with my own and translating them into the competence of another type of performance; writing their lives. A tension between my voice and the women's, between the emic and the etic, as well as between the different aspects of my own identity—Israeli, Tunisian, native, ethnographer—exists in this style of writing. Perhaps this is why it is easier to transmit all these variables into a foreign language—not that of authority, modernity, or tradition, but that of the intellectual world, English.

Just as the narrative texts bear signs of different cultures, their representation gives a voice to the different layers comprising them.

The resulting text, this book, combines the individual voices, attempting to avoid an authoritative stance. The dialogue between the narrators and me, and our mutual attempts to negotiate identities, surface in the writing of the book as well. This mode of writing presents ethnography as a co-production of knowledge, a verbal mediation bridging self and others (Conquergood 1992; D. Tedlock 1983; B. Tedlock 1991). This book attempts to erase the line separating conventional and experimental modes of writing ethnography, turning it into the hybrid formats which allow the voices of the "natives" to be heard without silencing the voice of the ethnographer (Behar 1995, 14; Abu Lughod 1993; Narayan 1995).

Postscript

In June 1999 my mother broke her femur and died two weeks later. Her friends, the older women whose stories are included in this book, kept repeating during their condolence visits: *la yineshikem fiha,* literally meaning, "May He not cause you to forget her." The year following her death brought many changes in Gilat. Miḥa's husband died in March 2000, and Thérèse died in April 2000. Ghaliya broke her leg in March 2000 and subsequently her family is considering bringing in a Philipina to help her recover. Jeani felt that her health was failing and also brought in a Philipina to help her. The continuing demise of this generation emphasizes the urgency of collecting and analyzing their accounts and the need to add my own contribution to the ethnic survival of my motherline.

ma qaˤdu kan ləxrayef.
What is left are only stories.
But these are the stories that shape our lives.

Appendixes: Full Narrative Texts

The following are the complete texts, of which segments are
analyzed throughout the book. The texts are translated from
Arabic (unmarked), *French*, and HEBREW.
The order of the texts follows their appearance in the book.

APPENDIX 1: BIYA IN SCHOOL

Taped conversation, segments 1988/30:16, 30:17.

Setting: Saturday night, July 23, 1988, at the front yard of Biya and Shimon. Participants: Biya, Shimon, his father Ḥayim, Rachel (a neighbor), Esther S-N.

In Arabic, *French,* and HEBREW.

1. Biya: *I was a very good student, a brilliant student at school. The teacher,*
2. what did she do
3. *I was studying in school,*
4. and when I finished classes she would send me to her mother to clean for her.
5. *That teacher. Miss Sitbon*
6. Shimon: *There, in Fran—in Tunisia, whoever had money could be something.*
7. Esther/Biya: *Yes.*
8. Shimon: *Not here. If you're smart, even if you don't have money, they'll help you.*
9. *But not there. Poor—*
10. Biya [overlapping]: By God, if I had been in Israel, I would have turned out SOMETHING SPECIAL.
11. Shimon: *Because she was always first in her class.*
12. Biya: *Always first in class.*
13. [solemnly]: BY THE TRUTH OF THE TORAH

165

14. Shimon: *She was—*
15. Biya: *A very, very good student.*
16. THEN the teacher, may she be cursed,
17. I would finish the—
18. *in the middle of the day she would send me off.*
19. *Tells me go to mommy and help her.*
20. I would work in her house, being maybe *twelve or thirteen* [years old].
21. I would go clean for her, wash dishes, do everything.
22. *She gave me good grades,* the truth I was . . . *no. and it is true.*
23. Esther: *Yes, yes.*
24. Biya: *She gave me notebooks and books,* WITHOUT CHARGING ME
25. *we didn't have. I had a friend*
26. Shimon: *There, whoever doesn't have money stays—*
27. Biya (overlapping): Yes, and I had, Rachel, I had A FRIEND *who was very, very rich.*
28. *She was an only child, Denise, daughter of the Yishay's.*
29. *She was very, very rich and we were very, very poor people.*
30. Esther: *The Yishay family from here?*
31. Biya: *Yes, it's a cousin, but not them.*
32. *We were very friendly, me and them, Lizette, and her sister Lucienne. She lives in Beersheva now.*
33. *We were in the same class. We were very close friends.*
34. SO this Denise Yishay says to me, I would go to her house in the morning so we go together *to walk to school*
35. SO *she prepares a sandwich for me;*
36. *No, my mother was too poor to prepare a snack for me.*
37. *So she fixes a* SLICE OF BREAD *with* A PIECE OF CHOCOLATE *for me to go to school and I would carry her* BAG *and prepare her homework.*
    (Shimon and I laugh)
38. *Yea, and she would get up in the morning, she sleeps in a very nice bed there was that* MARIANTUANET *(a dresser??) in her room*
39. She says *"Mother . . ."*
40. Shimon: And you, where did you sleep in Moknine?
41. Biya [in singsong]: ya diwani ʿaliya (woe is me!)
42. THEN SHE [says] what does she tell her? *"Mommy prepare me a dress. What will I put on today?"*
43. And I say to myself, "Damn her, look how many dresses she has, and she DOESN'T EVEN *give me one.*"
44. and she says: *"What dress should I put on, Mommy??"*
    Biya tells of Denise's whereabouts in the present, and concludes:

55. And that's it. The world is all stories.
56. BY MY LIFE, *but I did suffer a lot.*
57. Possibly *I began working when I was ten years old,* I swear to God.

APPENDIX 2:
THÉRÈSE IN THE WELL

Taped conversation, segment 1987/20:4.

Setting: In my parents' house, July 7, 1987. I asked Noro to tell me about the history of the community. My mother Fortuna was both listening and narrating.

In Arabic, *French,* and HEBREW.

1. Fortuna: Alas, alas, what he did to them!
2. Noro: ONE DAY ABROAD, WHEN Thérèse WAS LITTLE, SHE FELL INTO A WELL.
3. Esther: REALLY?
4. Fortuna: She tells about it.
5. Noro: YES, SHE TELLS ABOUT IT.
   At this point I went to bring my notebook and the story continued in a polyphonic manner:
8. Fortuna: A well, without water, in Sfax. An empty well.
9. SHE WAS A YEAR AND A HALF, I think or TWO YEARS OLD.
10. They say SHE FELL INTO A WELL.
11. Noro: FELL INTO A WELL.
12. Fortuna: They started looking for her, didn't find her.
13. Some Arab man found her—
14. Noro [overlaps]: —THEN THEY FOUND AN ARAB WHO TOLD THEM,
15. "YOU WANT ME TO TAKE HER OUT OF THE WELL—

169

16. Fortuna [overlaps]: —said, "do you want me TO TAKE HER OUT?"
17. Noro: "GIVE ME FIVE FRANCS."
18. Fortuna [corrects]: Duro, duro [rising tone].
19. Noro: Duro [old Tunisian currency].
20. Esther: IT'S A LOT OF MONEY.
21. Fortuna: Duro, *it's nice* [the sound of the word].
22. Esther: WAS THAT A LOT OF MONEY?
23. Noro: At THE TIME, YES.
24. Fortuna: YES. Five francs IT'S A LOT.
25. Noro: THEY HAD NO CHOICE, HE TOOK HER OUT OF—
26. [unclear comment]
27. SO WHEN HER FATHER CAME—
28. Fortuna: No, not like that.
29. *You don't know how to tell it.*
30. *The grandmother was with them.*
31. SHE SAID, "WHAT'S THAT? HE ASKS FOR duro FOR SUCH A—"
32. Esther: GIRL?
33. Fortuna: "LITTLE, LIKE THIS, WE GIVE A duro? THAT'S TOO MUCH."
34. NO. HER MOTHER said
35. "YES, YES, WHY, WHY, I WANT TO BRING HER OUT, ENOUGH."
36. WHEN HER FATHER CAME they told him, WHAT'S A duro
37. Esther: ISN'T IT A WASTE OF MONEY?
38. Fortuna: YEH, A WASTE OF MONEY.
39. *The grandmother* told them.
40. Noro [turns to another subject]: I USED TO DO ALL SORTS OF NONSENSE.
41. Fortuna [continues the story]:
    He told them, "YES, YES, IT'S OK, TAKE HER OUT."
    [two-second pause]
42. Esther [addresses Noro]: THERE WERE OTHER THINGS YOU DID WITH THEM, WITH THE MELONS?
    [Another story unfolds.]

APPENDIX 3:
BIYA WINS SHIMON

Taped conversation, segment 1988/30:22.

Continuation of the conversation in appendix 1.

Setting: Saturday night, July 23, 1988, at the front yard of Biya and Shimon. Audience: Shimon, his father Ḥayim, Rachel, Esther.

In Arabic, *French,* and HEBREW.

1. Biya: It was like in the stories.
2. When I heard about it [the relapse] I came running
3. BECAUSE *I was in love with him.*
4. Esther: THAT IS WHY HE WAS ILL AGAIN? HE MISSED YOU?
5. Biya: *No, he did not love me.*
6. He loved me as a cousin, but it was not love.
7. BUT *for me it was* THE OTHER WAY AROUND.
   Biya, Shimon, and Ḥayim repeat how the word got to Biya about the relapse, since there were no telephones.
31. Biya: It was a Saturday, Rachel, we were there
32. and who doesn't come to visit and ask about him?
33. *When my aunt came*
34. My aunt, my father's sister
35. came to visit.
36. She came to their house.
37. She told Ḥayim, "So, what PRESENT are you going to give my niece?"

38. She is the one who struggled on my behalf,
39. God helping from above and she down below.
40. She loved and he too loved her very much.
41. My uncle [Ḥayim] told her, "All the stores are waiting for her.
42. She can go into any one and get what she wants."
43. She told him, "No, she does not need things.
44. She has the whole world.
45. My niece NEEDS NOTHING.
46. Her trousseau is READY.
47. She fought for him; he will take [marry] her."
48. Like that.
    [Biya laughs.]
49. *I was glad.* [pause]
50. *and he, he did not want to,*
51. BUT *he was embarrassed, so he said nothing.*
52. *He tried . . .*
53. Esther: (overlap) TO GET AWAY?
    Ḥayim interjects another example of Shimon's mischievous behavior, but Biya returns to the personal subject, overlapping with Ḥayim:
65. Biya: Yes, the world is but stories, Rachel, I SWEAR TO YOU
66. *And when he kissed me for the first time, oh, oh*
    [laughter].
67. *But he—no. He did not love me.*
68. Rachel: HOW LONG WAS IT BEFORE YOU GOT MARRIED?
69. Biya: *I did not want* [to get married] *we stayed* [engaged] *at least a year and a half a year and a half.*
70. *I didn't want to.*
71. *I said maybe he was mocking me?*
72. *Maybe I would remain* like this?
73. Until finally . . .
74. Shimon : *It is destiny.*

APPENDIX 4: BREAD, SHABBAT, AND MISCARRIAGE

Taped conversation, segments 1989/27:22–26

Setting: July 17, 1989, afternoon hours. During an interview with Miḥa and her husband Fradji.

Jeani, the neighbor, was the main narrator.

Narrated mainly in Arabic and HEBREW. French words are italicized, transliterated words are underlined.

1. Jeani: Miriam, daughter of D. GOT DIVORCED.
2. NO ONE KNOWS WHY.
3. SHE HAS TWO BOYS AND A GIRL.
4. Miḥa: And the girl she adopted that year.
5. Jeani: Woe on her, that thing she did.
6. Esther: Why? What did she do? Why did she adopt?
7. Miḥa: She adopted a blind girl, *blind.*
   [Mention of occasions of seeing the mother and girl.]
13. Miḥa: That's the way of the world. [two-second pause]
14. Jeani: MY MOTHER, God have mercy on her, used to say
15. One IS all in a mess, a woman all messed up.
16. She used to tell me, by God,
17. She is going to a funeral while she herself is like a funeral.
18. She is like a funeral, why should she go to another one?
19. Esther: What does it mean?
20. Jeani: FROM TIME TO TIME WHEN SOMETHING HAPPENS, Devora [a neighbor] tells me "look here, Jeani,

21. God have mercy on you, Jeani, she is a funeral, why is she going to a funeral?
22. Miḥa: Yes, if she is a funeral, why go to another one?
23. Esther: What does it mean zenaza?
24. Jeani (repeats the proverb): She is a funeral—
25. Miḥa: *There is a funeral and this woman wants to go, and her house is in a mess*
26. Esther: ah, ah,
27. Miḥa: *So* she says to her, the whole place is like a funeral and you are going to a funeral.
    [all laugh]
28. Jeani: Devora tells me, God have mercy on you Jeani,
29. I tell her, this is my *legacy* to you.
30. Miḥa: Really, those people of yesteryear
31. Jeani: ya ḥasra ʿaliem, ya ḥasra ʿaliem
32. Miḥa: My aunt used to live with us, she was something.
33. Jeani: MY MOTHER ALSO, NOT MY MOTHER, MY GRANDMOTHER, SHE WAS CHARMING.
34. Miḥa: If you sit near my aunt, you won't be bored.
35. Jeani: How many stories I heard from her, oh, oh,
36. See if now you can hear even a word from me.
37. They ask me: TELL US GRANDMA
38. and I say, ya ḥasra.
39. Miḥa: No, those stories and the parallel words naxwi
40. Esther: Right.
41. Jeani: And there was the story of Shif-el-Ajal, the books of Shif el Ajal ["Sword of Power," an epic tale of early Islam, popular in North Africa. Translated into Judeo-Arabic, it was printed in chap-books, to be read in installments].
42. Jeani: My brother would sit and read to us, and we would WAIT FOR THE STORY TO END.
43. Fradji: Every night, every night.
44. Jeani: A little bit every night so he wouldn't get tired and the story would continue.
45. Esther: Like "A Thousand and One Nights."
46. Miḥa: During winter, my uncle would read to us every night.
47. Jeani: Roasting chestnuts on the fire [overlap]
48. Fradji: [overlap] and peanuts.
49. Jeani: We had nuts and roasted chickpeas.
50. Peanuts were VERY EXPENSIVE in our area.
51. Peanuts came from Tripoli, Devora's town. Only chickpeas and nuts.

52. We'd all be sitting in bed, wrapped in a heavy blanket, BUT ONLY ONE NIGHT [a week].
53. Miḥa: Exactly. In our town, too, just one night.
54. Esther: Friday night?
55. Jeani: No, Thursday night.
56. Thursday night when we prepare bread at home and took it to bake in the <u>kusha</u>.
57. Everyone did it.
58. FROM TWO A.M. UNTIL THE MORNING AND WE. . . .
59. Fradji [laughing, overlap]: They had no time, had no time.
60. Jeani: We'd knead until the grains of salt put on the dough fell off
61. And we'd SHAPE THE LOAVES or MARK them,
62 and my mother would take them on her head to the <u>kusha</u>.
63. The <u>kusha</u> was not far from us.
64. She would open the oven and put in the bread.
65. Later they'd put in peanuts for sale.
66. She'd put in the bread and wait.
67. She could figure out the time when it would be ready.
68. If it came out nice and shiny, she'd return happy.
69. Miḥa: They'd say to her, happy Shabbat.
70. Jeani: Tell her, blessed Shabbat.
71. But if it came out yellow or ugly [claps hand] she'd beat her heart.
72. Esther: WHAT WOULD COME OF HER?
73. Jeani [singsong]: Woe to the Shabbat, woe to the Shabbat.
74. Miḥa: They'd say, "If the bread comes out well the entire Shabbat will be a good day."
75. Fradji: Bread is essential, bread is essential.
76. Jeani: She'd say, "Oh Father God, isn't it enough that I'm working ALL NIGHT?
77. Aren't you satisfied?"
78. All that worry about a bit of bread we don't even need.
79. Fradji: RIGHT.
80. Miḥa: Our children used to go on Friday night,
81. late at night to their grandparents.
82. They make a <u>kusha</u> for them under the blanket.
83. The children find there shelled nuts and peanuts, pistachio and chickpeas.
84. Grandfather prepares and tells them, this came out the <u>kusha</u>.
85. Jeani: NICE.
86. Fradji: Yeh.

87. Miḥa: Every Saturday they woke up early and went there.
88. Jeani: Remember Shushan Damri, who lived with us over there [in the moshav]?
89. Miḥa: Yes
90. Jeani: She, may you hear only good tidings, had MANY children, and they died.
91. Miḥa: Oh, Levitil's mother.
92. Jeani: Yes, Levitil's mother.
93. Until she was able to keep these boys and girls alive, GOD KNOWS.
94. She bore MANY MANY AND THEY DIED.
95. So once they said she was pregnant.
96. The woman tending the oven was a Jew named Leah.
97. She went and prepared
98. one prepares the bread during the day and put the harisha and tfina in the afternoon [Saturday lunch, left cooking overnight because according to Jewish law it is forbidden to cook on Shabbat].
99. Fradji confirms: Yes, the tfina.
100. Jeani: Everyone writes his name on the pot,
101. and the attendant tells them that at ELEVEN people come out of the SYNAGOGUE
102. people come to take their pots, until all is gone.
103. That's how it is.
104. She kneaded the bread like we do until two A.M..
105. No, her name was not Leah, Lahlouha.
106. And she put the bread in.
107. She put the bread in and waited until it baked to take it home on a platter carried on the head
108. or on a board LIKE THIS.
109. Fradji: Yes, they put it on a wooden board.
110. Jeani: AND IT HAS, IT HAS A SPECIAL COVER.
111. Miḥa: A wooden board, a wooden board.
112. Jeani: and SPECIAL matter (not clear)
113. Miḥa [overlap]: we had someone taking the bread
114. Jeani [overlap]: we were living in the Jewish quarter not far from the kusha
115. EVERYONE WAS TOGETHER.
116. They said that she—and her luck, the (hesitates)
117. Miḥa [helping]: The bread slipped.
118. Jeani: No, the first oven, when she opened it, the first loaves were Esther's.

119. Miḥa: Yeh.
120. Jeani: The attendant gave the bread to Esther, who looked at it,
121. and she was FIVE MONTHS pregnant.
122. Miḥa: Woe!
123. Jeani: They say that she scratch her face,
124. hitting her heart and beating her face,
125. beating her heart, till she miscarried the child on the spot.
126. She miscarried it, FIVE MONTHS OLD.
     [Miḥa, Fradji, and I exclaim our astonishment.]
127. Jeani: And the date remained FOR LIFE
128. UNTIL I GREW UP TO BE TWENTY-THREE
129. and whenever I went to Lahlouha's oven I was told
130. this is where Esther, Shushan's wife, miscarried her child.
     [The audience make overlapping remarks]
131. Esther: Why? Because the bread was not right?
132. Miḥa: She was a very nervous woman.
133. Jeani: Nervous, and was also afraid of Shushan.
134. Women feared their husbands a lot because of the bread.
135. If it did not come out well they'd tell them "IT'S YOUR
     FAULT."
136. NOT THE FAULT of the oven attendant.
     [Miḥa laughs.]
137. Jeani: The poor one she miscarried it ON THE SPOT and that's
     it.
138. That's what happened because of the bread.
     [almost three seconds pause]
139. Jeani: When I tell that to my daughters-in-law, they die of
     laughter.
140. I tell them EVERYTHING WAS SO DIFFICULT THERE.
141. very difficult.
142. Miḥa: Everything DIFFICULT.
143. Jeani: EVERYTHING WAS VERY DIFFICULT, EVERYTHING.
144. Fradji: Everything was DIFFICULT and they used to—
145. Miḥa [overlap]: Here everything is easy, with washing
     machines.
146. Jeani: AND HOW DO WE FEEL TODAY? WE DON'T FEEL IT.
147. Miḥa [overlap]: —the machines and gas stove we have—
148. Jeani: [overlap] WHOEVER HAS [money] CAN ENJOY LIFE
149. THOSE WHO DON'T, have nothing.
150. [Over there] people work and live day to day.
151. IF HE DOES NOT HAVE, THE COMMUNITY GIVES HIM HIS
     NEEDS.

152. Fradji: They were not worried about tomorrow, would not worry about a thing.
153. Miḥa: There were treasurers of the community, this was their responsibility.
     The conversation continues, describing how the community took care of the poor people.

APPENDIX 5:
WOMEN AND GUNS 1

Taped conversation, segments 1987/20:16–17

Setting: In my parents' house, July 7, 1987. This segment begins with a request to tell about a specific event.

In Arabic, *French,* and HEBREW.

1. Esther: [Tell me] the one who shot out of the window, or something . . .
2. Fortuna: Noro MAY know it.
3. Noro: What is it?
4. Fortuna: Do you know it?
5. Esther: You said something about someone shooting her husband . . .
6. Fortuna: One day a man went on GUARD DUTY. He told his wife.
7. She said, "I'm afraid to stay [home] alone."
8. He told her, "If someone comes and makes noises or something, shoot, it's okay."
9. Noro: Yeh.
10. Fortuna: She told him, "No, no." He said, "It's okay. Shoot." Yeh.
11. That same night, AS IT HAPPENED, her husband unexpectedly came back.
12. She heard steps.
13. She quickly took the Sten gun and shot.

179

14. It turned out to be her husband.
15. Esther: Oh, oh, was she on bad terms with her husband?
16. Fortuna: No, no, she wasn't.
17. Esther: FATHER, wasn't she on bad terms with her husband, this woman?
18. Noro: I don't know. I DON'T REMEMBER THE STORY EXACTLY.
19. Esther: In what *moshav?* BUT WHAT DO YOU REMEMBER EXACTLY?
20. Noro: NOTHING, I DON'T REMEMBER ANYTHING OF THIS CASE
21. Fortuna: *No, I heard people, like that.*
22. Esther: *And in what moshav did it happen, do you know?*
23. Noro: In Gilat, in Gilat, that woman who was shot in the legs.
24. Fortuna: No, this was another one.
25. Esther: That's another one.
26. Fortuna: That's another one.
27. [In] this story she shot. She was not shot in the legs.
28. Esther: And who is that one who was shot in her legs?
29. Fortuna: May we not witness those days. All that happened during that time.
30. Noro: THOSE WERE THE DAYS.
31. Fortuna: What was going on.
32. They gave us weapons, *and we did not know how to use them.*
33. And there were people, well, how to say that
34. Noro: THERE WERE MANY CASES . . .
35. Fortuna: There were CASES.
36. People did not know how, and they were scared.
37. OUT OF FEAR they would hold the Sten gun and shoot, without knowing where.
38. Esther: Who was that woman shot in the legs?
39. Fortuna: On the other side of the community. Noro knows bout it.
40. Noro [overlap]: On the other side of the community.
41. Esther: Do you know it [the story]?
42. Noro: Friday night. IT WAS FRIDAY NIGHT. I REMEMBER IT.
43. WITH A FLASHLIGHT THE LADY WENT OUT.
44. Fortuna [overlap]: with the FLASHLIGHT.
45. Noro: THE GUARDS THOUGHT, DANI G., NO. DANI B. IF I REMEMBER CORRECTLY
46. Esther: WELL . . .

47. Noro: WAS ON GUARD DUTY AND HE SAW A FLASHLIGHT on Shabbat.
48. SURE, WE HAD NO ELECTRICITY IN THE HOUSES.
49. SO HE SHOT AT HER LEGS.
50. Fortuna: Woe, woe, woe.
51. Esther [laughing]: HE IS RIGHT, A LIGHT ON SHABBAT.
52. Noro: YES, NOW THAT WE ARE TALKING ABOUT IT, I REMEMBER EXACTLY.
53. Fortuna: He thought it was a Muslim.
54. Esther: That woman PROBABLY WENT OUT TO THE TOILETS.
55. Noro: Yeh.
56. Esther: She wanted to pee or something.
57. Noro: IT IS POSSIBLE, IT IS POSSIBLE.
58. Fortuna: Yes, they [the toilets] were outside.
59. Esther: I know they used to be outside. I REMEMBER THAT.
60. Noro: THE TOILETS WERE OUTSIDE THERE WAS NO ELECTRICITY AND MISSIS WHATS-HER-NAME GOES OUT
61. WITH A FLASHLIGHT TO LOOK FOR THE TOILET.
62. THE SENTRY THOUGHT IT MUST BE A CRIMINAL LOOKING TO BREAK INTO A HOUSE OR SOMETHING.
63. HE SHOT AT HER LEGS.
64. YES, I REMEMBER IT
65. ONLY I DON'T REMEMBER HER NAME. SHE WAS MARRIED.
66. Esther: THEY DON'T LIVE IN THE MOSHAV ANY MORE OR ELSE YOU WOULD KNOW WHO IT WAS.
67. Noro: THEY USED TO LIVE HERE.

APPENDIX 6:
WOMEN AND GUNS 2

Taped conversation, segments 1989/37:8,9,10.

Setting: In Kibbutz Lavie (northern Israel). Conversation with Fortuna. Audience included Noro (unable to actively participate in the conversation because of a stroke), my sister Miriam, and her children Ronit and Roi.

We were talking about the early years in Gilat and Fortuna told the story about the woman who was shot in her legs. She continued, without being asked, to tell another story about the use of guns.

In Arabic, *French,* and HEBREW.

1. Fortuna: There was one woman, wait. On another moshav, listen.
2. Esther: Yes.
3. Fortuna: In Brosh *in a* MOSHAV LIKE THAT.
4. *Her husband told her, if you a hear noise, shoot. If you hear noise, shoot.*
5. Esther: Yes. [to Miriam] LISTEN AND TELL ME IF YOU KNOW THIS ONE.
6. Fortuna: *If you hear a noise, shoot.*
7. AND HE WENT, TO GUARD DUTY OR SOMETHING LIKE THAT.
8. *Then he came back,* understand?
9. *She heard a noise—he knocked on the door* I THINK AND *she shot him.*

183

10. Miriam: WHO WAS IT?
11. Fortuna: Her husband.
12. Esther: *Which moshav was it?*
13. Fortuna: *On another* moshav, say Brosh. Put Brosh.
14. Noro: *It's true, it's true.*
15. Fortuna: She shot him.
16. Thought he was an Arab, she shot him, shamʿu ǝl xir (God forbid), it turned out to be her husband.
17. Esther: Oh oh, did she kill him or just injure his legs? [joking remarks about shooting]
20. Esther: Did you shoot too?
21. Fortuna (laughs): No, listen to this.
22. I—Once—Noro went on guard duty.
23. You understand, went to the other side (of the moshav).
24. He was late. Baḥla my sister was with me, and I aid, "Oh (claps hands), Noro is not back yet."
25. It was almost 1:00 A.M., and I had a gun.
26. I told her, "I am going to shoot."
27. Baḥla my sister said, "No, no, don't shoot, who knows who's walking by?"
28. I told her, "Who can be walking by at 1:00 A.M.?
29. No, I'm going to shoot so Noro will hear me from the other section" [and return home].
30. Miriam: YEH, WITH MARGO. WITH RACHEL [Baḥla, Fortuna's sister, who lived with us for some time].
31. Fortuna: Rachel. She says to me, "No," and I say . . .
32. I climbed to the window on a bed, because we had a bed.
33. Esther: RIGHT, SHE HAD TO CLIMB ONTO THE WINDOW.
34. Fortuna: From the window, and put the gun out, and wanted to shoot. I was ready.
35. She tells me "Don't shoot, there must be . . ."
36. I told her, "At one after midnight? Who is going to pass by after midnight?"
37. Finally I say, "Yes," and she says, "No."
38. In the end I did not shoot. I did not shoot [all laugh].
39. After fifteen minutes Noro came home.
40. Esther: HE HEARD, HOW DID YOU KNOW?
41. Miriam: *How did you know how to shoot? Who taught you to shoot?*
42. Fortuna: *Noro taught me to shoot. Before he went on* GUARD DUTY. *I shot two or three times.*
43. Miriam: TRAINING, THERE WERE TRAININGS.
[all laugh]

44. Esther: YOU WERE TRAINING MOTHER?
45. Fortuna: *No, I knew.*
46. No, but Noro was on guard duty every night, and you were little, sleeping.
47. He told me, "If you hear a noise . . ."
48. He tells me, "You hear a noise or scratching on the door, or something, shoot!"
49. I learned to shoot! I would put the GUN near my head, upright like that.
50. Esther: LOADED?
51. Fortuna: You understand, and I stayed awake, when I heard some scratching, I get up.
52. *No, I sleep very lightly.*
53. I lay on the bed sleeping, like this, and the kids sleeping here, and I stood near the window.
54. No, lying or standing.
55. When I hear scratching, I shoot. What! the truth, I never shot.
56. Esther: SINCE THEN SHE LEARNED TO LOCK THE DOOR.
57. Fortuna: I did not shoot.

APPENDIX 7:
MAMA KUKA'S STORY

Taped conversation, segment 1987/26:28.
Setting: December 24, 1987. In the evening. In the house of Ghaliya.
Her children, Yudit, Dina, Ariyeh, and Roni were present. Audience's
minimal responses appear in parenthesis.
Narrated in Arabic and HEBREW.

1. Your father and Lalu Uzan used to plant
2. they had in the field (yes) cucumbers
3. and bell peppers
4. and hot peppers
5. and tomatoes
    (YES, right)
6. and they transport full carts
7. like this
8. and we were A LARGE FAMILY (RIGHT)
9. and my husband works in Sollel Boneh
10. we could HARDLY buy anything
11. just hardly (yeah)
12. (in a low voice): I say
13. oh God I wish I had a bit of that
14. to prepare dinner for my kids (yeah)
15. your mother never gave us [anything]
16. and I never asked (yeah)
17. and I cannot say "give me"

18. but mother Kuka
19. may God lighten the heavy earth on her
20. that mother Kuka how good she was
21. her husband
22. God forgive them all
23. [was] A MISER
24. may God forgive them all
25. only one's character remains (yeah)
26. Yes
27. SO when mother Kuka
28. may God forgive her,
29. came [to Israel]
30. what a wonderful woman (yeah)
31. what sweet speech
32. and what eloquence
33. and what company
34. being with her was better than in a café
35. SO your father used to give her bags and bags of peanuts
36. and when she had nothing to do in the afternoon
37. she dresses
38. makes herself pretty
39. combs her hair and makes coffee (yeah)
40. she thought much of herself
41. and he
42. God forgive him
43. her husband
44. what he had done to her
45. in Sfax he left her for five years and went to France
46. Yudit: YES ALWAYS [overlap]
47. Ghaliya: In France
48. and left her with three children
49. Yudit [overlap]: Noro ALWAYS TELLS THAT
50. Ghaliya: and then when his daughter got married she sent a message to him saying
51. just come just come
52. so people won't say she has no father
53. don't bring anything.
54. Well,
55. that was then
56. that's what he did in his youth
57. and later when he got older
58. he was peeling bananas for her

59. because now he turned old
60. he is good for nothing.
    [Yudit and Esther laugh]
61. Ghaliya: Yeah, God forgives her
62. she told me everything
63. Esther: REALLY when they lived here when I knew them
64. when they came here
65. what a love was between them (yeah)
66. you'd say they have never . . .
67. Yudit: TO COMPENSATE HER
68. Ghaliya: yeah she told me the poor woman
69. otherwise how would I know
70. she is from Sfax
71. and I am from Gabes
72. Esther: yeah
73. Ghaliya: SO I would come [to see her]
74. she knows the SITUATION (yeah)
75. may God forgive you oh my mother Kuka
76. she'd fill up a pillow case
77. a pillow case
78. fill it up with everything
79. sweet peppers
80. hot peppers
81. tomatoes
82. and cucumbers
83. and she waits until her husband goes inside
84. and tells me
85. take my dear take
86. go my child go
87. go and prepare dinner for your children go.
88. So that her husband wouldn't see her (yeah)
89. he does not want.
90. A diamond she was
91. how good she was
92. what a big heart
93. Ariyeh: WHO'S THAT
94. Yudit: Esther's GRANDMA
95. Ghaliya: MOTHER—
96. Esther (overlap): MY FATHER'S MOTHER
97. Ghaliya: FATHER'S MOTHER how she—
98. Esther (overlap) THEY USED TO LIVE HERE
99. Ghaliya: because she tells me

100. tells me
101. I have suffered too
102. I also had children and have suffered
103. take my dear take
104. God forgive her

NOTES

Introduction

1. See Coupland and Nussbaum 1993; Gergen and Gergen 1988; Josselson and Lieblich 1999; Lawless 1991; Lieblich, Tuval-Mashiach, and Zilber 1998; Linde 1993; Ochs 1997; Ochs and Capps 1996; Paoletti 1998; Rosenwald and Ochberg 1992; and Sawin 1999.

2. Bauman and Sherzer 1989; Hymes 1996; Langellier 1989; Langellier and Peterson 1993; Moerman 1988; Peterson and Langellier 1997; Saville-Troike 1989; Sawin 1999.

3. This statement was specifically repeated in a series of conversations with the women held in September and October 1997.

4. The interactions between individual and communal memories have been studied in a variety of contexts, for example, Katriel 1997; Zerubavel 1995. See Ben-Amos and Weissberg 1999.

5. The idea of "cultural symbiosis" between Muslim and Jewish cultures was suggested by Goitein ([1955] 1974) and has been further elaborated by Patai (1986).

6. According to the census of 1936, there were 27,345 Jews living in the capital, Tunis. Their occupational breakdown was: 2,196 merchants, 1,827 artisans, 1,710 day workers, 1,427 professionals, and 33 farmers. In Sousse there were no farmers in a population of 3,741, and in Sfax there was only one among 3,466 Jews (Abramski-Bligh 1997).

7. There were cases where entire communities were transplanted in Israeli *moshavim*. See Goldberg (1972) or Shokeid (1971).

8. This distinction is not accurate but informative, as the issue here is group perceptions and stereotypes (see also Shohat 1990). The term "Sephardim" applied originally to Jews who traced their ancestry to fifteenth-century Spain (Sepharad), and "Ashkenazim" referred only to

German Jews. In ordinary use today, however, "Ashkenazim" defines Israelis of European roots, and "Sephardim" stands as the most inclusive opposing category, to include Middle Eastern Jews, or 'edot hamizraḥ (communities of the East). See Goldberg (1996) for an extensive analysis of the different groups.

9. The viability of ethnic tension can be seen in the public apology in September 1997 of Ehud Barak, then head of the opposition Labor Party, to the Sephardi population in Israel for their having been robbed of their cultural heritage during the early years of the state. In July 1998, Ori Orr, a Knesset member from the Labor Party, was quoted in a newspaper interview as claiming that Moroccan Israelis were easily offended and that one could not talk to them the way one could talk to other Israelis. His comments raised a public outcry, and he was removed from his position in the party.

10. In *Moshav* Gilat, where I grew up, women always participated in the elections for local committees, but the elderly women admit that they voted according to their husbands' instructions.

11. On February 11, 2000, *Kol Ha'ir*, a local newspaper, announced that for the first time in fifty years women had been elected to a major committee in *Moshav* Nes Harim, in the vicinity of Jerusalem. The same newspaper published three weeks earlier a story about inaccessibility of local government to women in moshavim in the same area (Hadar 2000).

12. Similar functions are found in the poetry of Bedouin women, a venue for expressing a range of emotions in a normative mode (Abu-Lughod 1986).

13. The women watch television news as well as movies and soap operas. The lives of media personae, fictive or real, are a favorite topic of conversation.

14. This word play is borrowed from Assia Djebar, *l'amour, ses cris (s'écrit)* ([1985] 1993).

15. Specific details were obtained on October 1, 1997. Biya insisted that her real name be used.

16. When I interviewed him in 1984, he was proud to tell me about his contact with academic folklorists and about his methods for keeping an audience alert.

17. Specific details were collected on October 1, 1997.

18. Interviewed on May 25, 1995, and again on June 5, 1995.

Chapter 1

1. The *martba* is a specially arranged corner in the house with sacred books, for the protection of the mother and the newborn.

2. Cohen does not specify whether the informants were women or men. The texts are in Judeo-Arabic transcript and translated into French.

3. Even in women's recollections the birth of a boy takes precedence over that of a girl. Madeline Duwek, whose childhood memories were published in Hebrew in 1979, does not mention celebrations for girls, only the elaborate ceremonies for boys (1979, 30–31).

4. Financial support may be provided by sons, but care in old age is usually given by daughters. This point is stressed over and over again in stories about old age. See chapter 5.

5. Another Arabic proverb simply puts it: "The father of daughters does not sleep well" (Lunde and Wintle 1984, 122).

6. Cohen (1975, 148) notes that while *bint* and *sbiyya* are common terms among the Jews, *tofla* is mainly used in Jewish interactions with Muslims.

7. This is typical of Muslim society. A Palestinian student of mine related that her sixty-year-old unmarried aunt is still referred to as *bint* (February 1999).

8. Abu-Lughod (1993, 167–202) describes a similar situation among the Bedouin she studied. Weddings are a time for great excitement, not only for the bride but for other females of all ages as well.

9. My conversation with Biya about this event took place in the summer of 1998, following my specific question about the onset of menarche.

10. Ghaliya's story contradicts Valensi's findings about the Jewish girls in Jerba, that "neither birth nor puberty were marked by any ritual at all" (1989, 66). The Jewish population in Gabes, where Ghaliya grew up, is closely tied to the customs and traditions of Jerba.

11. Support for this belief is found in the story of Uzan, who found a piece of mirror in the wedding mattress. His wife explains, "I will forever look to you as you saw me on that night" (Awret 1984, 213).

12. A discussion of a Judaic studies group on the Internet (January–February 2000) indicates that the custom of slapping is still practiced.

13. This information was provided by Jocelyn, an Algerian woman in her early fifties residing in Jerusalem. Playing the role of an adult in a rite of passage is also seen in the bar mitzvah celebration for boys: it is the first time that boys wear long pants and a tie (Cohen 1964, 27).

14. My curiosity was piqued by anthropologist Harvey Goldberg, who noticed the mention of oil in connection with menarche in his research and inquired if I had supporting data.

15. There were some professional Jewish women in Tunisia, but they were mostly from middle-class or European families, rather than working-class Tunisians, as are the women described here.

16. Fortuna told me how upset her grandfather was to hear her recite as part of history lessons *nos pères les gaullois . . .* (our fathers the Gualles . . .). She quotes him as saying *adi sla taʿ ʾl bibassa* (these are monks' prayers).

17. Djebar's description of the girl going to school in Algeria echoes similar concerns: "The jailer who guards a body that has no words—and written words can travel—may sleep in peace: it will suffice to brick up the windows, padlock the sole entrance door, and erect a blank wall rising up to heaven. And what if the maiden does write? Her voice, albeit silenced, will circulate. . . ." (Djebar [1985] 1993, 3). Similar concerns existed in Tunisia as well, as suggested by Zamiti-Horchani (1986, 112–13), who notes that opposition to girls' education was based on principle rather than practical matters (e.g., a need for the child to support the family), and voiced mainly by males in the family.

18. Interview from July 5, 1995. The story was narrated in Hebrew.

19. The collection of Arabic proverbs compiled by Lunde and Wintle (1984) includes a slight variation of the proverb, "after puberty, a husband or a grave" (p. 52). The origin is marked simply "Arabic" and no examples are given. A Muslim-Tunisian colleague informed me that the proverb is no longer common among young Tunisians (personal communication, February 2000).

20. Telephone conversation, February 16, 2000.

21. Other narrators did not specifically distinguish between mother and father's attitude toward school. The choice between male and female role models is particularly significant in Odette's life story as it unfolds (see chapter 4).

22. Ethnicity was (and still is) an important marker of identity in the stories. Fortuna always identifies the other two top girls in her class as being Italian and Greek.

23. The Ben Zvi Institute for the Study of Jewish Communities in the East (located in Jerusalem) has a vast collection of texts in Judeo-Arabic. Other texts are held in private collections (see Attal 1980, 1989, 1996; Avivi 1993; Tobi 1996; Tobi 2000). The large number of newspapers and other secular texts in these collections is an indication of their popularity and the level of literacy among Tunisian Jewish men.

24. The Hebrew University, March 29, 1999. Odette referred to the students as her children several times during the talk. At the end of the class she blessed each and every one, including the video camera operator. See further discussion in chapter 5 on the role of "everyone's grandmother."

25. July 23, 1988. The participants in the interaction knew that I was taping the conversation.

26.   July 7, 1987. See Schely-Newman (1997, 407) for another example of a joint competitive narration from that same interaction.

27.   During a condolence visit (a *shiva* call) after Thérèse's death, one of her daughters repeated the same story. In the family version, however, it was a neighbor who complained about the price for such a little girl. The grandmother insisted that the girl be rescued nevertheless (*Moshav Gilat*, April 18, 2000).

Chapter 2

1.   Interview from November 23, 1998.

2.   The worldwide Jewish custom of breaking a glass during the wedding ceremony is explained as a sign of mourning for and commemoration of the destruction of the Temple. Tearing the garment is a Jewish sign of mourning for a parent, spouse, child, or sibling. Goldberg (1990, 65–66) provides other examples of Libyan wedding customs with added explanations that make them "Jewish."

3.   Raphael Uzan, whose life in Tunisia is depicted in Awret (1984), tells about his own wedding: "My share in all that was a red dot on the tip of my little finger" (p. 273).

4.   According to Valensi (1989, 71), there seems to be no Jewish element in or explanation for this ritual, which is closely related to the first ritual in Muslim weddings, called ʿutriya.

5.   The women were unaware of the sexual symbolism of the shoe, as seen in folktales such as Cinderella.

6.   The use of chicken wings as symbolizing girls' future is found in Jewish rabbinic literature in a sequence of riddle tales from *Lamentation Rabbah* praising the wisdom of Jerusalem inhabitants (Hasan-Rokem 2000, 46).

7.   It is worth noting that although Cohen (1964) mentions the first custom, he makes no reference to the second. Nor does it appear in Valensi (1989), even though among Israelis of Jerban origin this event continues to be celebrated; older women are especially invited to lead the singing of Tunisian wedding songs.

8.   The use of *henna* for marriage has acquired a Jewish religious meaning for North African Jews, as explained by an elderly Moroccan rabbi. The Hebrew letters of the word are an acronym for the three women's duties, which construct Jewish female identity: *Hallah, Niddah,* and *Hadlaka* (Sered, Kaplan, and Cooper 1999, 158). See further discussion on these duties in the next chapter.

9.   The collection of articles edited by Wasserfall (1999b) includes in-depth discussions on the history and current practices of *niddah*. For an extensive discussion of religious development, see Fonrobert (2000).

10. Raymonde still remembers with indignation being displayed naked in front of relatives and friends, including her future mother-in-law, during the visit to the *mikvah*. Like other women now in their fifties and sixties, she made sure that her own daughters would not go through the same experience, and took them to the bath in private.

11. Among other Jewish ethnic groups it is customary for friends and relatives to invite the newlyweds and some friends for a festive dinner on each of the seven nights following the *ḥuppa*. The seven blessings are recited during the after-meal grace.

12. Thérèse and Rachel told this version of the tragic shooting in an interview on December 16, 1987. Another version was less dramatic, and does not include the *mikvah* or a prediction of disaster. According to Shula and Malka (both born in 1946), the groom's parents objected and the wedding was postponed again and again. The couple was finally married, but had a very unhappy marriage (related on July 19, 1988).

13. Israeli celebrities of Moroccan or Yemenite origins have been celebrating the *ḥenna* ceremony with great opulence. The media coverage might also be a reason for the growing popularity of ethnic celebrations in weddings.

14. Interview in October 1998, in the *moʿadon* of Moshav Givat Yearim, near Jerusalem.

15. Telephone interview, February 16, 2000. Odette's mother prepared a festive meal and announced to the groom that the bride was now mature enough to be married.

16. Narrated by a non-Tunisian counselor who worked in Gilat in 1956–57 (July 1989).

17. Told in December 1987 by Thérèse's husband, this was believed to have happened during the 1980s.

18. Told in May 1996, and again in October 1998, during a visit to the *moʿadon* in Moshav Givat Yearim.

19. Initial data recorded in May 25, 1995, and again on February 17, 2000.

20. Sara (born 1945, in Tunis) told me about her grandmother, who complained to the end of her days that she had lost a good husband because her family was unable to buy the sewing machine promised as part of her dowry (May 1997). My great-grandmother had to plead with her relatively well-to-do daughter to help buy a special garment for her sister, so that she could be married. Raphael Uzan tells about a bride left under the *ḥuppa* because her parents did not provide the groom with a prayer shawl; an Algerian Jewish soldier (it was in 1942) offered to marry her right then and there. He turned out to be wealthy (Awret 1984, 160).

21. Interview July 5, 1995.

22. July 23, 1988. Narrated in a mixture of Arabic, French, and Hebrew.

23. Ḥayim and Biya's mother are siblings. Marriage between first cousins is a preferred choice among Tunisian Jews, as it is among Muslims.

24. July 5, 1995. See Schely-Newman 1999a for discussion about Odette's representation of her public and private selves.

25. Cohen (1964, 39) describes the procedure in the capital, Tunis. The matchmaker suggests a potential pairing, based on the knowledge of the people involved. Then it is time for financial bargaining about the *dotta*. When all is agreed upon, the matchmaker arranges for the couple to see each other, usually in a quasi-accidental manner, for example, on the beach.

26. The name Sandriella is probably a combination of the French Cendrillon and the Hebrew Cinderella.

27. As noted earlier, Biya and Shimon are first cousins. Their siblings are married to each other, and their two older children are also married to first cousins. Common in Tunisia, this pattern has been changing in Israel and is no longer as frequent.

Chapter 3

1. Mishnah Shabbat, chapter 2:6. Fonrobert (2000) suggests that there are two directions of rabbinical readings of this passage: as punishment for women because they brought death to the world, or as punishment by death at a young age for not fulfilling divine destination of human beings, men and women alike.

2. Dairy and meat products are not to be mixed, or eaten together. Only certain types of meat are allowed, and the animals must be slaughtered and prepared in special ways and meat thoroughly cooked before being consumed.

3. Sexual relations on Friday night (Shabbat) are seen as mirroring the spiritual union between God and the people of Israel and are considered a *mitzvah*.

4. The conversation took place in August 1990, when I stopped by at Biya's house. As I did not initiate the conversation, it was not taped. For a fuller analysis of this story see Schely-Newman 1996b.

5. Men may also use the *mikvah* for ritual purification, but they are not required to do so. Men's immersion may derive from a personal commitment to piety or may be performed in preparation for a deed requiring a high degree of sanctity, such as making ritual objects.

6. Education in general has been expropriated from the family by the state, emphasizing the right of the collective over that of the family, as shown by Handelman (1998, 163) in his study of holiday celebrations.

7. In ultra-Orthodox Jewish (European) communities, visiting the *mikvah* was (and is) a woman's duty that did (and does) not depend on the husband (personal communication, Harvey Goldberg).

8. Fonrobert (1999) provides interesting examples from the Talmud of women's words and rabbinical rulings in the matter of deciding the woman's state of purity. In all cases the rabbis ruled according to the woman's declaration.

9. I also have heard of a woman being raped in a town near Gilat following her immersion, and consequently being divorced (described to me in July 1988).

10. Though Weissler makes this point regarding devotional prayers of Eastern European Jewish women, evidence from North Africa indicates similar concerns.

11. In the 1950s a cash prize was awarded to women who had ten children. The state now provides child support, and the amount given for the fourth child and subsequent children is substantially larger than that for each of the first three children. See further discussion in Sered 2000.

12. Avoiding intercourse or using contraceptives were not options for the women, nor was birth control an issue with which they were familiar.

13. Information about childbearing was collected in *moʿadonim* in the vicinity of Jerusalem during 1993. One Yemeni woman told me that she chose to have her last child in the hospital because she wanted to have this experience.

14. Narrated (in Hebrew) by Odette on January 6, 1993, in the *moʿadon*. The audience included other elderly women, from Yemen, Kurdistan, and Morocco.

15. Honey as a symbol for women also appears in biblical verses; for example, "I have come to my garden, my own, my bride; I have plucked my myrrh and spice, eaten my honey and honeycomb" (Song of Songs 5:1) and "For the lips of the forbidden woman drip honey" (Proverbs 5:3).

16. Wasserfall (1995, 1999a) analyzes a particular ceremony among Moroccan-Israeli women in which the bride's sexuality is transferred from mother to mother-in-law through the use of white and green ribbons.

17. Yemeni Women raised in Israel do attempt to discuss sexual matters with their daughters. This may be the result of a combination of factors, including exposure to sex in the media and in school and the relative freedom of unmarried women in Israel with regard to schooling and work, together with the mothers' feelings of frustration over their own inadequate preparation for sexual life (Gilad 1989, 112).

18. Biya claimed that the subject of childbearing and the story of the honey plate had been discussed, even in Tunisia, in the presence of men.

At the same time, she was embarrassed to notice that her friend's husband was nearby.

19. Susan Sered, who studies older Israeli-Kurdish women, suggests this distinction between rejecting the social order and resisting individual abuse. (Personal communication, August 1998).

Chapter 4

1. Narrated on March 16, 1989. I remember hearing the story from Leah herself when I was a child. The image of Rachel being carried on angels' wings, smiling to Leah and saying, "I'm going back to Jerusalem," is part of my own memories. Leah joined her daughters Fortuna and Rachel in the *moshav* in 1956.

2. With the exception of oral folklore systematically collected from every Jewish group, other folkways were neglected (cf. Noy 1963). Nevertheless, some cultural practices were preserved, particularly Yemenite dance and craftsmanship (embroidery, silversmithing, pottery). Yemenites were singled out among non-European groups as being the "authentic" bearers of the purest Jewish tradition. Is this a case of "Orientalism?" See Dominguez (1989) and Ram (1993) for a critical view of Israeli ethnography.

3. Tunisian folktales collected and published by Israel Folklore Archives (IFA) support this tendency. Although men did tell folktales, most of their repertoire consists of moral tales or sacred legends. In women's tales, the proportions are reversed (see Noy [1966] 1968).

4. Rabbi Ḥuri migrated to Israel in 1955 and died in Beersheba two years later. His grave is now a popular pilgrimage site known for its efficacy in helping people in need (see Weingrod 1990).

5. Interviewed on May 25, 1995.

6. I heard of several other cases in which women claim to have threatened to divorce their husbands if they did not agree to join them in immigrating to Israel.

7. Yehudit was the Hebrew name given to Odette in Israel. It was a practice of the *Sochnut* to change names of immigrants into more Jewish-Israeli names.

8. Babylonian Talmud, tractate Sotah, page 37a: "R. Judah said: . . . each tribe was unwilling to be the first to enter the sea. Then sprang forward Nahshon son of Aminadav and descended first into the sea."

9. The Hebrew expression "Go to Gaza" is not just a geographical marker; *lex le-ʿaza* is a euphemism for *lex la-ʿazazel* (go to hell). This allusion makes the destination more menacing.

10. Narrated on December 24, 1987, during an hour-long taped interview. Four of Ghaliya's children were present; they all knew the

stories and helped the narration by adding details and asking for more information.

11. Narrated during an interview with her daughter, Shula, and her friend Malka, July 19, 1988.

12. Recorded by a student researching personal histories in *moshavim,* June 1993.

13. Compare to the description in an ethnography of a Moroccan *moshav* established in the mid-1950s in the Negev: "Disembarking from the boat the forty families climbed into trucks and began the journey from Haifa to the Negev. They traveled at night and therefore saw little of the landscape. The immigrants later recalled the cold of the night on an open truck and what seemed like an unending journey" (Weingrod 1966, 52–53).

14. See Goldberg's discussion on the role of community leaders in the establishment of the Alliance Israelite schools (1996, 22–24) and Tsur's analysis of correspondence relating to Jewish schools in the town of Mahdia, Tunisia (Tsur 1996, 146–67).

15. Interview on December 24, 1987.

16. Interview with my parents on July 7, 1987.

17. April 2, 1989. Interview conducted in Kibbutz Lavie, where we were staying on the occasion of my niece's wedding.

18. July 19, 1988. Alice was referring to events like immigrating to Israel, going to the ritual bath, and about plumbing problems in her house.

19. July 17, 1988, during the interview with Miha and Fradji, joined by Jeani, who told the story about the miscarriage near the *kusha* (see chapters 3 and 5). Ghaliya came for a short visit, and then Yossi, Miha and Fradji's son, also arrived to see his parents.

20. Odette says, "Am I better than Aminadav?" but it was actually Nahshon, son of Aminadav, who jumped into the Red Sea.

21. With teary eyes Odette told me of the last night in Tunisia: Her mother was sleeping with her in the same bed and she noticed her mother kissing her toes. Odette said that if her mother had shown her this kind of affection earlier, she would have never left her mother in Tunisia.

Chapter 5

1. Gilat, July 19 1988. The awkwardness of talking about the *mikvah* was evident in another case: when Odette spoke to my students at the university and mentioned the women's ritual bath, she broached the topic by saying, "You'll excuse me, but I am like a mother to you" (March 29, 1999).

2. Kennedy International Airport, New York City, May 26, 1999. Reḥana was pleased to find a Tunisian-Arabic and Hebrew speaker who

could help her. She gladly shared some of her life stories over a cup of coffee waiting for our connecting flights to the West Coast.

3. During my latest visit to Aminadav (April 2000) the counselor proudly showed me the new building for the center, but women complained that it is too far from the grocery store and the clinic. They were not so happy with the structure, saying they preferred one large assembly room rather than several small rooms for different activities.

4. When I visited Aminadav shortly after the excursion, the women told me about the pilgrimages in great detail, while the visit to the waste-disposal site was mentioned only by the counselor, who commented that they were now familiar with the "entire Israeli garbage scene."

5. Men participate in games (dominoes, cards, bingo), but not in arts and crafts classes. Women take part in all types of activities, including mixed groups.

6. Israeli women in general seem to be more prone to sickness than men. Their constant complaints may be interpreted as a mode of resistance: on the one hand being sick gives them "time out" from daily chores, but on the other hand the poor health deepens their dependence on male institutions (Sered 2000, 156–57).

7. For example, two of Odette's children invited their parents to spend Passover 1999 in a hotel. Odette surprised all of her eight children by preparing traditional dishes in advance and giving each one his or her share.

8. The center is closed on Fridays and during the week before Passover. No woman would "waste" her time in the center when she should be preparing what is necessary for a forthcoming event.

9. Narrated on July 22, 1984, in the center for the elderly in Gilat by Yosef (in his eighties) and repeated (with slight variations) by Thérèse.

10. A family requesting to employ a non-Israeli worker must provide documents to prove the need for live-in help, as well as pay an agency for the service, and must have money in escrow to ensure that the worker will be able to leave the country after the assigned period of work.

11. When Odette told her life story to my class in March 1999, she brought pictures, amulets, and a certificate awarded to her for reaching second place in a quiz on religious matters held in the mo'adon for the elderly population of the area.

12. Shula Keshet, a single thirty-nine-year-old artist born in Israel to parents who emigrated from Iran, presents a similar case. In a newspaper interview she is quoted as saying: "I would like to have seven children. Now it seems too late. . . . My mother suggests that I have a child. Not to wait" (Peled 2000).

13. Visits to Egypt were made possible after the peace treaty between

the two countries in 1982; visits to Morocco were limited to groups of Moroccan-born with a laissez-passer (Levy 1997). The impact of the 2000–2001 Israeli-Palestinian tensions on these trips cannot be estimated as yet.

14. The video documenting this scene (shot by the husband) shows that the house was demolished some time prior to the visit, but the story as told is more dramatic.

Conclusion

1. Shlomo, whom I interviewed about the history of Gilat, was pleased to have the transcript of the interview included in the Hebrew University's oral history archives. Other women mentioned in this book inquired why I did not collect their life stories to write about.

2. January 24, 1996. I should add that my dark complexion, language use, and Hebrew pronunciation identified me as ʿedot hamizraḥ, thus perhaps facilitating my acceptance as "a daughter."

3. Tunisian women's folktales emphasize the importance of other women in the lives of their heroines. In a version of "Snow White," the princess is revived by a group of women who appear as the "significant other," supporting and helping her achieve full life (Schely-Newman 1990; see also Alexander 1993).

4. Miriam proudly reported to Noro that she was part of a target shooting team and mentioned that training took place on Shabbat. Our father immediately removed her from the school that egregiously disregarded religious laws. Because it was the middle of the school year, it took an extensive search and some effort to have her relocated in another school.

5. Compared to boys, who were frequently left home to help support the family, girls were allowed to continue their education. See Shokeid's (1971) discussion on education in the Moroccan moshav he studied.

BIBLIOGRAPHY

Abramski-Bligh, Irit. 1997. *Pinkas Hakehillot: Libya. Tunisia: Encyclopaedia of Jewish Communities from Their Foundation till after the Holocaust.* Jerusalem: Yad Vashem, Hebrew.

Abu-Lughod, Lila. 1986. *Veiled Sentiments.* Berkeley and Los Angeles: University of California Press.

———. 1988. "Fieldwork of a Dutiful Daughter." In *Arab Women in the Field: Studying Your Own Society,* ed. Soraya Altorki and Camillia Fawzi El-Solh, 139–61. Syracuse, N.Y.: Syracuse University Press.

———. 1990. "The Romance of Resistance: Tracing Transformations of Power Through Bedouin Women." *American Ethnologist* 17:41–45.

———. 1993. *Writing Women's Worlds: Bedouin Stories.* Berkeley and Los Angeles: University of California Press.

Tamar, Alexander. 1993. "Hanintallah—the Yemenite Jewish Version of the Story of Cinderella and Its Parallels." *Peʿamim* 53: 124–28. Hebrew.

Alexander, Tamar and Galit Hasan-Rokem. 1989. "Spacial Elements in the Proverbs of Jews of Turkey." *Peʿamim* 41: 112–33. Hebrew.

Andezian, Sossie, and Jocelyne Streiff-Fenart. 1986. "Neighborhood Relations and Social Control: The Role of Women in Maghrebian Communities in Southern France." In *Women of the Mediterranean,* ed. Monique Gadant, trans. A. M. Berrett, 164–69. London: Zed Books.

Attal, Robert. 1980. *Périodiques juifs d'Afrique du Nord.* Inventory of Ben Zvi Institute Archives. Jerusalem: Ben Zvi Institute.

———. 1989. "Jewish Press in Tunisia." *Kesher* 5:87–96. Hebrew.

———. 1996. *La Presse Périodique Juive d'Afrique du Nord*. Tel Aviv: Tel Aviv University. Hebrew and French.

Avivi, Joseph. 1993. *Manuscripts Des Juifs Du Maghreb à L'Institut Ben-Zvi*. Jerusalem: Ben Zvi Institute. Hebrew and French.

Avneri, Ariyeh. 1983. *David Levi*. Tel Aviv: Revivim. Hebrew.

Awret, Irene. 1984. *Days of Honey: The Tunisian Boyhood of Rafael Uzan*. New York: Schocken Books.

Azmon, Yael. 1995. "Introduction: Judaism and the Distancing of Women from Public Activity." In *A View into the Lives of Women in Jewish Societies, Collected Essays*, ed. Yael Azmon, 13–43. Jerusalem: Zalman Shazar Center for Jewish History. Hebrew.

Bahloul, Joelle. 1983. *Le Culte de la Table Dressée: Rites et Traditions de la Table Juive Algérienne*. Paris: Édition A-M Metailie.

———. [1992] 1996. *The Architecture of Memory: A Jewish-Muslim Household in Colonial Algeria, 1937–62*. Translated by Catherine Du Peloux Menage. Cambridge: Cambridge University Press.

Bakhtin, Mikhail M. 1986. *Speech Genres and Other Late Essays*. Translated by Vern W. McGee. Austin: University of Texas Press.

Bamberg, Michael. 1997. "Positioning between Structure and Performance." *Journal of Narrative and Life History* 7:335–42.

Bar Yosef, Rivka. 1968. "Desocialization and Resocialization: The Adjustment Process of Immigrants." *International Migration Review* 2, no. 3: 27–45.

Bascom, William R. [1954] 1965. "Four Functions of Folklore." In *The Study of Folklore*, ed. Alan Dundes, 279–98. Englewood Cliffs, N.J.: Prentice Hall.

Bauman, Richard. 1986. *Story, Performance, and Event*. Cambridge: Cambridge University Press.

———. 1992. "Disclaimers of Performance." In *Responsibility and Evidence in Oral Discourse*, ed. Jane H. Hill and Judith T. Irvine, 182–96. Cambridge: Cambridge University Press.

Bauman, Richard, and Charles L. Briggs. 1990. "Poetics and Performance as Critical Perspectives on Language and Social Life." *Annual Review of Anthropology* 19:59–88.

Bauman, Richard, and Joel Sherzer, eds. 1989. *Explorations in the Ethnography of Speaking*, 2nd edition. Cambridge: Cambridge University Press.

Behar, Ruth. 1995. "Introduction: Out of Exile." In *Women Writing Culture*, ed. Ruth Behar and Deborah A. Gordon, 1–29. Berkeley and Los Angeles: University of California Press.

Ben-Amos, Dan. 1993. "'Context' in Context." *Western Folklore* 52: 209–26.

Ben-Amos, Dan, and Lillian Weissberg, eds. 1999. *Cultural Memory and the Construction of Identity*. Detroit: Wayne State University Press.

Ben-Rafael, Eliezer. 1994a. *Language, Identity, and Social Division*. Oxford Studies in Language Contact. Oxford: Oxford University Press.

———. 1994b. "A Sociological Paradigm of Bilingualism: English, French, Yiddish, and Arabic in Israel." *Israel Social Science Research* 9, no. 1–2: 181–206.

Bentolila, Yaacov. 1994. "Bilingualism in a Moroccan Settlement in the South of Israel." *Israel Social Science Research* 9, no. 1–2: 89–108.

Bilu, Yoram, and Galit Hasan-Rokem. 1989. "Cinderella and the Saint." *Psychoanalytic Study of Society* 14:227–66.

Blum-Kulka, Shoshana. 1997. *Dinner Talk: Cultural Patterns of Sociability and Socialization in Family Discourse*. Mahwah, N.J. and London: Lawrence Erlbaum Assoc. Publishers.

Briggs, Charles L. 1988. *Competence in Performance: The Creativity of Tradition in Mexicano Verbal Art*. Philadelphia: University of Pennsylvania Press.

Briggs, Charles L., and Richard Bauman. 1992. "Genre, Intertextuality, and Social Power." *Journal of Linguistic Anthropology* 2:131–72.

Brunvand, Jan Harold. 1984. *The Choking Doberman*. New York and London: W. W. Norton.

Burt, Susan Meredith. 1994. "Code Choice in Intercultural Conversation: Speech Accommodation Theory and Pragmatics." *Pragmatics* 4:535–59.

Chafets, Zeev. 1986. *Heroes and Hustlers, Hard Hats and Holy Men*. New York: William Morrow.

Coates, Jennifer. 1997. "One-at-a-Time: The Organization of Men's Talk." In *Language and Masculinity*, ed. Sally Johnson and Ulrike Hanna Meinhof, 107–29. Oxford, England, and Cambridge, Mass.: Blackwell.

Cohen, David. 1964. *Le Parler Arabe Des Juifs de Tunis. Textes et Documents Linguistiques et Ethnographiques*. Paris et La Haye: Mouton & Co.

———. 1975. *Le Parler Arabes Des Juifs de Tunis. Vol. 2: Etude Linguistique*. Janua Linguarum #161. Paris et La Haye: Mouton & Co.

Conquergood, Dwight. 1991. "Rethinking Ethnography: Towards a Critical Cultural Politics." *Communication Monographs* 58:179–94.

———. 1992. "Review Essay: Ethnography, Rhetoric, and Performance." *Quarterly Journal of Speech* 78:80–123.

Cooper, Robert. 1985. "Language and Social Stratification among the Jewish Population in Israel." In *Readings in the Sociology of Jewish Languages*, ed. Joshua A. Fishman, 65–81. Leiden: E. J. Brill.

Coupland, Nikolas, and Jon F. Nussbaum, eds. 1993. *Discourse and Lifespan Identity.* Newbury Park and London: Sage Publications.

Crapanzano, Vincent. 1980. *Tuhami: Portrait of a Moroccan.* Chicago and London: University of Chicago Press.

Crawford, Lyall. 1996. "Personal Ethnography." *Communication Monographs* 63:158–70.

Davis, Fred. 1979. *Yearning for Yesterday: A Sociology of Nostalgia.* New York: Free Press.

Delaney, Carol. 1987. "Seeds of Honor, Fields of Shame." In *Honor and Shame and the Unity of the Mediterranean,* ed. David D. Gilmore, 35–48. American Anthropological Association Special Publication #22. Washington, D.C.: American Anthropological Association.

———. 1988. "Mortal Flow: Menstruation in Turkish Village Society." In *Blood Magic: The Anthropology of Menstruation,* ed. Thomas Buckley and Alma Gottlieb, 75–93. Berkeley and Los Angeles: University of California Press.

DellaPergola, Sergio. 1992. "Sources of Jewish Population Data: Present and Future, Preliminary Inventory." In *World Jewish Population: Trends and Policies,* ed. Sergio DellaPergola and Leah Cohen, 154–56. Jerusalem: The Institute of Contemporary Judaism.

Deshen, Shlomo. 1989. *The Mellah Society: Jewish Community Life in Sherifian Morocco.* Chicago and London: University of Chicago Press.

———.1997. "Near the Jerba Beach: Tunisian Jews, the Anthropologist, and Other Visitors." *Jewish Social Studies* New Series 3(2):90–118.

Djebar, Assia. [1985] 1993. *Fantasia: An Algerian Cavalcade.* Translated by Dorothy S. Blair. Portsmouth, N.H.: Heinemann.

Dominguez, Virginia R. 1989. *People as Subject, People as Object: Selfhood and Peoplehood in Contemporary Israel.* Madison: University of Wisconsin Press.

Duranti, Alessandro. 1997. *Linguistic Anthropology.* Cambridge: Cambridge University Press.

Duwek, Madeline. 1979. *Days in the Tunis Ghetto.* Jerusalem: Ministry of Education. Hebrew.

Dwyer, Daisy H. 1978. *Images and Self-Images: Male and Female in Morocco.* New York: Columbia University Press.

Elazar, Daniel. 1989. *The Other Jews: Sephardim in Israel.* New York: Basic Books.

Elor, Tamar. 1994. *Educated and Ignorant: Ultra Orthodox Jewish Women and Their World.* Boulder, Colo.: Lynne Rienner Publishers.

Fernandez, James W. 1986. *Persuasions and Performances: The Play of Tropes in Culture.* Bloomington: Indiana University Press.

Fine, Gary Alan. 1980. "The Kentucky Fried Rat: Legends and Modern Society." *Journal of the Folklore Institute* 17:222–43.

Fonrobert, Charlotte Elisheva. 1999. "Yalta's Ruse: Resistance against Rabbinic Menstrual Authority in Talmudic Literature." In *Women and Water,* ed. Rahel R. Wasserfall, 60–81. Hanover and London: Brandeis University Press.

———. 2000. *Menstrual Purity.* Stanford: Stanford University Press.

Gal, Susan. 1988. "The Political Economy of Code Choice." In *Code-switching: Anthropological and Sociolinguistic Perspectives,* ed. Monica Heller, 245–63. Berlin, New York, and Amsterdam: Mouton de Gruyter.

———. 1991. "Between Speech and Silence: The Problematics of Research on Language and Gender." In *Gender at the Crossroad of Knowledge: Feminist Anthropology in the Postmodern Era,* ed. Micaela di Leonardo, 175–203. Berkeley and Los Angeles: University of California Press.

Georgakopoulou, Alexandra. 1997. *Narrative Performance: A Study of Modern Greek Storytelling, Pragmatics and Beyond.* Amsterdam and Philadelphia: John Benjamins Publishing Company.

Gergen, Kenneth, and Mary Gergen. 1988. "Narrative and Self as Relationship." In *Advances in Experimental Social Psychology,* ed. L. Berkowitz, 17–56. New York: Academic Press.

Gergen, Mary. 1992. "Life Stories: Pieces of a Dream." In *Storied Lives: The Cultural Politics of Self-Understanding,* ed. George C. Rosenwald and Richard L. Ochberg, 127–44. New Haven, Conn.: Yale University Press.

Gilad, Lisa. 1989. *Ginger and Salt: Yemeni Jewish Women in an Israeli Town.* Boulder, Colo.: Westview Press.

Glazer, Mark. 1981. "The Dowry as Capital Accumulation among the Sephardic Jews of Istanbul, Turkey." In *Jewish Societies in the Middle East,* ed. Shlomo Deshen and Walter P. Zenner, 299–309. Washington, D.C.: University Press of America.

Goffman, Irving. 1981. "Footing." In *Forms of Talk,* 124–59. Philadelphia: University of Pennsylvania Press.

Goitein, S. D. [1955] 1974. *Jews and Arabs: Their Contacts through the Ages.* New York: Schocken Books.

Goldberg, Harvey E. 1972. *Cave Dwellers and Citrus Growers: A Jewish Community in Libya and in Israel.* Cambridge: Cambridge University Press.

———. 1990. *Jewish Life in Muslim Libya: Rivals and Relatives.* Chicago and London: University of Chicago Press.

———, ed. 1996. *Sephardi and Middle Eastern Jewries: History and Culture in the Modern Era.* Bloomington: Indiana University Press.

Goodwin, Charles, and Alessandro Duranti. 1992. "Rethinking Context: An Introduction." In *Rethinking Context,* ed. Alessandro Duranti and Charles Goodwin, 1–42. Cambridge: Cambridge University Press.

Goodwin, Marjory H. 1997. "Toward Family Histories in Context." *Journal of Narrative and Life History* 7:107–12.

Gumperz, John J. [1968] 1972. "The Speech Community." In *Language and Social Context,* ed. Pier Paolo Giglioli, 219–31. New York: Viking Penguin.

———. 1982. *Discourse Strategies.* Cambridge: Cambridge University Press.

Hadar, Alon. 2000. "Isha Bamakom (Woman in Her Place)." *Kol Ha'ir,* January 21, 56–60. Hebrew.

Hall, Deanna L., and Kristin M. Langellier. 1988. "Storytelling Strategies in Mother-Daughter Communication." In *Women Communicating: Studies of Women's Talk,* ed. Barbara Bates and Anita Taylor, 107–26. Norwood, N.J.: Ablex Publishing Corporation.

Handelman, Don. 1998. *Models and Mirrors: Towards an Anthropology of Public Events.* New York and Oxford: Berghahn Books.

Harshav, Benjamin. 1993. *Language in the Time of Revolution.* Berkeley and Los Angeles: University of California Press.

Hasan-Rokem, Galit. 2000. *Web of Life: Folklore and Midrash in Rabbinic Literature.* Stanford, Calif.: Stanford University Press.

Haviland, John B. 1979. "Guugu Yimidhirr Brother in Law Language." *Language in Society* 8:365–93.

Hejaiej, Monia. 1996. *Behind Closed Doors: Women's Oral Narratives in Tunisia.* New Brunswick, N.J.: Rutgers University Press.

Hertz, Dan G. 1994. "The Stress of Migration: Adjustment Problems of Migrant and Displaced Families." In *Family Issues: An Interdisciplinary View on Family Stresses and Their Consequences,* ed. Dan G. Hertz, 67–93. Jerusalem: Gefen Publication House.

Hill, Jane H. 1992. " 'Today There Is No Respect': Nostalgia, 'Respect,' and Oppositional Discourse in Mexican (Nahuatl) Language Ideology." *Pragmatics* 2:263–80.

Hines, Caitlin. 1999. "Rebaking the Pie: The Woman as Dessert Metaphor." In *Reinventing Identities: The Gendered Self in Discourse,* ed. Mary Bucholtz, A. C. Liang, and Laurel A. Sutton, 145–62. New York and Oxford: Oxford University Press.

Hirschberg, H. Z. 1974. *A History of the Jews in North Africa.* Leiden: Brill.

Hollway, Wendy and Tony Jefferson. 1999. "Gender, Generation, Anxiety, and the Reproduction of Culture." In *Making Sense of Narrative,* ed. Ruthellen Josselson and Amia Lieblich, 107–139. Thousand Oaks, London and New Delhi: Sage Publications.

Hymes, Dell. 1972. "Models of the Interaction of Language and Social Life." In *Directions in Sociolinguistics: The Ethnography of Communication,* ed. John J. Gumperz and Dell Hymes, 35–71. New York: Holt, Rinehart and Winston.

———. 1974. "Toward Ethnographies of Communication: The Analysis of Communicative Events." In *Language and Social Context,* ed. Pier Polo Giglioli, 21–44. New York: Penguin Books.

———. 1996. *Ethnography, Linguistics, Narrative Inequality: Toward an Understanding of Voice.* London: Taylor and Francis.

———. 1998. "When Is Oral Narrative Poetry? Generative Form and Its Pragmatic Conditions." *Pragmatics* 8:475–500.

Interpreting Women's Lives. 1989. Edited by Personal narrative group. Bloomington: Indiana University Press.

Irvine, Judith T. 1996. "Shadow Conversations: The Indeterminacy of Participant Roles." In *Natural Histories of Discourse,* ed. Michael Silverstein and Greg Urban, 131–59. Chicago and London: University of Chicago Press.

Jackson, Bruce. 1988. "What People Like Us Are Saying When We Say We're Saying the Truth." *Journal of American Folklore* 101, no. 401:276–92.

Josselson, Ruthellen and Amia Lieblich, eds. 1999. *Making Sense of Narrative.* Thousand Oaks, London and New Delhi: Sage Publications. (*Narrative Study of Lives,* vol. 6).

Kalčik, Susan. [1975] 1986. " ' . . . Like Ann's Gynecologist or the Time I Was Almost Raped': Personal Narratives in Women's Rap Groups." In *Women and Folklore,* ed. Claire R. Farrer, 3–11. Prospect Heights, Ill.: Waveland Press.

Kapchan, Deborah. 1996. *Gender on the Market: Moroccan Women and the Revoicing of Tradition.* Philadelphia: University of Pennsylvania Press.

Kapchan, Deborah A., and Pauline Turner Strong. 1999. "Introduction: Theorizing the Hybrid." *Journal of American Folklore* 112:239–53.

Katriel, Tamar. 1986. *Talking Straight: Dugri Speech in Israeli Sabra Culture.* Vol. 2 of *Studies in the Social and Cultural Foundations of Language.* Cambridge and New York: Cambridge University Press.

———. 1993. " 'Our Future Is Where Our Past Is': Studying Heritage Museums as Ideological and Performative Arenas." *Communication Monographs* 60:69–75.

———. 1994. "Performing the Past: Presentational Styles in Settlement Museum Interpretation." *Israel Social Science Research* 9:1–26.

————. 1997. *Performing the Past: A Study of Israeli Settlement Museums.* Mahwah, N.J. and London: Laurence Erlbaum Associates.

Katriel, Tamar, and Aliza Shenhar. 1990. "Tower and Stockade: Dialogic Narration in Israeli Settlement Ethos." *Quarterly Journal of Speech* 76:359–80.

Katzir, Yael. 1976. *The Effects of Resettlement on the Status and Role of Yemeni Jewish Women: The Case of Ramat Oranim, Israel.* Ph.D. diss., University of California at Berkeley.

————.1984. "Yemenite Women as Agents of Social and Cultural Change in a Moshav." In *Jews in the Middle East: Anthropological Perspectives on Past and Present,* ed. Shlomo Deshen and Moshe Shokeid, 221–30. Tel Aviv: Schocken Publishing House. Hebrew.

Keddie, Nikki R. 1991. "Introduction: Deciphering Middle Eastern Women's History." In *Women in Middle Eastern History,* ed. Nikki R. Keddie and Beth Baron, 1–22. New Haven, Conn. and London: Yale University Press.

Kimmerling, Baruch. 2001. *The End of Ashkenazi Hegemony.* Jerusalem: Keter Publishing House. Hebrew.

Kirshenblatt-Gimblett, Barbara. 1989. "Authoring Lives." *Journal of Folklore Research* 26:123–49.

Kugelmass, Jack. 1993. "The Rites of the Tribe: The Meaning of Poland for American Jewish Tourists." *YIVO Annual* 21:395–454.

Labov, William, and Joshua Waletzky. 1967. "Narrative Analysis: Oral Versions of Personal Experiences." In *Essays in the Verbal and Visual Arts,* ed. June Helms, 12–44. Seattle: University of Washington Press.

Langellier, Kristin M. 1989. "Personal Narratives: Perspectives on Theory and Research." *Text and Performance Quarterly* 9:243–76.

————. 2000. "Heroic Mothers and Good-Enough Daughters in Ethnic Family Storytelling." Paper presented at the National Communication Association Annual Meeting, November. Seattle, Wash.

Langellier, Kristin M. and Eric E. Peterson. 1993. "Family Storytelling as a Strategy of Social Control." In *Narrative and Social Control: Critical Perspectives,* ed. Dennis K. Mumby, 49–76. Newbury Park, Calif.: Sage Publications.

Lawless, Elaine J. 1991. "Women's Life Stories and Reciprocal Ethnography as Feminist and Emergent." *Journal of Folklore Research* 28:35–60.

Lees, Susan. 1995. "The Moshav: An Introduction." In *Rural Cooperative in Socialist Utopia: Thirty Years of Moshav Development in Israel,* ed. Moshe Schwartz, Susan Lees, and Gideon M. Kressel, xiii–xx. Westport, Conn.: Praeger.

Levy, André. 1997. "To Morocco and Back: Toursim and Pilgrimage among Moroccan-Born Israelis." In *Grasping Land: Space and Place in Contemporary Israeli Discourse and Experience,* ed. Eyal Een-Ari and Yoram Bilu, 25–46. Albany: State University of New York Press.

Lieblich, Amia, Rivka Tuval-Mashiach and Tamar Zilber. 1998. *Narrative Research: Reading, Analysis and Interpretation.* Newbury Park, London and New Delhi: Sage Publications. Applied Social Research Method Series, vol. 47.

Linde, Charlotte. 1993. *Life Stories: The Creation of Coherence.* New York and Oxford: Oxford University Press.

Loshitzky, Yosefa. 1996. "Authenticity in Crisis: Shur and the New Israeli Forms of Ethnicity." *Media, Culture and Society* 18:87–103.

Lowenthal, David. 1985. *The Past Is a Foreign Country.* Cambridge, London, and New York: Cambridge University Press.

———. 1989. "Nostalgia Tells It Like It Wasn't." In *The Imagined Past: History and Nostalgia,* ed. Christopher Shaw and Malcolm Chase, 18–32. Manchester, England: Manchester University Press.

Lunde, Paul and Justin Wintle. 1984. *A Dictionary of Arabic and Islamic Proverbs.* London and Boston: Routledge and Keagan Paul.

Martin, Joann. 1990. "Motherhood and Power: The Production of a Women's Culture of Politics in a Mexican Community." *American Ethnologist* 17:470–90.

Maschler, Yael. 1994. " 'Appreciation Haʿaraxa 'o Haʿaratsa?' (Valuing or Admiration?): Negotiating Contrast in Bilingual Disagreement Talk." *Text* 14:207–38.

Mernissi, Fatima. [1975] 1987. *Beyond the Veil: Male-Female Dynamics in Modern Muslim Society.* Revised edition. Bloomington: Indiana University Press.

Moerman, Michael. 1988. *Talking Cultures: Ethnography and Conversation Analysis.* Philadelphia: University of Pennsylvania Press.

Myerhoff, Barbara. 1988. " 'Life Not Death in Venice': Its Second Life." In *The Anthropology of Experience,* ed. Victor W. Turner and Edward M. Bruner, 261–86. Urbana: The University of Illinois Press.

Myers-Scotton, Carol. 1993. *Social Motivation for Codeswitching: Evidence from Africa.* Oxford: Clarendon Press.

Narayan, Kirin. 1993. "How Native Is a 'Native' Anthropologist?" *American Anthropologist* 95:671–85.

———. 1995. "Participant Observation." In *Women Writing Culture,* ed. Ruth Behar and Deborah A. Gordon, 33–48. Berkeley and Los Angeles: University of California Press.

Nora, Pierre. 1989. "Between Memory and History: Les Lieux de Memoire." *Representations* 26:7–25.

Noy, Dov, ed. 1963. *Folktales of Israel.* Chicago: University of Chicago Press.

————. [1966] 1968. *Contes Populaires Racontés par des Juifs de Tunisie.* Jerusalem: Organisation Sionist Mondiale.

Ochs, Elinor. 1997. "Narrative." In *Discourse as Structure and Process,* ed. Tuen A. van Dijk, 185–207. London and Thousand Oaks, Calif.: Sage Publications.

Ochs, Elinor, and Lisa Capps. 1996. "Narrating the Self." *Annual Review of Anthropology* 25:19–43.

Oring, Elliott. 1990. "Legend, Truth, and News." *Southern Folklore* 47:163–77.

Ortner, Sherry B. 1974. "Is Female to Male as Nature to Culture?" In *Women, Culture and Society,* ed. Michelle Zimbalist Rosaldo and Louise Lamphere, 67–87. Stanford, Calif.: Stanford University Press.

Paoletti, Isabella. 1998. *Being an Older Woman: A Study of Social Production of Identity.* Mahwah, N.J. and London: Lawrence Erlbaum Associates.

Patai, Raphael. 1986. *The Seed of Abraham—Jews and Arabs in Contact and Conflict.* Salt Lake City: University of Utah Press. 1986. Reprint, New York: Charles Scribner's Sons.

Peacock, James L., and Dorothy C. Holland. 1993. "The Narrated Self: Life Stories in Process." *Ethos* 21:367–83.

Peled, Assepa. 2000. "From the East with Love and Disgust." *Maariv,* 11 February, 68–74. Hebrew.

Pelias, Ronald J., and James VanOosting. 1987. "A Paradigm for Performance Studies." *Quarterly Journal of Speech* 73:219–31.

Peterson, Eric, and Kristin Langellier. 1997. "The Politics of Personal Narrative Methodology." *Text and Performance Quarterly* 17:135–54.

Philipsen, Gerry. 1992. *Speaking Culturally: Explorations in Social Communication.* Albany: State University of New York Press.

Ram, Uri, ed. 1993. *Israeli Society: Critical Perspectives.* Tel Aviv: Breirot Publishers. Hebrew.

Reinharz, Jehuda. 1991. "The Transition from Yishuv to State: Social and Ideological Changes." In *New Perspectives on Israeli History: The Early Years of the State,* ed. Laurence J. Silberstein, 27–41. New York and London: New York University Press.

Reinharz, Shulamit. 1994. "Feminist Biography: The Pains, the Joys, the Dilemmas." In *The Narrative Study of Lives* vol. 2: Exploring Identity and Gender. Sage Publications. 37–82.

Rosen, Lawrence. 1984. *Bargaining for Reality.* Chicago and London: University of Chicago Press.

Rosen, Rahel. 1981. *Perceptions of Femininity among Moroccan Women in an Israeli Moshav.* Master's thesis, The Hebrew University. Hebrew.

Rosenthal Gabriele. 1993. "Reconstruction of Life Stories: Principles of Selection in Generating Stories for Narrative Biographical Interviews." In *The Narrative Study of Lives,* ed. Ruthellen Josselson and Amia Lieblich, 59–91. Newbury Park, Calif., London, and New Delhi: Sage Publications.

Rosenwald, George C. 1992. "Conclusion: Reflections on Narrative Self-understanding." In *Storied Lives: The Cultural Politics of Self-Understanding,* ed. George C. Rosenwald and Richard L. Ochberg, 265–89. New Haven, Conn. and London: Yale University Press.

Rosenwald, George C., and Richard L. Ochberg, eds. 1992. *Storied Lives: The Cultural Politics of Self-Understanding.* New Haven, Conn. and London: Yale University Press.

Saadon, Haim. 1999. "The Struggle for Jewish Education in Tunisia 1878–1939." In *Education and History: Cultural and Political Contexts,* ed. Rivka Faldahi and Emmanuel Etkes, 305–28. Jerusalem: Zalman Shazar Center for Jewish History. Hebrew.

Saville-Troike, Muriel. 1989. *The Ethnography of Communication: An Introduction.* 2nd edition. Oxford: Blackwell Books.

Sawin, Patricia E. 1999. "Gender, Context, and the Narrative Construction of Identity: Rethinking Models of 'Women's Narrative.' " In *Reinventing Identities: The Gendered Self in Discourse,* ed. Mary Bucholtz, A. C. Liang, and Laurel A. Sutton, 241–58. New York and Oxford: Oxford University Press.

Schely-Newman, Esther. 1990. "Zin el Gamra: A North African Snow White." *Jerusalem Research in Jewish Folklore* 11–12:76–101. Hebrew.

———. 1993. "The Woman Who Was Shot: A Communal Tale." *Journal of American Folklore* 106:285–303.

———. 1995a. "Role Changes of Tunisian Women in Israel." In *Active Voices: Women in Jewish Culture,* ed. Maurie Sachs, 157–70. Urbana and Chicago: University of Illinois Press.

———. 1995b. "Sweeter Than Honey: Discourse of Reproduction among North African Women in Israel." *Text and Performance Quarterly* 15:175–88.

———. 1996a. "The Nightly Voyage: Encounters between Immigrants and Their New Place." In *Veterans and New Immigrants, 1948–1952,* ed. Dalia Ofer, 285–98. Jerusalem: Ben Zvi Institute. Hebrew.

———.1996b. "The Peg of Your Tent: Narratives of North African Women." In *Sephardi and Middle Eastern Jewries: History and Culture in the Modern Era,* ed. Harvey E. Goldberg, 277–87. Urbana and Chicago: University of Illinois Press.

——. 1997. "Finding One's Place: Locale Narratives in an Israeli Moshav." *Quarterly Journal of Speech* 83:401–15.

——. 1998. "Competence and Ideology in Performance: Language Games, Identity and Israeli Bureaucracy in Personal Narrative." *Text and Performance Quarterly* 18:96–113.

——. 1999a. "I Hear from People Who Read Torah: Reported Speech, Genre and Gender Relations in Personal Narrative." *Narrative Inquiry* 9:49–68.

——. 1999b. "Mothers Know Best: Construction of Meaning in a Narrative Event." *Quarterly Journal of Speech* 85:285–302.

——. 2001. "Remember Shushan?: Counter-Nostalgia in Gendered Discourse." *Text* 21(3)411–36.

Schiffrin, Deborah. 1994. *Approaches to Discourse.* Oxford: Blackwell.

Segev, Tom. 1986. *1949: The First Israelis.* New York: Free Press.

Sered, Susan Starr. 1992. *Women as Ritual Experts: The Religious Lives of Elderly Jewish Women in Jerusalem.* Oxford and New York: Oxford University Press.

——. 2000. *What Makes Women Sick? Maternity, Modesty, and Militarism in Israeli Society.* Hanover, N.H. and London: Brandeis University Press.

Sered, Susan Starr, Romi Kaplan, and Samuel Cooper. 1999. "Talking about *Miqveh* Parties, or Discourse of Gender, Hierarchy, and Social Control." In *Women and Water,* ed. Rahel R. Wasserfall, 145–65. Hanover, N.H. and London: Brandeis University Press.

Shohat, Ella. 1990. "Master Narrative/Counter Readings: The Politics of Israeli Cinema." In *Resisting Images: Essays on Cinema and History,* ed. Robert Sklar and Charles Musser, 251–78. Philadelphia: Temple University Press.

——. 1997. "Sephardim in Israel: Zionism from the Standpoint of Its Jewish Victims." In *Dangerous Liaisons: Gender, Nation and Post-colonial Perspective,* ed. Anne McClintock, Aamir Mufti, and Ella Shohat, 15–68. Minneapolis and London: University of Minnesota Press.

Shokeid, Moshe. 1971. *The Dual Heritage—Immigrants from the Atlas Mountains in an Israeli Village.* Manchester: Manchester University Press.

Shotter, John. 1993. "Becoming Someone: Identity and Belonging." In *Discourse and Lifespan Identity,* ed. Nikolas Coupland, 5–27. Newbury Park, Calif. and London: Sage.

Shuman, Amy. 1993a. "Gender and Genre." In *Feminist Theory and the Study of Folklore,* ed. Susan Tower Hollis, Linda Pershing, and Jane M. Young, 71–88. Urbana and Chicago: University of Illinois Press.

214

———. 1993b. " 'Get Outa My Face': Entitlement and Authoritative Discourse." In *Responsibility and Evidence in Oral Discourse,* ed. Jane H. Hill and Judith T. Irvine, 135–60. Cambridge: Cambridge University Press.

Shuval, Judy. 1989. "The Structure and Dilemmas of Israeli Pluralism." In *The Israeli State and Society: Boundaries and Frontiers,* ed. Baruch Kimmerling, 216–37. Albany: State University of New York Press.

Siegel, Jeff. 1995. "How to Get a Laugh in Fijian: Code Switching and Humor." *Language in Society* 24:95–110.

Silverstein, Michael. 1976. "Shifters, Linguistic Categories, and Cultural Description." In *Meaning in Anthropology,* ed. Keith H. and Henry A. Selby Basso, 11–55. Albuquerque: University of New Mexico Press

———. 1985. "On the Pragmatic 'Poetry' of Prose." In *Meaning, Form, and Use in Context: Linguistic Applications,* ed. Deborah Schiffrin, 181–99. Washington, D.C.: Georgetown University Press.

———. 1992. "The Indeterminacy of Contextualization: When Is Enough Enough?" In *The Contextualization of Language,* ed. Peter Auer and Aldo Di Luzio, 55–76. Amsterdam: John Benjamins.

———. In press. "Translation, Transduction, Transformation: Skating "Glossando" on Thin Ice." In *Translating Culture,* ed. Abraham Rosman and Paula Rubel. New York: Routledge.

Silverstein, Michael, and Greg Urban. 1996. "The Natural History of Discourse." In *Natural Histories of Discourse,* ed. Michael Silverstein and Greg Urban, 1–17. Chicago and London: University of Chicago Press.

Smooha, Sammy. 1993. "Class, Ethnic and National Cleavages and Democracy in Israel." In *Israeli Democracy under Stress,* ed. Larry Diamond and Ehud Sprinzak, 309–42. Boulder, Colo.: Lynne Rienner Publishers.

Stahl, Sandra Dolby. 1989. *Literary Folkloristics and the Personal Narrative.* Bloomington: Indiana University Press.

Stone, Elizabeth. 1988. *Black Sheep and Kissing Cousins: How Our Family Stories Shape Us.* New York: Time Books.

Tedlock, Barbara. 1991. "From Participant Observation to the Observation of Participation: The Emergence of Narrative Ethnography." *Journal of Anthropological Research* 47:69–94.

Tedlock, Dennis. 1983. *The Spoken Word and the Work of Interpretation.* Philadelphia: University of Pennsylvania Press.

Tobi, Yosef. 1996. "Judeo-Arabic Literature in North Africa." In *Sephardi and Middle Eastern Jewries: History and Culture in the Modern Era,* ed.

Harvey E. Goldberg, 213–25. Bloomington: Indiana University Press.

Tobi, Yosef and Zivia Tobi. 2000. *Judeo-Arab Literature in Tunisia.* Lod, Israel: Orot Yahadut Ha-Maghreb. Hebrew.

Tölölyan, Khachig. 1989. "Narrative Culture and the Motivation of the Terrorist." In *Texts of Identity,* ed. John Shotter and Kenneth J. Gergen, 99–118. London: Sage Publications.

Tsur, Yaron. 1996. "Haskala in a Sectional Colonial Society: Mahdia (Tunisia) 1884." In *Sephardi and Middle Eastern Jewries: History and Culture in the Modern Era,* ed. Harvey E. Goldberg, 146–67. Bloomington: Indiana University Press.

Udovitch, Abraham L., and Lucette Valensi. 1984. *The Last Arab Jews.* London: Harwood Academic Press.

Valensi, Lucette. 1989. "Religious Orthodoxy or Local Tradition: Marriage Celebration in Southern Tunisia." In *Jews among Arabs: Contacts and Boundaries,* ed. Mark R. Cohen and Abraham L. Udovitch, 65–84. Princeton, N.J.: Darwin Press.

van Langenhove, Luk, and Rom Harre. 1993. "Positioning and Autobiography: Telling Your Life." In *Discourse and Lifespan Identity,* ed. Nikolas Coupland and John Nusbaum, 81–99. Newbury Park, Calif. and London: Sage Publications.

Voloshinov, V. N. [1929] 1986. *Marxism and the Philosophy of Language.* Translated by Ladislav Matejka and I. R. Titunik. Cambridge, Mass.: Harvard University Press.

Vromen, Suzanne. 1993. "The Ambiguity of Nostalgia." *YIVO Annual* 21:69–86.

Walters, Keith. 1996. "Gender, Identity and the Political Economy of Language: Anglophone Wives in Tunisia." *Language in Society* 25:515–55.

———. 1999. " 'Opening the Door of Paradise a Cubit': Educated Tunisian Women, Embodied Linguistc Practices, and Theories on Language and Gender." In *Reinventing Identities: The Gendered Self in Discourse,* ed. Mary Bucholtz, A. C. Liang, and Laurel A. Sutton, 200–217. New York and Oxford: Oxford University Press.

Wasserfall, Rachel. 1992. "Menstruation and Identity: The Meaning of Niddah for Moroccan Women Immigrants to Israel." In *People of the Body,* ed. Howard Eilberg-Schwartz, 309–27. Albany: State University of New York Press.

———. 1995. "Fertility and Community: The White Ribbon and the Green Ribbon Ceremony among Moshav Residents of Moroccan Descent." In *A View into the Lives of Women in Jewish Societies,* ed.

Yael Azmon, 259–71. Jerusalem: Zalman Shazar Center for Jewish History. Hebrew.

———. 1999a. "Community, Fertility and Sexuality: Identity Formation among Moroccan Jewish Immigrants." In *Women and Water,* ed. Rachel R. Wasserfall, 187–97. Hanover, N.H. and London: Brandeis University Press.

Wasserfall, Rachel, ed. 1999b. *Women and Water: Menstruation in Jewish Life and Law.* Hanover, N.H. and London: Brandeis University Press.

Webber, Sabra. 1984. "Between Two Folklores." In *Connaissance Du Maghreb—Sciences Sociales et Colonisation,* ed. Jean Claude Vatin, 291–307. Paris: CNRS.

———. 1985. "Women's Folk Narratives and Social Change." In *Women and the Family in the Middle East,* ed. Elizabeth Warnock Fernea, 310–16. Austin: University of Texas Press.

———. 1991. *Romancing the Real: Folklore and Ethnographic Representation in North Africa.* Philadelphia: University of Pennsylvania Press.

Weingrod, Alex. 1966. *Reluctant Pioneers.* Ithaca, N.Y.: Cornell University Press.

———. 1990. *The Saint of Beersheba.* Albany: State University of New York Press.

Weissberg, Liliane. 1999. "Introduction." In *Cultural Memory and the Construction of Identity,* ed. Dan Ben-Amos and Liliane Weissberg, 7–26. Detroit: Wayne State University Press.

Weissler, Chava. 1992. "Mizvot Built into the Body: Tkhines for Niddah, Pregnancy and Childbirth." In *People of the Body,* ed. Howard Eilberg-Schwartz, 101–15. Albany: State University of New York Press.

———. 1998. *Voices of the Matriarchs: Listening to the Prayers of Early Modern Jewish Women.* Boston: Beacon Press.

Woolard, Kathryn A., and Bambi B. Schieffelin. 1994. "Language Ideology." *Annual Review of Anthropology* 23:55–82.

Yetive, Isaac. 1987. *1,001 Proverbs from Tunisia.* Washington, D.C.: Three Continents Press.

Zamiti-Horchani, Malika. 1986. "Tunisian Women, Their Rights and Their Ideas about These Rights." In *Women in the Mediterranean,* ed. Monique Gadant, trans. A. M. Berrett, 110–19. London: Zed Books.

Zborowski, Mark, and Elizabeth Herzog. 1952. *Life Is with People: The Culture of the Shtetl.* New York: Schocken Books.

Zerubavel, Yael. 1995. *Recovered Roots: Collective Memory and the Making of Israeli National Tradition.* Chicago and London: University of Chicago Press.

INDEX

Abandonment, 130, 144, 145, 148

Abstinence, 58

Algeria, 32, 194n.17

Alice, 26, 82, 105, 117, 121, 122, 200n.18

Alliance Israélite Française, 34, 36. *See also* Education

Aminadav (biblical figure), 104, 115, 200n.20. *See also* Moshav Aminadav

Amuri (courting), 53

Anthropology, 154, 155. *See also* Esther (researcher); Ethnography

Arab countries, 101, 134. *See also* Tunisia

Arabic: and contentious narration, 48, 49; and Israeli-Arab conflict, 39; and joint narrative, 46; Judeo-Tunisian, 38; and Kuka story, 140; and *Moshav* Gilat, 40; and nostalgia, 134, 136, 137, 138, 139; and tradition, 42; Tunisian, 37, 38; use of, 18; value of, 41–42; and women, 39. *See also* Language

Arab-Israeli conflict, 39

Arrival, narrative of, 104–6, 115–16. *See also* Immigrant/immigration

Ashkenazim, 15, 191n.8. *See also* Ethnicity

Assault. *See* Violence

Audience, 43; and conversational narrative, 19; dialogue with, 9; and elderly, 122; Esther (researcher) as, 76, 157; and gender, 117; and Kuka

story, 140, 148; mixed, 154; role of, 72; and text production, 160

Autonomy. *See* Independence

Bar mitzvah, 33, 193n.13. *See also* Ritual

Bat mitzvah, 33. *See also* Ritual

Beautification, of bride, 53, 57, 60–61. *See also* Marriage; Ritual

Beersheba, 107, 115, 124

Bible, 104

Bilingualism, 37, 39. *See also* Language

Bint (girl), 30, 193n.6

Birth. *See* Childbearing/childbirth

Biya: and aunt, 69, 70; background of, 23, 24; and cohort, 152; and contention, 48; and daughter, 33; and education, 24, 37, 43–44, 45; and entitlement, 70–71; and Esther (researcher), 24; and immigration, 23; and joint narration, 43–45, 48; and language, 42, 44; and marriage, 23, 64–66, 69, 70–71, 72, 75–76; and menarche, 31, 33; and nostalgia, 134; performance at, 73–75; and Shabbat story, 80; sisters of, 73–75, 155, 158; as talking chief, 74; and work, 23, 43–44

Blessing, 58, 59, 60, 196n.11. *See also* Ritual

Blood, 57, 58, 81

Boy, 29, 33, 34, 193n.3, 193n.4. *See also* Childhood; Men

219

Dowry, 30, 53, 55, 63, 70, 196n.20.
  See also Marriage
Dream, 67, 68, 71
Dress. *See* Clothing

Economy/finances, 36–37, 44, 63,
  64, 68, 70, 125, 130, 135. *See also*
  Dowry
'edot hamizrah, 12, 202n.2
Education: Arab, 35, 36; and Biya,
  24, 37, 43–44, 45; and family,
  81, 197n.6; and Fortuna, 37, 159;
  French, 34, 35; and French, 41,
  153; and Ghaliya, 24, 107–8, 159;
  and girls, 34–37, 194nn.17, 21; and
  individual, 37; and Israel, 40, 81,
  197n.6; and menstruation, 33; and
  Miriam, 202n.4; and modernity,
  153; and modesty, 159; and
  narration, 17, 34, 35, 36, 37; and
  Odette, 25, 37, 66; and religion, 34;
  role of, 153; and sexuality, 33; and
  tradition, 35, 36; and Tunisia, 34;
  and women, 37, 49, 87–88, 107–8;
  and work, 34
Elderly, 121–50; care for, 30, 125,
  126–28, 149, 193n.4; and childcare,
  126; and criticism, 11, 121, 137,
  139, 149–50, 155; and holidays,
  125–26; and language, 40, 41;
  and narration, 121–22, 127–28,
  129–30, 133, 135–49, 150; respect
  for, 136; role of, 126, 149; as term,
  13; and voice, 149–50
Election, 16, 98, 192n.11
Emancipation, narrative of, 114–15,
  154. *See also* Independence
Emigration. *See* Immi-
  grant/immigration
English, 40. *See also* Language
Entextualization, 160. *See also* Text
Entitlement, 14; and Biya, 70–71;
  and elderly, 121, 122; and gender,
  149; and Ghaliya, 148; and
  immigrant narratives, 100, 101;

and joint narration, 46, 48; and
  personal narrative, 12; and shooting
  narrative, 109, 110
Esther (researcher): as audience, 76,
  157; and Biya, 23; and Biya's sisters,
  73–75, 155, 158; and bread baking
  narration, 89, 90; and Ghaliya,
  25; and identity, 18, 73–75, 155,
  160; and menarche, 32; method
  of research, 18; and Odette, 25;
  and privacy, 154, 155; role of, 10,
  151–52, 154, 155–56, 157–58; and
  shooting narratives, 108, 110, 111,
  112; text production, 160; and well
  story, 46, 47
Esther (Shushan's wife), 80, 87, 89,
  92–95, 130, 137–38, 139, 149
Ethnicity: and Ashkenazim, 15,
  191n.8; and competition, 36; and
  identity, 135; and Israel, 15–16, 33,
  39, 135, 192n.9; and Sephardim,
  15, 191n.8, 192n.9; and weddings,
  60; and Yemenites, 199n.2. *See also*
  Culture
Ethnography, 158–59. *See also*
  Anthropology; Esther (researcher)
Eurocentrism, 15, 39. *See also*
  Ethnicity
Europe/Europeans, 34, 36, 38, 53, 58,
  99
Evil eye, 57, 58, 59
Exclusion, 33, 73, 84–87, 96, 149. *See
  also* Private sphere; Public sphere
Exodus, 104

Factuality, 43, 48, 98, 99. *See also*
  Truth
Family: and education, 81, 197n.6;
  and elderly, 125–26; extended, 13,
  14, 107, 128; and immigration,
  101, 106–7; importance of, 155–56;
  and *moshavim*, 14; and narration,
  43; reliance on, 74; and residence,
  14; and society, 156; supervision
  by, 35; as theme, 18; and women,

Family (*continued*)
35, 107, 155; and work, 22. *See also*
Kin/kinship
Farming, 14, 106
Fate. *See Maktub* (fate); *Shaʿad*
(fortune, fate)
Father: and chastity, 62, 63; and child
support, 131; and identity, 36; and
marriage, 70; and Odette, 35, 37,
66, 67, 68, 69, 72, 156; role of,
156–57; and women's work, 98. *See
also* Men; Parent
Fertility, 77–78, 78, 82. *See also*
Childbearing/childbirth; Sexuality
Fiction. *See* Narrative/narration;
Truth; *Xurafah/Xurayef*
Fieldwork, 18, 23. *See also* Esther
(researcher)
Finances. *See* Economy/finances
Folktale, 17–18, 51, 70, 71, 72,
199nn.2, 3. *See also* Narra-
tive/narration
Food: and bread baking, 79, 80,
87, 88, 89, 90, 91, 92, 93, 94,
137, 138; and dietary law, 79,
197n.2; and elderly, 125–26; and
identity, 79, 91; and menarche,
32; and weddings, 53, 55,
58, 60, 61. *See also* Cooking;
Nurturance
Fortuna: and Arabic, 40; background
of, 21–23; and childbirth, 22;
and cohort, 152; and contention,
46–49; and daughter, 33; death of,
23, 161; and education, 35, 37, 159;
and Ghaliya, 142, 146–47, 149;
and health, 22; and immigration,
21; and joint narration, 46–49; and
Kuka story, 142, 146–47, 149; and
language, 40, 41, 46; and marriage,
21, 64, 69; and menarche, 31, 33;
and *mikvah* (bath), 82; and nostalgia,
133; and shooting narratives, 108,
109, 110, 111, 112, 113, 114; and
weddings, 54

Fortune. *See Maktub* (fate); *Shaʿad*
(fortune, fate)
Fradji, 88, 89, 90, 91, 92, 94, 136,
137, 138, 139, 200n.19
France, 34, 36, 38, 58
French: and *amuri* (courting), 53;
and education, 36, 41, 153; and
intelligence, 37, 44; and love, 71;
and modernity, 37, 44; and *Moshav*
Gilat, 40; prestige of, 41; and
Tunisia, 37, 38; use of, 18, 42; and
women, 39. *See also* Language

Gabes, 24, 53, 86, 144, 148, 193n.10
Gabriel, 25, 66, 68, 69, 71, 72
Gender: and audience, 117;
construction of, 93–94; and
entitlement, 149; and identity, 30;
and illness, 201n.6; and immigrant
narratives, 99; and Israel, 16;
and male interference, 138; and
narration, 101, 117, 149, 158,
199n.3; and role, 16, 33, 144, 145;
and segregation, 78; and shooting
narratives, 112, 113; and text,
151; and work, 107. *See also* Men;
Women
Genre, 17–18, 101, 117–18, 154,
199n.3. *See also* Narrative/narration
Ghaliya: and arrival narrative, 115–
16; background of, 24–25; and
children, 25; and cohort, 152; and
daughter, 33; and education, 24,
107–8, 159; and emancipation, 115;
and entitlement, 148; and Esther
(researcher), 25; and Fortuna, 142,
146–47, 149; and husband, 129;
and illness, 161; and immigration,
25, 104–5; and Kuka story, 140,
142–49; and marriage, 24, 62;
and menarche, 31, 33, 193n.10;
and narration, 117, 200n.19; and
nostalgia, 133; and voice, 116
Gift, 55, 68
Gilat. *See Moshav* Gilat

bread baking, 137; of shooting incidents, 80, 108–14; stability, 71; and structure, 145, 148; and symbol, 153; and textual coherence, 94–95; and tradition, 153, 154; transmission of, 156; and truth, 43, 48, 98, 99, 100; and Tunisia, 101; and well story, 46–49; and women, 17–18, 101, 117–18, 149, 154, 156

Narrator, 19, 160

Niddah (menstruation laws): and childbearing, 84; and ḥenna, 81, 195n.8; and marriage, 57, 79, 81. *See also* Menstruation

Noro: background of, 21–22; and contention, 46–49; and illness, 22; and immigration, 21; and Israel, 21–22; and joint narration, 46–49; and Kuka, 140, 141, 146, 148; and language, 46; and marriage, 21, 64; and Miriam's education, 202n.4; and narration, 22; and shooting narratives, 108, 109, 111, 112, 113, 114; and weddings, 54; and work, 22

North Africa/North African, 13, 34, 57, 81, 192n.8, 195n.8

Nostalgia, 89, 133–36, 137, 138, 139, 152. *See also* counternostalgia

Nurturance, 79, 80, 87, 88, 91, 125. *See also* Food; Mother/motherhood

Odette: and Arabic, 40; background of, 25; and cohort, 152; and daughter, 33; and dowry, 63; and education, 25, 35–36, 37, 66; and emancipation, 114–15; and Esther (researcher), 25; as family representative, 107; and father, 35, 37, 66, 67, 68, 69, 72, 156; and Ḥuri, 72, 102, 103, 104, 119, 124; and husband, 129; and immigration, 102–4, 114–15; and language, 41; and male role, 118; and marriage, 25, 62, 63, 66–69, 70, 71–72, 103,

104; and menarche, 33; and *mikvah* (bath), 200n.1; and modesty, 132, 133; and mother, 69, 119, 156, 200n.21; and narration, 117–18; and travel, 124; and work, 25, 67

Oil, 31–32, 193n.14

Opposition, binary, 145, 147

Oral narrative, 140. *See also* Narrative/narration

Oral tradition, 79, 93

Otiyya, 55

Outsider, 73–75, 114, 138

Parent: and identity, 74, 155; and marriage, 69, 75; and tradition, 74. *See also* Father; Mother/motherhood

Past, 95–96, 135, 136. *See also* Memory; Nostalgia; Tradition

Patriarchy, 18, 91, 93–95, 154. *See also* Men

Performance, 11, 18–19, 20, 41, 42, 72–75, 158

Personal sphere, 19, 43, 45, 100. *See also* Private sphere

Pilgrimage, 124, 129, 134, 201n.4. *See also* Travel

Pollution, 29. *See also* Menstruation; Purity

Position/positioning (in narrative), 21, 52, 69, 76, 118, 140

Poverty, 63, 70, 135. *See also* Economy/finances

Pregnancy, 83, 87

Prejudice, 15–16. *See also* Eurocentrism; Xenophobia

Present, 96. *See also* Past

Privacy, 154, 155

Private sphere, 17, 32, 33, 78–79, 87, 100–101, 114. *See also* Personal sphere

Procreation. *See* Childbearing/childbirth

Property, 78, 85. *See also* Economy/finances

www.ingramcontent.com/pod-product-compliance
Lightning Source LLC
Chambersburg PA
CBHW050237270326
41914CB00034BA/1962/J

BOOKS IN THE
RAPHAEL PATAI SERIES IN
JEWISH FOLKLORE AND ANTHROPOLOGY

The Myth of the Jewish Race, revised edition, by Raphael Patai and Jennifer Patai, 1989

The Hebrew Goddess, third enlarged edition, by Raphael Patai, 1990

Robert Graves and the Hebrew Myths: A Collaboration, by Raphael Patai, 1991

Jewish Musical Traditions, by Amnon Shiloah, 1992

The Jews of Kurdistan, by Erich Brauer, completed and edited by Raphael Patai, 1993

Jewish Moroccan Folk Narratives from Israel, by Haya Bar-Itzhak and Aliza Shenhar, 1993

For Our Soul: The Ethiopian Jews in Israel, by Teshome G. Wagaw, 1993

Book of Fables: The Yiddish Fable Collection of Reb Moshe Wallich, Frankfurt am Main, 1697, translated and edited by Eli Katz, 1994

From Sofia to Jaffa: The Jews of Bulgaria and Israel, by Guy H. Haskell, 1994

Jadid al-Islam: The Jewish ANew Muslims@ of Meshhed, by Raphael Patai, 1998

Saint Veneration among the Jews in Morocco, by Issachar Ben-Ami, 1998

Arab Folktales from Palestine and Israel, introduction, translation, and annotation by Raphel Patai, 1998

Profiles of a Lost World: Memoirs of East European Jewish Life before World War II, by Hirsz Abramowicz, translated by Eva Zeitlin Dobkin, edited by Dina Abramowicz and Jeffrey Shandler, 1999

A Global Community: The Jews from Aleppo, Syria, by Walter Zenner, 2000

Without Bounds: The Life and Death of Rabbi Ya=akov Wazana, by Yoram Bilu, 2000